Praise for *Stanley*

'Poet, explorer, irresistibly funny ...
This lovely book reflects its author's delightful personality.'

– Esther Rantzen

'Stanley Johnson's life sparkles with a joy of living.
He writes with the wit and humour of a true raconteur.
Stanley, I Presume is a fascinating read of a fascinating life.'

– Zoë Wanamaker

'A wonderful, jaw-dropping account of a rollercoaster life.
Johnson senior does not disappoint ... the book is a triumph.'

– Anne Robinson

'*Stanley, I Presume* is funny and engaging. It reveals not only
the person but also his many talents, passions and adventures, from
novelist to secret service agent, poet to population activist and explorer
to Eurocrat. And it also reveals why the Mayor of London is called Boris.'

– Tony Juniper

'Hearty and humorous ... an enjoyable yarn, full of tall stories ...
yet contains real achievements.'

– *TLS*

'A hilarious memoir.'

– *Sunday Times*

'Illuminating ... Tells Johnson senior's life story without pretension and
is full of the literary, historical and social confidence that goes with real
erudition ... A happy book about a happy life, tempered with poetry and
sadness ... We could do with much more of this sort of writing.'

– *Country Life*

'A very funny book and quite often made me laugh out loud.'

– Andrew Gimson, *Daily Telegraph*

'When asked to review my father's memoir ... I was thrilled.
My father has had a rip-roaring life, created countless cock-ups on all
four continents and writes like a dream ... Highly enjoyable reading.'

– Rachel Johnson, *Evening Standard*

'Laugh-out-loud funny – once you've read it you'll understand a lot more

Also by Stanley Johnson

Gold Drain (1967)

Panther Jones for President (1968)

*Life without Birth: A Journey Through the Third World
in Search of the Population Explosion* (1970)

The Green Revolution (1972)

The Population Problem (1973)

The Politics of Environment (1973)

The Urbane Guerilla (1975)

Pollution Control Policy of the EEC (1978)

The Doomsday Deposit (1979)

The Marburg Virus (1982)

Tunnel (1984)

Antarctica: The Last Great Wilderness (1985)

The Commissioner (1987)

Dragon River (1989)

*The Earth Summit: The United Nations Conference on Environment and Development
(UNCED)* (1993)

World Population: Turning the Tide (1994)

The Environmental Policy of the European Communities (1995)

The Politics of Population: Cairo, 1994 (1995)

Icecap (1999)

Stanley, I Presume (2009)

Survival: Saving Endangered Migratory Species (with Robert Vagg) (2010)

Where the Wild Things Were: Travels of a Conservationist (2012)

UNEP: The First 40 Years: A narrative by Stanley Johnson (2012)

STANLEY, I RESUME

STANLEY JOHNSON

The Robson Press

941.085092

First published in Great Britain in 2014
This edition published in 2015 by
The Robson Press (an imprint of Biteback Publishing Ltd)
Westminster Tower
3 Albert Embankment
London SE1 7SP
Copyright © Stanley Johnson 2014, 2015

ISBN 978-1-84954-837-3

10 9 8 7 6 5 4 3 2 1

A CIP catalogue record for this book is available from the British Library.

Set in Baskerville by five-twentyfive.com

Printed and bound in Great Britain by
CPI Group (UK) Ltd, Croydon CR0 4YY

MIX
Paper from
responsible sources
FSC® C020471

Contents

Chapter One

My Forty-First Year to Heaven

My forty-first year to heaven, as Dylan Thomas might have put it if he had lived just a few weeks longer, did not begin auspiciously. For a start, I was on my own. I hate being on my own. I am not good at it. But that morning, 18 August 1980, the very morning of my fortieth birthday, I was definitely the only one sitting down for breakfast in the kitchen of our Exmoor farmhouse.

I hadn't planned it that way. My American girlfriend, Bobby, with her two young children, aged four and two, had been staying on the farm with me for the past few days. Bobby never travelled light. She had brought with her a staff of three Nepalese ladies and a vast quantity of baggage. She planned to stay on for the big four-zero event.

I should have realised things were not going well when I came down to the kitchen in the middle of the night a couple of days earlier to find all three Nepalese hunched over the old oak table, studying some document intently by the light of a candle. Caravaggio? Georges de la Tour?

There are several things I should explain about this scenario.

The first is that in 1980, West Nethercote, our Exmoor home, still didn't have mains electricity. The breakthrough on that front didn't occur till halfway through the '90s when our nearest and dearest neighbours, Antony and Jenny Acland, clubbed together with us to bribe the local power company. I use the term 'bribe' figuratively, of course. SWEB, the South Western Electricity Board, charged a premium rate – tens of thousands of pounds – to bring a line in over the hills. Irritatingly, a year or two later, an EU grant enabled deprived houses and farms like ours on Exmoor to be linked to the modern world for a nugatory fee. We didn't exactly miss the boat. We embarked too early and missed the discount!

The second thing I should point out is that the document the three Nepalese ladies were studying turned out to be the railway timetable.

When they saw me walk into the kitchen in my dressing gown, torch in hand, the three women 'started like a guilty thing' like the ghost in *Hamlet*, and scurried off, taking their candle with them.

I shone my torch on the book. It was still open. I could see that Bobby's inhouse team had been studying Table 56: Weekend Trains from Taunton to London.

Were the three Nepalese already planning to leave, I wondered? Was Exmoor too much for them? In that case, were Bobby and her kids going to leave with them?

I was, I admit, alarmed. I was keen on Bobby. We had been an 'item', as the saying goes, for several months. I had met her soon after I was elected to the European Parliament in June 1979. When I wasn't in Brussels, Strasbourg or Luxembourg (in those days the European Parliament had three seats and we visited each more or less in turn), I stayed in lovely Bobby's lovely listed seventeenth-century house in Hampstead, looking out onto Hampstead Heath. Though Bobby still worked with her husband – they dealt in primitive art and had a gallery in Cork Street – he had moved out of the marital home and, as I understood it, they were in the process of separating.

Looking back almost thirty-five years later, I can see that, from Bobby's point of view at least, I was not necessarily an ideal partner. I was a divorced father of four. I spent most of my time on the train or plane, heading off to or returning from meetings of the European Parliament. I didn't really pull my weight. I didn't, for example, make any useful contribution to the running of her large household, apart from once helping to resurface her tennis court. Nor did I really put in the time I should have with her young children, Redmond and Sarah.

Even before we left London for Somerset, I could tell she was giving some thought to the situation. You don't have to have super-sensitive antennae to pick up on these things. But with the European Parliament in recess over the summer, I knew I had a chance to 'raise my game', as the saying goes. And I wasn't just talking about tennis.

'Come to Exmoor for my fortieth birthday,' I said to Bobby. 'You can stay as long as you like. The kids will love it.'

The third thing I need to explain is the actual physical layout of the farmhouse, because that proved to be a key aspect of the ensuing drama.

West Nethercote is a fine example of a traditional West Somerset long-house. And by 'long', I really mean long. Think Borneo! As far as the upstairs sleeping arrangements were concerned, Bobby and I were at one end of the house. Her staff and the two young children were at the other. The distance that separated us was at least the length of a cricket pitch.

I was quite happy about this in the sense that I felt confident that if Redmond or Sarah woke up in the night, Bobby's staff would rise to the occasion and Bobby and I would not be disturbed.

Bobby, I could see, was doubtful. On arrival, she had gazed at the gloomy passage that separated one end of the house from another.

'Isn't that an awfully long way for little kids to come and find their mother when it's dark as pitch?' she commented. 'Can't you leave the light on at least?'

I explained patiently that I could hardly leave the 4 kilowatt Lister Diesel Startomatic chugging away all night in the engine shed beyond the barn. (Startomatic was a total misnomer. In order to get that particular engine going you had to whirl away with the crank while simultaneously squirting 'Easystart' into the cylinder block. Once the engine fired, you had to pull the heavy crank away swiftly, otherwise it would spin round too, before literally flying off the handle, endangering life and limb.)

'I am sure the kids will be fine,' I added.

Well, they weren't fine. On more than one occasion, in the middle of the night, that first week of Bobby's stay on Exmoor, I would hear the patter of tiny feet in the long passage. I would slip out of bed, without waking Bobby up, and gently shoo the owners of those tiny feet back to their end of the house.

I think Bobby knew what was happening. Maybe she was half-awake and realised what was going on. Or maybe the Nepalese told her that the kids had been wandering round in the dark at night, looking for their mother. Anyway, on the Sunday before the birthday Monday she told me firmly at breakfast in her no-nonsense American way, 'My children must have access to me at all times.'

I wanted to say 'not in my house, they don't', but I hate confrontations, so I kept quiet. Instead, claiming urgent business at the top of the farm, I eased out of the kitchen to start the Land Rover.

While I was out 'up-over' that morning in the Land Rover, fetching wood from a pile stacked in a field where we had been hedging, Bobby summoned the village taxi, which duly bounced its way up the two-mile track to the farm. By the time I got back down with a load of logs, the whole party – Bobby, her two children, the three Nepalese staff and all their baggage – had gone.

I found a note on the kitchen table. 'Gone back to London. Happy birthday! Bobby.'

So that is why, when I woke up the next day, having turned forty overnight, I had no one but my own chastened self for company.

Forty years earlier, cows had munched their way through their own breakfasts in the very room where I was now sitting. In a bad winter, and winters were often bad on Exmoor, the cows were brought into the byre at the east end of the house. This was quite convenient, since the hay was stored on the floor immediately above the byre. To feed the cows, you simply dropped the hay down into the manger below.

Even today, in many parts of the world (Bhutan, for example), cows still 'live in' on the ground floor of the houses. It makes a lot of sense, if you think about it. You don't have to trudge out into the fields to feed them, and their body heat, rising up through wooden or wattle structures, helps to keep a place warm.

I think my father would have been quite content to leave the cows in situ as it were when we took over West Nethercote from the previous owners but my mother, not at all a pushy woman, insisted on having a kitchen, so the cows went off to a newly restored cowshed some distance away.

My mother pressed home her advantage.

'Surely, Johnny,' – she always called my father Johnny – 'now the cows have gone, we don't need to store the hay in the house. Can't we have a bathroom instead of the hayloft?'

I remember that hayloft well. It had a warm, comfortable smell. But, even as a ten-year-old (we moved to Exmoor in 1951), I could see my mother's point. There was no bathroom at all at West Nethercote when we arrived, though there was an Elsan in one of the outbuildings.

But back to the present. After that solitary breakfast, there being no other convenient distractions, I decided I would trim a large ash tree that hung over the eastern gable of the house. The tree not only cast a deep, almost excessive, shade over the front garden, but some of the branches looked quite rickety and might have done considerable damage to the roof if they became detached from the trunk.

I went out to the stable across the yard to fetch the chainsaw. Strictly speaking, it is not really a stable nowadays. We haven't kept horses for twenty years. It's more of a toolshed than a stable.

Clad in shorts and sandals (it was high summer on Exmoor), I climbed up the tree holding the chainsaw. I found a good perch and yanked on the cord. The chainsaw started on the first pull.

It would have been better if it hadn't. After clearing some foliage and twigs, I decided to attack a large solid branch some twenty feet above the ground. Unfortunately, it happened to be the branch I was sitting on.

The extraordinary thing about falling out of a tree is how quickly it happens. One minute you are up in the air, hacking away. A split second later you are lying on your back, totally winded, and the chainsaw is roaring away an inch or two from your jugular vein.

Later that week, my (then) four children, viz. Boris, Rachel, Leo and Jo – all of them in the middle of their summer holidays – arrived at the farm. A day or two later we set off for Cornwall in the Land Rover.

It proved to be a long journey. In the course of travelling from Exmoor to Penzance, the Land Rover developed not just one but a whole series of punctures. It was totally bizarre.

A garage man in Lostwithiel had his own theory.

'Basically,' he said, 'the tyres are all bruised internally.'

Truth to tell, I was feeling fairly bruised internally at that particular juncture of my life, but I let it pass.

'What do you mean?' I asked.

The man explained, 'Maybe you've been doing some rough work on the farm. At low speeds, that doesn't matter. But you start driving at 50 or 60 miles an hour on the highway for long distances, those bruises will blow out. How many new tyres do you say you've had?'

'Three,' I sighed. 'The near front tyre is the only one I haven't had to change so far.'

The man walked round to the front of the car and gave the relevant tyre a reflective kick.

'It might last you, but I wouldn't bet on it.'

My almost-fifteen-year-old daughter, Rachel, clambered out of the back of the vehicle to stretch her legs. It had been a long journey.

'You just have to roll with the punctures,' she said.

Happily, the sun sets late in the far west of England. It was still daylight when, around Penzance, the near front tyre decided to join the club, deflating suddenly and forcing me to swerve to the roadside. I had bought a spare 'spare' at the last pit stop in Lostwithiel and I fitted the last new tyre by the roadside in the fading light.

I wondered at the time whether that epic journey from Exmoor to the furthest extremity of Cornwall was in some way symbolic. Was the transition to a new and different life (*'newly elected Euro MP, newly single, still blonde or blonde-ish, father of four, GSOH, seeks change of direction, maybe more'*) always going to be fraught with unexpected hazards?

I took my hat off to the children, then as always. It had taken more than ten hours to get from Exmoor to Land's End, but I hadn't heard a single whine or squeal of protest.

Next morning, we all woke up, checked the tyres on the Land Rover (no overnight punctures!), had breakfast and went out into the garden of Minack House.

'Wow!' I said.

'Wow!' the children chorused.

Whoever said 'the journey not the arrival matters' got it wrong. The arrival is what counts.

Minack House, which I had rented for a couple of weeks that summer, is built right on top of the cliff. A steep footpath takes you down to Porthcurno Beach. On the far side of the bay you can see the magnificent granite cliffs, which are (to me) Cornwall's most distinctive feature. From the garden, and from almost every window of the house, you have a clear view of the great Logan Rock, an 80-ton monster, so precariously balanced that it looked as though every gale might dislodge it.

I was working that summer on my fourth novel. It was called *The Marburg Virus* and it was about the outbreak of a mysterious and fatal epidemic. I like to think I foresaw the AIDS epidemic, at least in fictional terms, before the event itself.

Strictly speaking, I was rewriting the book. I had completed most of it on holiday in Rhodes the previous year. In those days, I prided myself that I could knock off a novel in a few weeks. Give me an uninterrupted month or two and it was a done deal.

Gillon Aitken, my then literary agent, was more concerned with quality than speed. He was tremendously tall and tremendously grand. He rang me up, after I had sent him the first draft, suggesting that I might like to come to see him in his house in Chelsea.

'I think this needs a bit more work, Stanley,' he told me over a glass of *Pouilly-quelque-chose*. 'Every time a cliché rears its ugly head, you've got to take it out. Ruthlessly.'

Amazingly, Gillon had actually started to rewrite the first few chapters. But I could tell that he was beginning to regret it. He was looking pale and drawn.

'You may have bitten off more than you can chew,' I suggested.

He pounced immediately. 'That's exactly what I mean, Stanley. For heaven's sake, try to avoid the clichés.'

My first season as a newly elected Member of the European Parliament had been fairly busy. But I promised my agent that I would work on the book in Cornwall.

So I sat in the garden of Minack House while the children scrambled down the cliff path to spend the day on the beach, and basically rewrote *The Marburg Virus* from top to toe. The only real problem was the wind. With the house's breezy location, I was constantly running to reclaim pages, and sometimes whole chapters, from the edge of the cliff.

Did those Cornish gales dispose of all the offending clichés? I suppose they must have done, because when Heinemann, the firm that had published my first three novels, published *The Marburg Virus* too, the response of the literary critics was quite positive. Stephen Glover, for example, reviewing the book in the *Daily Telegraph*, wrote: 'There are some novelists who, whether by accident or design, understand perfectly the ingredients of a thriller. Stanley Johnson is one of these.'

When I meet Stephen Glover nowadays, I sometimes remind him of the good review he gave to my fourth novel. I am not sure he remembers it as clearly as I do. He probably reviews quite a few books.

One night during that summer holiday in Cornwall, we went to the famous Minack Theatre, set in the cliff-face just below Minack House. The play was Edmond Rostand's *Cyrano de Bergerac*. With the wind blowing strongly, and the waves almost crashing over the rocks onto the stage, the actors had to shout their lines.

I carried my youngest child, Jo (aged eight at the time, now an MP), back to the house during the interval and handed him over to Candy, a solid Lancastrian girl whom I had employed to cook and housekeep during our Minack vacation.

'The main thing I want you to do, Candy,' I had told her when I picked her up from Penzance Station the day after our own traumatic arrival at Minack, 'is to provide plenty of binge meals.'

Well, she certainly did that even if she was a touch heavy on the carbohydrates.

Chapter Two

The Pope Gives His Approval

Summers always have to come to an end. As the children went back to their respective schools, I realised I needed a London base.

I thought it would be best to avoid Hampstead so I wrote off to some estate agents serving the Paddington area. Paddington, I felt, was convenient. There were good trains to the West Country from Paddington.

In any case, I already had use of a *pied-à-terre* in Paddington.

When I left the European Commission on being elected to the European Parliament in June 1979, Crispin and Penelope Tickell had very kindly lent me their flat in Blomfield Road, which runs alongside the Union Canal near Paddington Basin. Crispin served as Roy Jenkins's chef de cabinet when Jenkins took over the presidency of the Commission and was still *en poste* in Brussels. Penelope, who happened to be in London that day, volunteered to come with me to inspect a maisonette on Maida Avenue, the road that runs along the canal on the opposite side from Blomfield Road.

We met outside the house. It was a large, imposing, stucco-fronted building, looking out onto the canal. Boatmen glided past on barges. They didn't call it Little Venice for nothing. My spirits soared after the débacle on Exmoor. Perhaps I could survive living on my own in a place like this.

The house was three storeys high, with the maisonette occupying the second and third floors. According to the particulars, it had three bedrooms and a large L-shaped sitting room looking out over the water. Just the ticket, I thought.

The maisonette was empty, but the agent had given me the keys. I suppose we had been looking around inside for about twenty minutes when the flat's own doorbell rang. Though the maisonette was reached through the main entrance, as was the ground-floor flat, it had its own door at the top of the stairs leading up to the first floor.

I ignored it. It sounded again. More urgently.

'I wonder who that can be,' Penelope said.

I opened the door, and looked down the stairs into the hall to see a slim, dark-haired woman gazing up at me with a cross look on her face.

'What are you doing?' she asked.

I don't know why I didn't give the obvious answer. I could have told the cross young lady that I was a potential tenant on a tour of inspection. But there was something about the whole situation that irked me. I didn't like being put on the spot.

'Actually, I'm a burglar,' I said. 'I've just broken in, and quite soon, I'm going to start a fire.'

Fast forward several weeks. I have made my apologies to Jenny, the young lady from downstairs. As a matter of fact, I have fallen for her. But I don't think she has fallen for me.

Before Christmas, Jenny fled to Barbados. But I tracked her down, flying out to the Caribbean myself on the next available plane.

I went windsurfing that first afternoon. I am not particularly good at windsurfing. I crashed heavily on some rocks. When I dragged the windsurfer back in to shore after a disappointing stint, Jenny pointed out that the little toe on my left foot was sticking out at right angles.

'You must have dislocated it.' She didn't sound very sympathetic. I think my sudden appearance in Barbados, when she thought I was safely back in London, had rather thrown her.

Having a dislocated little toe is surprisingly debilitating. You can't wear normal shoes, for example. Your feet look odd, even in sandals, because there is this solid lump of flesh sticking out at one side.

'Stop worrying about how it looks,' Jenny advised. 'You need to have that seen to soon, otherwise they'll have to break it and reset it.'

I realised then that Jenny, apart from being an absolute stunner as far as looks were concerned, was an extremely practical person. She helped me (hobbling) into her rented car and drove off at speed.

'Where are we going?' I asked.

'There's a vet's surgery halfway to Sandy Lane.'

'A vet?'

'No time to lose,' she said.

Half an hour later, after a couple of quick, if painful, wrenches from a man who obviously knew what he was doing, I was right as rain.

After a few more days together, we flew back from Barbados to London. Jenny, recently widowed, had two dogs. Douglas was a large chocolate Labrador; Jimmy was a Cairn terrier.

I carried my bags upstairs to my maisonette. Jenny went straight into her downstairs flat and firmly shut the door.

Most days, as I looked out of my first floor window onto the canal when I was in London (which wasn't often since the Euro parliamentary term had begun again), I would hear the front door slam and, seconds later, see Jenny stride down the path into the street, being – literally – pulled by the two dogs. Jenny clearly gave the dogs their money's worth because it would often be more than an hour before she returned.

I met her once on the doorstep. Douglas slobbered over me, while Jimmy nipped at my heels.

'Where do you take them?' I asked.

'Hyde Park, usually,' Jenny said. 'I have to keep an eye on them though.'

'I'll take them tomorrow, if you like. I don't have to go to Strasbourg till Tuesday this week.'

Jenny looked doubtful.

'No, I mean it,' I insisted. 'I'll be delighted.'

Truthfully, when I made the offer, I didn't for a moment foresee any problems. I had grown up with dogs. There were always dogs on the farm. They were a basic part of my parents' life and of my own childhood. At mealtimes, if you didn't want to eat the fatty bits, you could surreptitiously flip them onto the floor for the dogs.

Next day I set off in the car with Jimmy and Douglas. I parked near the Serpentine. It was a bright, sunny day.

Jimmy and Douglas, once released from the leash, took off and disappeared into the distance. Within seconds of letting them out of the car, I had managed to lose both of them.

I wouldn't say I panicked, but it certainly wasn't a happy moment. I headed off on foot in the direction I thought the two dogs had taken. I asked passers-by, 'I say, you haven't by any chance seen two dogs, Jimmy and Douglas? Chocolate Labrador and Cairn terrier?'

Two fruitless hours later, I drove back to the house on Maida Avenue and parked the car on the concrete pad in front of the garage.

I rang Jenny's doorbell. I wasn't quite sure how I was going to break the news.

Jenny opened the door just a crack. This wasn't Penelope welcoming Odysseus on his return from Troy.

'I hear you lost the dogs.' She sounded cool, if not icy. 'Someone rang up. They were both of them found in Hyde Park earlier today. Near Park Lane, actually. Not the best place for them.'

Jimmy and Douglas obviously had no hard feelings. They pushed their way out into the hall and greeted me enthusiastically.

One morning, only a few days after I had returned with Jenny from the Caribbean, I went downstairs to the front hall to collect the morning mail. On the mat I found an extraordinary communication. It was from James Scott-Hopkins, a former MP, now an MEP, whom Mrs Thatcher had asked to serve as the leader of the sixty-one Conservatives MEPs.

> During the course of the discussions to be held in Rome later this month with Italian colleagues from the Christian Democratic Party, Members of the European Democratic Group will have the honour of being received by His Holiness the Pope in the Vatican. Wives are also invited. Mantillas should be worn.

By then, Jenny had forgiven me for losing her dogs in Hyde Park. She had even driven down to the farm with me for the weekend with the dogs in the back. She had met my parents, who approved of her enormously.

The dogs as well as Jenny were a total success. When Douglas killed a duck on the pond at West Nethercote, my father patted him approvingly.

'Every dog is allowed his duck,' he had said.

I was still in the hall, mulling over Scott-Hopkins's intriguing message, when Jenny came out of her ground-floor flat to pick up her own post.

'Do you have a mantilla?' I asked.

Strictly speaking, the invitation to meet the Pope applied to MEPs and their *wives*. It didn't say anything about 'partners' or 'girlfriends'. And anyway, Jenny, when I invited her to join me on the trip to Rome, said she wasn't sure that she wanted to meet 'a whole load of 'Tories'. She hadn't met a lot of Tories in the past. I had a feeling she disapproved of them.

'Do come,' I urged her. 'How often are you going to have an audience with the Pope?'

Two weeks later we found ourselves in Rome, being ushered into the gilded papal reception rooms in the Vatican.

Scott-Hopkins, a tall, imposing man, made the introductions.

'This is Lord Bethell, Holy Father,' Scott-Hopkins said. 'This is Lady Douro. This is Sir Fred Warner and this is Lady Warner. This is Sir Henry Plumb and this is Lady Plumb. This is Sir Jack and Lady Stewart-Clark. This is Sir David Nicholson and Dame Shelagh Roberts…'

Jenny and I shuffled slowly forward while the Pope greeted the grandees. Eventually, it was the turn of the 'plebs', to use that now fashionable term.

I saw Scott-Hopkins look at me and then look at Jenny. He seemed doubtful. He had obviously forgotten her name.

'This is … er … Mr Johnson, Holy Father,' Scott-Hopkins mumbled, 'and this is, er, in point of fact…'

When Jim lost the thread, as he sometimes did, he 'in point of fact'ed quite a lot.

The Holy Father looked at our puzzled leader. He looked at me. He peered at Jenny under her mantilla. He obviously decided to help Scott-Hopkins out.

'Well, this is Mrs Johnson, I suppose,' he said.

The Pope was not speaking *ex cathedra* but he might as well have been. When it was all over, and the Pope had gone back to the papal apartments, and the Conservative MEPs and their wives had dispersed in various directions, Jenny and I scooted off to have a pizza in the piazza.

Jenny tucked the mantilla into her bag.

'Well, what do you think?' I asked.

She studied the menu. 'I'll go for the pizza napolitana but with extra anchovies.'

'No,' I persisted, 'what do you feel about being "Mrs Johnson"? The Pope seems to think it's a good idea.'

Jenny and I were married on 27 February 1981, which, at the time of writing (June 2014), is more than thirty-three years ago. I have a lot to thank the Pope for.

Chapter Three

Roman Remains

The Parliament's Environment Committee was meeting in Rome towards the end of July 1981 when I received an invitation to lunch at the exclusive Circolo della Caccia, in the Palazzo Borghese in the heart of Rome.

My host, a charming silver-haired gentleman, Mr Pio Teodorani Fabri (who, as it happened, was married to the sister of Giovanni Agnelli, founder of Fiat) insisted on calling me '*Onorevole*', Italian for 'honourable'.

'The problem, *Onorevole*,' he explained, as the game course succeeded the pasta (it is not called Circolo de la Caccia – the Hunting Club – for nothing), 'is that the planners are proposing to divert water from the River Po by building an irrigation canal hundreds of kilometres across the plains of northern Italy to the Adriatic Coast. And the route they have selected goes directly through the famous "centuriations", which are to be found in the vicinity of present-day Cesena. As you may know, these are possibly the best-preserved "centuriations" in the whole of Italy, indeed in the whole world. Not only do the *centuriationi* in Cesena cover a large area, not only are they among the oldest in Italy, they are also unique in that they have a precise north–south orientation. There is no other such example in the whole of Italy.'

'*Dio mio!*' I exclaimed, 'A precise north–south orientation!'

Teodorani Fabri poured me a glass of some delicious dessert wine. It could have been ambrosia. Then he went on to explain that he, and people like him, who were keen to preserve a unique part of Italy's heritage, had run into a brick wall in their attempts to stop, or at least divert, the proposed canal. The authorities were determined to proceed with the project.

'We need help at the European level. That's why we are appealing to you, both as a Member of the European Parliament and as the vice chairman of the Parliament's Environment Committee.'

I telephoned the Mayor of Cesena from London a few days later. Pio Teodorani Fabri had obviously given him a glowing account of our recent encounter.

The mayor pleaded with me to come to Cesena in person.

'*Veni subito, Onorevole Signor Johnson.*' Come at once!

Before ringing the mayor, I had looked up Cesena on the map. I could see that the town was situated in the Emilio-Romagna region of Italy, in the province of Cesena-Forli, a few miles from the Adriatic, about 40 miles south of Ravenna.

I was already planning to drive through Italy to Greece for a long-arranged family holiday in Corfu.

'I'll stop off in Cesena on the way,' I said.

We agreed that I would come to Cesena on Sunday 2 August. The mayor suggested we should meet in the parking area of Cesena's best hotel, the Hotel Casali.

It only remained to agree on the precise time of the RV.

'How about six o' clock?' I suggested. To be sure that the mayor had understood, I repeated myself in Italian. '*A la sei de la tarde. A la sei, pronto.*'

That, at least, is what I thought I had said.

I still have my engagement book in front of me as I write these words. The entry for 2 August 1981 reads: 'Meet Mayor of Cesena, Hotel Casali, Via Benedetto Croce, 6 p.m.'

Jenny, already pregnant with Julia, wisely decided to fly, rather than drive, to Corfu. My mother, whom we had invited to join us in our rented villa there, would accompany her. This was a load off my mind. Well into her seventies, I didn't like the idea of my mother making the journey by herself. For one thing, since she was quite deaf by then, I doubted if she would be able to hear the boarding announcements. She might board a plane to New Zealand by accident.

There was also the question of space. My Volvo estate could easily handle four children and their luggage, but we planned to pick up a Belgian friend, Camille de Wouters. Camille, with a lively and engaging personality, was the same age as my daughter, Rachel, then a few weeks short of her sixteenth birthday.

'It would be marvellous,' I said to Jenny, 'if you could bring Granny Butter with you on the plane.'

My mother's nickname was Buster. Acquired decades earlier when my mother was a vigorous lacrosse player at Cheltenham Ladies College, the nickname had stuck with her in later life. My children, though, called her 'Granny Butter'.

I have to hand it to Jenny. When she said 'yes' to my marriage proposal over that pizza napolitana ('with extra anchovies') in St Peter's Square, the day we met the Pope in Rome, she could have had no idea what she was letting herself in for.

I was, as I have already indicated, a recently divorced man with four children. I was frequently absent and not very rich. On the face of it, I wasn't much of a catch. And now I was asking her to look after my elderly mother as well.

But Jenny made it all right at once. 'I love your mother,' she told me. 'I really do. We can play Scrabble at Gatwick while we're waiting for the plane.'

As a matter of fact, my mother, even then, when some of her faculties had begun to fade, was a more than competent Scrabble player. She was also very good at anagrams.

'Can you think of an anagram of SPINE, Granny Butter?' the children would ask.

My mother didn't fall for that one. 'PINES,' she would say firmly.

Sometimes, when my parents came to lunch, my mother would insist on doing the washing up and the kids would pass her the same saucepan time and time again. Lovingly, of course. Granny Butter played the game. She knew they were pulling her leg.

The four children and I left England on the last day of July 1981, driving down in my Volvo estate car to Dover, with luggage piled high on the roof rack. We took the afternoon ferry to Calais, picked up Camille in Brussels, and then drove through the night through Germany and Austria, before coming down out of the mountains via Cortina d'Ampezzo. As we reached the plains I saw a sign that said: 'VENICE – VENEZIA 220 kilometers'!

'Hey, kids,' I called out. 'What do you say to lunch in St Mark's Square?'

I don't know if anyone else has 'done Venice' in two hours but that is what we did that day. We parked up by the station and whizzed down the Grand Canal on the *vaporetto* to see St Mark's Square and the Doge's Palace and we still had time for a meal in a nearby trattoria.

At 3 p.m. we were back on the road.

By then I was going for gold. It was 140 kilometres to Ravenna and only another 60 kilometres to Cesena. 'Why don't we take in Ravenna, too?' I called out. 'It's right on the way to Cesena.'

So we stopped in Ravenna to gawp, wonderstruck, at the mosaics.

We swept into the *parcheggio* of the Hotel Casali, in Cesena's Via Benedetto Croce, at precisely five minutes to six. I reckoned I still had time to change. I was an *Onorevole*, after all. And I didn't want to 'diss' the Mayor of Cesena by looking too casual.

While the kids stayed put, I dashed round to the back of the car to whip off my shirt and shorts. I was still in my underpants when I heard excited cries coming from the hotel, on the far side of the parking lot. Moments later, I found myself surrounded by half a dozen smartly dressed Italians. One of them wore a mayoral chain of office.

'*Finalmente! Eccolo-qui!*' the mayor exclaimed.

I thought I detected a note of irritation in his voice. Did he think I was late? I jolly well wasn't. I was right on the dot!

Well, it turned out that, by the Mayor of Cesena's reckoning, I really was late. I had noted 6 p.m. as the time of the RV because I thought I had clearly said '*a la sei*'. Six o'clock. But the mayor and his team had been waiting two hours because they thought I had said '*a la seidici*'. Sixteen hundred hours, or *four o'clock*!

'Quick,' the mayor cried, when we had sorted out the confusion. '*Andiamo molto presto, per favore.*'

It seemed that even though we would not have time that evening to see the famous *centurationi*, it would not be too late for me to deliver my speech!

Speech? What speech? Nobody had told me about a speech.

We screeched out of the car park onto the highway, following the mayoral cavalcade, with blue lights flashing.

The mayor had reserved seats for all of us in the grandstand of the Cesena racecourse. He bounced up to the podium to seize the mike.

'*Signore e signori*,' his voice echoed over the stand. 'I am delighted to welcome to Cesena tonight Mr Stanley Johnson, the Vice President of the European Parliament. Senor Johnson, *Onorevole Johnson*, we are honoured to have you! Senor Johnson is here to help us save Cesena's famous Roman *centuriationi*!'

There was a roar of applause from the crowd as the mayor handed me the mike.

In my view, speaking Italian is basically a piece of cake. *Un pezzo di torta.* You just need a bit of self-confidence. It helps, of course, if you have a bit of Latin. As a matter of fact, I have a lot of Latin. Several decades' worth.

Still, it was a strange experience. I could hear my voice booming about the ground as I spoke. The floodlights came on.

I began by saying what an honour it was to be in Cesena and that I was sorry to be a bit late. My fault entirely. I went on to say that the mission of the European Community was not just to shovel money at French or even Italian farmers. It also had a mission to save the environment and culture.

'*La politica ambientale e molto importante,*' I cried. '*Anche la preservatione degli bene culturale.*'

When it came to the matter of most immediate concern, the preservation of the Roman legionnaires' hard-won homesteads, I could not have been clearer.

'*Questa canale Padana –* the Po Canal *– no e una problema locale di Cesena; no e una problema regionale di Emilio-Romagna; no e una problema nationale – di Italia. No e solamente una problema europea!*'

After all these '*no e*'s, I had to deliver a punchline and I did. '*La preservatione degli centuriationi Romani di Cesena e una problema INTERNATIONALE! GLOBALE!*'

There was another roar of applause from the crowd. The starter waved his flag, the horses bounded from the gates and I subsided gratefully into my seat. It had been a long day.

It turned out to be a profitable day as well. I won 188,000 lire on the tote, having to my amazement correctly bet on the results of three of the five races. That may sound like a lot of money. Actually, at 3,000 lire to the pound, the then current exchange rate, it was about £60.

Just enough, I thought, as I pocketed my winnings, to buy a decent present for Leonard and Rosalind.

I should explain that Leonard Ingrams was Boris's godfather and that Rosalind, his wife, was a contemporary of my former wife, Charlotte, at Lady Margaret Hall, Oxford. The Ingrams owned a magical villa called Rufena, not far from Gaiole in Chianti. John Mortimer, who often hired Rufena from them for the summer, used it as a setting for his novel *Summer's Lease*.

A few weeks earlier I had telephoned Rosalind in Italy and had asked whether we might 'drop in', given that we were going to be in her neck of the woods.

I realise that I was using the expression 'drop in' rather loosely. We were, after all, a party of six (me plus five) and we planned to stay three nights before catching the ferry from Ancona, on Italy's Adriatic coast, to Patras.

Weighing things up as we headed for Tuscany after our eventful time in Cesena, I decided that our 'house gift' should indeed be a generous one.

So we stopped at a 'super-mercato' on the autostrada en route to the Ingrams' Tuscan villa, where I spent all the money I had won at the races the previous evening on a huge wheel of Parmesan. It was so heavy I could barely lift it.

To my sorrow, there was no sign of that splendid cheese at dinner that first night, nor at lunch the next day. Not a hunk. Not a sliver. Certainly not the great wheel that I had seen Rosalind stow in the fridge the evening we arrived at Rufena. I had high hopes, however, that the cheese would make an appearance by the time we sat down for the second dinner, taken as always on the Ingrams' terrace in the long Tuscan evening, with the distant Castello de Brolio providing a wondrous backdrop. No such luck. There were plenty of other cheeses, but no Parmesan. It was clear to me that Rosalind, the most generous of hostesses, had forgotten all about it.

That night, when all the Ingrams and the Johnsons had gone to bed, I snuck into Rufena's huge rustic kitchen and padded across the old stone floor, towards the fridge.

I opened the fridge door. There was the giant cheese, utterly virgin, still taking up the whole of the top shelf.

It wouldn't hurt, I said to myself, to cut a bit off. I didn't want to lift the whole cheese out of the fridge since I didn't want to be caught *in flagrante*, as it were. So I decided to tackle the cheese without trying to lift it from the shelf. If I heard anyone coming I could quickly shut the fridge door and shuffle off into the night.

I found a knife, opened the fridge door and tried to hack off a modestly sized piece of cheese. Disaster! Parmesan is tough stuff. It's not like Dolcelatte or Gorgonzola. Even when it is fresh and tender, as 'my cheese' undoubtedly was, it still has a certain resilience.

I pressed harder, but to no avail. I was coming at it from a tricky angle and simply couldn't get the leverage I needed. I pressed even harder. Suddenly there was a tremendous noise in the kitchen. The fridge's top shelf had collapsed. The cheese had fallen through onto the second shelf and that in turn had collapsed onto the bottom shelf.

I shut the fridge door quickly, returned the knife to its drawer and scarpered back to bed, mission totally unaccomplished.

I was there next morning when Rosalind came into the kitchen and opened the fridge.

'Good heavens!' she exclaimed. 'All the shelves seem to have collapsed! It must have been the cheese. We had better have some for breakfast.'

I think Leonard suspected something. He was a brilliant classicist and a one-time fellow of Corpus Christi, Oxford.

'*Timeo Danaos,*' he muttered, '*et dona ferentes.*'

Replete, finally, with Parmesan and prosciutto, we headed on to Ancona.

I feel everlastingly grateful to Aristomenes Karageorgis, owner of the Karageorgis Shipping Line that *inter alia* operated the Ancona to Patras car ferry. He 'comped' us luxury cabins on board his splendid streamlined vessel as it made the overnight crossing of the Adriatic from Ancona on Italy's Adriatic coast to Patras, the principal harbour of the western Peloponnese. I have had a soft spot for Greek ship owners ever since.

In my youth, I have slept on deck under the stars on these Aegean ferries. This time, thanks to Mr Karageorgis's generosity, we had cabins aplenty and felt fighting fit when we landed at Patras. So much so that we headed off at once to Olympia, 130 kilometres to the east, where we spent a happy day among the ruins, returning to Patras in time to catch a late afternoon ferry to Corfu.

The White House, Kalami, on the east coast of Corfu, where we were to spend the next two weeks, was once owned or at least occupied by Gerald Durrell. As portrayed in the Corfu Villas brochure, it looks utterly superb: a large, square house, set right on the sea at the edge of a most enchanting bay. What I hadn't realised, when I signed on the dotted line, was that only the upper floor was available for holiday lets, the ground floor being taken over by a taverna.

We barely had time to settle in before I had to drive back from Kalami to Corfu airport to meet Jenny and my mother.

'How was your journey?' I asked.

'Fine,' Jenny replied. 'How was yours?'

I told her about the cheese.

'Did you see Venice?' she asked.

'Sort of.'

Even though, being by now a party of five children (ages ranging from Boris's seventeen to my youngest son, Jo's, eight and a half years) and three adults, we were fairly cramped on the top floor of the White House, Kalami, my mother thought it was all wonderful. That was her default position. Jenny was less convinced. Since we had been married only a few months and this was the first summer holiday *en famille*, she certainly had a lot to get used to.

But that was true for the children, too. If Jenny had acquired four stepchildren, they had acquired a stepmother. Was everything for the best in the best of all possible worlds? Well, maybe not absolutely totally, but pretty darn close. That was my view and I was sticking to it.

To celebrate my forty-first birthday, I hired a small fishing dinghy with an outboard motor for an afternoon's excursion.

My plan had been to chug up the coast towards the north-eastern tip of the island, somewhere around Agios Stefanos, then anchor in some idyllic cove for a swim and some 'birthday' drinks, which we had packed in a coolbox.

At first, all went to plan. We puttered north, keeping Albania on the right and Corfu on the left.

Unfortunately, the wind grew stronger by the minute.

The children finally put their life jackets on. Since there weren't enough life jackets to go round, my mother dramatically took hers off.

She thrust it at Camille.

'Here, darling,' she said. 'You take it. I don't need it. I've had a long life.'

My mother was a stickler for etiquette. If you've invited a friend on your boat, and you put that friend's life in danger, then that friend has to be saved first.

I was still at the helm. Time to make for home, I thought. Forget about that idyllic cove.

Unfortunately, just about then, the outboard motor fell off into the sea. Luckily, it didn't go to the bottom. It was attached to the boat by a rope. Trying not to fall in myself, I pulled the engine back up.

I yanked on the starting cord more than a dozen times to no avail. Water, I thought, must have got into the carburettor, if outboard motors had carburettors.

Frankly, I had absolutely no idea what to do. I gave another despairing tug on the lanyard (is that the right word?) and, amazingly, the motor fired and caught.

That wasn't the last of our misadventures on that Corfu holiday. One morning, Boris went windsurfing in the bay and headed straight for Albania. When we saw him, far out to sea, fall off the windsurfer and fail to restart, I said to Jenny, 'I'd better get out there.'

My swimming technique is slow but serviceable. 'Crawl' is *le mot juste*. It took me about twenty minutes to reach Boris.

I think Boris was pleased to see me when I finally caught up with him. The strait between Corfu and Albania is only about 2 miles wide at that point. If he had gone much further, he might have found himself in a Maoist prison.

'Leave it to me,' I panted.

While Boris swam back, I heaved the sail up in the approved fashion. Amazingly, I kept my balance. The windsurfer took off in a hurry, heading, of course, even closer to the Albanian coastline.

Half an hour later, I had given up all attempts to sail the windsurfer. Instead, I lay on the board face down, having jettisoned the sail, using my hands to try to paddle it back to Kalami.

I wasn't making much progress. In fact, I was wondering whether I might not have to swim back myself, when I heard a shout.

'I say, aren't you our Euro MP? Freddy, come over here and take a look. That's Stanley Johnson, isn't it?'

I'm not making this up. I looked up to see a group of holiday-makers, clearly English, gazing down at me from the taffrail of a largish pleasure boat. I recognised one of them at least.

'Oh my God!' What on earth was Freddy Emery Wallis, the Conservative leader of Portsmouth City Council, doing on that boat? Freddy was a key member of my Euro Constituency Council.

'Hello, Freddy!' I waved cheerfully, trying to give the impression that this was the way I normally operated a windsurfer, viz. prone and paddling.

Freddy had a gin and tonic in his hand.

'Can we get you a drink?' he shouted.

In the end, they picked up the windsurfer's sail, which was still floating in the water where I had discarded it. Then they threw me a line and towed me to shore. Phew!

Chapter Four

The Seal Campaign

My second daughter, and Jenny's first, Julia Lois Johnson, was born on 9 January 1982, in the Lindo Wing of St Mary's, Paddington. Nowadays mothers seem to leave hospital almost as soon as they have given birth. I am glad to say that at the beginning of the '80s they were allowed a little 'downtime'. Julia and Jenny didn't come back to 30 Maida Avenue, a stone's throw from St Mary's, until a decent interval had elapsed.

There was no question, of course, of 'paternity' leave. We had an au pair organised and, anyway, I was at that moment deeply involved in the Seal campaign.

If I had to point out the ten things that have most changed the course of my life, I would say that seals and, specifically, the great herds of harp and hooded seals that each spring migrate from the Arctic to Canadian waters to give birth to their young on the ice floes in the Gulf of St Lawrence and off the coast of Newfoundland, would certainly feature on that list – and quite high on it at that.

For me, at least, so much has flowed from the seal campaign that I initiated in the European Parliament in 1980, soon after being elected as an MEP, that it is hard to imagine my own personal direction of travel without it.

I stumbled into the seal campaign almost by accident. I was reading the *Daily Telegraph* one day in the plane coming back from

Strasbourg when I came across a story about the annual Canadian seal hunt. Of course, I knew about the hunt. Everyone did. Brigitte Bardot was trying to stop it. So were Greenpeace, the RSPCA and a host of other environmental and animal welfare organisations. More than 200,000 harp and hooded seals in Canadian waters, under quotas issued by the Canadian authorities, were slaughtered each year even though these animals were in no sense the exclusive property of Canada. On the contrary, they undertook an annual vast migration, arriving in Canadian waters only to take advantage of the ice floes as a place to give birth to their young.

What I didn't know, until I read the article, was that around 80 per cent of the skins resulting from the Canadian seal hunt were actually sold in, or through, the European Community.

In those days, the European Parliament was a fairly feeble body. Even though the Parliament would in due course acquire rights of 'co-decision' with the Council, the crucial right of initiative lay, as it still does, with the European Commission.

I had already spent six years with the European Commission. I knew how jealously that institution guarded its 'right of initiative'. Could the Parliament, I wondered, somehow force the Commission to act, even when it didn't want to?

The seal campaign, it seemed to me, was a wonderful test case, quite apart from being a 'good thing' in its own right. Was more blood to be spilled on the ice year after year, with the quotas of slaughtered animals being raised ever higher from one season to the next?

In April 1980, with the support of other MEPs, I had tabled a motion for a resolution calling for 'measures designed to regulate international trade in seal products and to prohibit entry into the Community of: (a) any products coming from seals which had not been humanely killed, and (b) any products coming from seal species whose stocks are recognised as being imperilled'.

Because the Canadian seal hunt focused especially on young harp seals (whitecoats) as well as young hooded seals, my resolution went on to call on the Commission to make 'proposals for a total ban on imports into the Community of products from whitecoat or blueback (hooded) seals and on all intra-Community trade in such products'.

Finally, my resolution called for 'negotiations with other countries involved in the trade in such products, and in particular with Norway and Canada, with a view to achieving international action'.

I knew perfectly well, when I put the motion down, that there was absolutely no obligation on the Commission to come forward with any proposals even if the Parliament adopted the resolution in precisely the form I had put forward. MEPs were always drafting resolutions. It was a way of letting off steam. We drafted resolutions on all kinds of subjects: Nicaragua, Afghanistan, washing powder, maternity leave – there would always be some individual or some group in the Parliament with strong views on a particular subject, ready to call on the Commission to 'take action'.

Ninety-nine times out of a hundred, the Commission politely, and sometimes not so politely, looked the other way.

My seals resolution fared rather differently.

It was referred to the Environment Committee, chaired by a Scottish Labour MEP, Ken Collins. In due course a rapporteur, a Dutch Christian Democrat called Johanna Maij-Weggen, was appointed. All this was perfectly normal. The general expectation – including, I have to say, my own prediction – was that the Environment Committee would eventually come out with a report, the matter would be referred to a plenary session of Parliament, a vote would be taken, the responsible commissioner would stand up and rattle off a prepared statement without committing the Commission to any action. And that would be the end of the matter.

It didn't turn out that way at all. Even if the Parliament didn't take itself seriously, in terms of expecting the Commission to act on its resolutions, there were apparently others who did.

One of those who did was a Welshman turned Canadian called Brian Davies. Davies had devoted much of his life to trying to stop the Canadian seal hunt. In 1969, he had founded an organisation – the International Fund for Animal Welfare (IFAW) – dedicated to that end. He had been arrested and imprisoned by the Canadian authorities. But the objective of ending the seal hunt seemed as elusive as ever.

I don't think Davies knew much about the European Parliament or indeed about the European Community as a whole. He had been forced by the Canadian authorities to move IFAW's headquarters from Canada to Cape Cod in the United States, but that move didn't bring him any nearer to his goal.

When Davies – far off in Cape Cod – heard that the European Parliament was considering my resolution, he was over the moon. As he saw it, if Europe banned the import of sealskins, the hunt would die, whatever action the Canadian authorities might take. Without the European market, it would simply be economically unsustainable.

Davies, naively, believed that the European Parliament was a real Parliament in the sense that it had 'teeth' (which, as I have explained, it patently didn't – at that time at least). IFAW launched an enormous publicity campaign. MEPs were urged by their constituents to back a seal import ban. Each MEP received hundreds, sometimes thousands, of letters. IFAW and other NGOs organised enormous petitions in support of the ban. In those days, there were no electronic sign-ins. Lorries trundled through the night to the headquarters of the European Parliament in Strasbourg, bearing boxes containing 2.5 million signed petitions. They would be stacked in the Parliament's grand atrium in anticipation of the Parliament's upcoming vote on the Maij-Weggen report and resolution.

I do not pretend that all my fellow MEPs were thrilled to be the recipients of so much unsolicited correspondence. Some of them were plainly annoyed. They were, at a trivial level, irritated by having to answer hundreds of letters. More seriously, some of them didn't like upsetting the Canadians. One day, a large piece of paper was pinned to the noticeboard by one of the entrances to the chamber. It depicted yours truly in the guise of a seal, with a huge message scrawled with a magic marker: 'I'M STANLEY. CLUB ME!'

The vast majority of MEPs, however, appeared to welcome the recognition they were suddenly receiving. If so many people, from all walks of life, had decided that the European Parliament might be able to do something about the seal hunt, maybe the Parliament wasn't just a toothless talking shop after all.

The Canadian authorities, belatedly, sensed that something was in the wind. They turned up in force one day in Brussels when the Parliament's Environment Committee was discussing Mrs Maij-Weggen's draft report and was on the point of approving a call to action. The Canadian Fisheries Department was represented, as well as the provincial authorities. A delegation of Inuits had been brought along to add weight.

I shall never forget the look of annoyance, even horror, on the faces of those Canadians when they saw Brian Davies sitting next to me in the meeting room. One of them raised a hand.

'Mr Chairman,' the leader of the Canadian delegation protested, 'I would like to know what Mr Davies is doing in the room at this time. I thought the Committee intended to have an objective discussion of this question.'

I intervened quickly. 'Mr Davies is my technical adviser.'

Once the Parliament's Environment Committee had voted in favour of Maij-Weggen's report, it only remained for the matter to go before the plenary. The plenary vote was scheduled for 10 March 1982, at a time when, on the other side of the Atlantic, the seal hunt would be in full swing.

I flew to Boston on Friday 26 February, then on via Halifax, Nova Scotia, to Prince Edward Island in the heart of the St Lawrence Basin. Deep snow lay in the streets and around the entrance to the Kirkwood Motel, Charlottetown, where we were staying. The IFAW team, and other seal-hunt activists, were anxious to get going. I wasn't exactly clear what the game plan was. Were they going to set down on the ice to try to intervene between the sealers and the seals? In that case, under the regulations in force, they risked arrest. Were they just going to observe as best they could within the rules? If so, how close could we get and what would we see?

Tension mounted over the weekend as the weather closed in and we were confined to quarters in the motel. But on Monday 1 March 1982, the weather cleared. IFAW's small fixed-wing plane was cleared for take-off.

Here are my notes, scribbled in my notebook on the plane, from that first flight out from PEI towards the Magdalen Islands, where we hoped to have a first view of the seal herds.

9.39 a.m. Take-off with Bob Walsh (IFAW's pilot) at the controls.

10.50 a.m. Flying north west. Still no sign of seals. Headed 310 degrees for 60 miles but no real sea ice.

11.38 a.m. We found the seals, hundreds, thousands of them on the ice. Some whelping. Amazing sight. Red splodges on the ice indicate they are pupping. If we found them, others will too. Did some tight

360-degree turns. Quota for the seal hunt in Gulf this year is 56,000. Imagine 56,000 deaths.

You can't land on the ice with a fixed-wing plane. The IFAW helicopter was out of action as a result of the heavy clubbing it had received from irate locals with their hakapiks. But the Canadian Fisheries Ministry kindly laid on a helicopter for me. They didn't have to, but they did. Full marks for that. Here, again, are my notes:

2 March 1982.
3.31 p.m. Flying off looking for the seals.

Round about 4.20 p.m. we at last found the herd of seals and set down on the ice. Seals all round, large grey and black adults, some newly whelped with pups beside them on the rafted ice. Baby seals mewing as we approach, scuttling after their mothers, mothers scrambling towards the safety of the waters, honking angrily. Blood on the ice where they have whelped.

In the helicopter on the way back, Brian Tobin who is Romeo Le Blanc's PPS (Le Blanc is Fisheries and Oceans Minister) tries to talk me into saying I have changed my mind. He doesn't.

The chartered ministry plane is standing by with engines running – it is a question of trying to make Halifax in time for the 6.35 p.m. flight to Montreal and a connecting flight to London.

I would like to be able to say that I still had snow on my boots when the overnight plane from Canada touched down at Heathrow next morning. But, of course, the snow and ice from the 'Maggies' had long since melted.

I made my way by taxi to the Hotel Astoria, in Aldwych, central London. Ian MacPhail, IFAW's UK representative, met me in the lobby and presented me with a large white furry toy baby seal. He then ushered me into an ornate 'salon' for a press conference.

MacPhail had a long history as a 'campaigning conservationist'. He had been involved, at the beginning of the '60s, in the establishment of the World Wildlife Fund (WWF), now the World Wide Fund for Nature. For the last several years he had been working with IFAW. He knew how to rally the troops.

A press statement, which Ian had drafted, was to be found on every gilt chair. There were copies on the dais as well.

As McPhail introduced me, I glanced at the headline: THE HUNT WITHOUT PITY MAY BECOME THE HUNT WITHOUT PROFIT. EURO MPs TO VOTE ON CANADIAN SEAL IMPORT BAN.

'Great stuff, Ian!' I said, as I took the floor to address the waiting journalists, still clutching that large white furry baby seal.

What happened in London that day was paralleled, to a greater or lesser extent, by similar actions in other countries of the European Community. The letter-writing campaign intensified and it was accompanied by full-page advertisements in the press. In the UK, IFAW, Greenpeace, Friends of the Earth, the RSPCA and several other NGOs formed a Seal Protection Group to coordinate action. National MPs were targeted as well as Euro MPs.

The European Parliament debated the Maij-Weggen report on 11 March 1982, exactly a week after that press conference in the Hotel Astoria.

Quite often, when MEPs rise to their feet to speak in the European Parliament, they find the place is half empty. That evening the Chamber was at least three-quarters full.

Mrs Veil, the first president of the new 'directly elected' European Parliament, had been succeeded at the beginning of 1982 by Piet Dankert, a Dutch Socialist MEP.

'Mr President,' I began, 'I returned last Thursday from Canada, more precisely from the Magdalen Islands in the Gulf of St Lawrence. I count myself privileged to have been able to witness on the ice floes the arrival of thousands of harp seals, which, together with the seals in the front ice off the coast of Newfoundland, make up the north-west Atlantic herd.

'These seals have travelled thousands of miles from the Arctic to reach their breeding grounds. While I was there, the pupping had begun and the females were congregating on the whelping patches with their white-coated pups beside them. I have travelled in many different parts of the world, but I would say that the arrival and migration of the harp seal to its breeding grounds off the Canadian coast is a natural spectacle whose magnificence rivals that of the movement of vast herds of wildebeest across the plains of the Serengeti in Africa...'

There were many speeches that night. Most of those who intervened supported the idea of a seal import ban.

A roll-call vote was held at the end of the debate. One hundred and ninety MEPs voted: for, 160; against, 10; abstentions, 20.

Frankly, this was an overwhelming victory, owing much not only to the MEPs who had backed the cause but also to tens of thousands of supporters and activists throughout the European Community.

The Commission, determined not to upset the Canadians, predictably refused to accede to the Parliament's request to propose a seal import ban. But we did not give up the fight. Over the coming months, the Commission faced a barrage of Parliamentary Questions, as MEPs queried the Commission's lack of action.

On 16 September 1982, for example, the European Parliament passed a motion 'noting that over 300 Members of the House of Commons in the United Kingdom have signed Early Day Motions calling for action in response to the European Parliament's resolution' and that in the United States 'no less than 51 Senators and 105 Congressmen have sent telegrams to the President of the Commission and the President of the Council urging them to ensure "swift and complete implementation of all points of the Parliament's resolution"'.

To help ensure that US senators and congressmen signed those telegrams, I had made a flying visit the previous week to Washington to attend a reception on Capitol Hill. I am not sure that many legislators actually turned out that night, but there were plenty of staffers who obviously did what was necessary to ensure that their bosses signed on the dotted line.

The European Parliament in its 16 September 1982 resolution went on to 'deplore' the Commission for its 'continued failure to bring forward the draft regulations requested by Parliament' and called upon it to do so 'before the October session'.

Karl-Heinz Narjes, a former German U-boat commander who was then serving as the EC's Environment Commissioner, was forced to make several appearances. At first, he blustered and prevaricated. He suggested that the Commission might possibly propose a 'labelling' scheme. Consumers could, for example, be informed in some way as to how the animal, whose fur they were keen to purchase, had met its death.

I remember my good friend the Dutch Socialist MEP Hemmo Muntingh (who would later serve as the rapporteur when the Commission finally gave up the fight and agreed to propose a ban) rising to his feet and asking, with icy scorn in his voice: 'Is the Commissioner proposing that sealskin items imported into the European Community should be labelled with the phrase "clubbed to death"?' In the end, the Commission surrendered to overwhelming pressure. I learned on the grapevine that there were those inside the Commission who feared that the 'seal issue' might develop into a full-blown inter-institutional row, with the Parliament actually censuring the Commission and even calling for its resignation *en bloc*.

On 20 October 1982, the Commission came forward with a proposal for a Council regulation 'concerning the importation into member states of skins of certain seal pups and products derived therefrom'.

The Commission proposed a two-year ban on seal imports into the European Community, to run from 1983 to 1985.

Of course, I – as well as many others – were disappointed that the Commission had not proposed a permanent ban, but just getting the Commission to make an official proposal for a ban, even a short-term ban, draft onto the table of the Council could be seen as an enormous achievement.

What counted now was to keep up the pressure.

Towards the end of November, I was invited onto the BBC's *A Week in Politics* programme. The presenter, Professor Anthony King, asked me to talk about my work as an MEP.

I kept it brief. Five minutes max.

When I finished, Professor King looked a bit bemused.

'Mr Johnson, I know that the survival of seals is extremely interesting and important and you want a permanent ban on the import of sealskins. But are you interested in anything else besides seals? Aren't there other issues of concern?'

'Of course there are,' I replied truculently (I still have the transcript the BBC sent me later). 'I care about whales and dolphins as well!'

A few weeks later, the BBC *Panorama* team came to Strasbourg to film the Parliament in session. They decided to attend, among other things, a ceremony at which the RSPCA presented to Johanna Maij-Weggen and myself the RSPCA's Richard Martin Award for Outstanding Services to Animal Welfare.

The chairman of the RSPCA Council, Mr Anelay Hart, had travelled to Strasbourg in person to make the presentation, which consisted of two beautifully carved statuettes of a harp seal and pup.

The action now shifted to the member states. The Commission had in the end made its proposal. The Parliament had approved that proposal. The Council now had to decide.

The EC's Environment Council, which would be handling the Commission's proposal for a sealskin import ban, was made up of environment ministers from the then twelve EU member states.

Each and every one of those ministers had to be persuaded to support the ban. Some countries, such as Denmark, Germany and the United Kingdom, were heavily involved in the fur trade.

The UK was in an especially difficult position. Not only was London an important trade centre, but Canada was also a fellow member of the British Commonwealth and the UK government's default position was not to give offence to a loyal ally.

There was another factor to be taken into consideration, at least as far as the UK was concerned. That was the question of *vires*.

Was this, officials asked, truly an 'environmental' issue? Was it not more of an 'animal welfare' issue? In that case, might it not be *ultra vires*, i.e. falling outside the legal competence of the European Community?

If the legal basis in the Treaty of Rome for environmental action was shaky, the case for EC animal welfare measures was surely even flimsier.

Giles Shaw, the Minister of State in Britain's Department of the Environment, was especially obstructive.

The environment ministers met two or three times before the end of 1982 on the fifteenth floor of the EC Council headquarters, the Charlemagne building on the Rue de la Loi. Though, as a Commission official, I was used to attending meetings of the environment ministers, as an MEP I had no such privileges.

That was all to the good. I was far more useful, it seemed to me, playing my part among the crowd of bystanders who crowded around the entrance to the Council building, carrying banners and chanting 'Save the Seals!' as the ministers arrived in their limousines and hurried up the steps.

Demonstrations matter. They are a manifestation of public opinion. I think the ministers welcomed our presence. Some of them stopped to have their photo taken among the crowd of waving placards.

I am not sure whether the ministers, when they finally got down to business on the fifteenth floor, could still hear our distant chanting. There was a glorious moment, so I was told later, when seal-shaped helium-filled balloons, procured by Greenpeace, were released on long strings around the Charlemagne building. The balloons apparently bumped against the glass windows of the Council chamber. Each balloon bore the message: 'Ministers, Please Save Us!'

In the end, Michael Heseltine, the Secretary of State for the Environment, intervened personally to overrule Giles Shaw, his junior minister, so as to ensure UK support for the two-year seal import ban, which the Council finally agreed on 28 February 1983. This was a tremendous victory. We held a rally in Trafalgar Square a few days later. I stood on the podium with Spike Milligan and Joanna Lumley, both warm supporters of the seal campaign.

The crucial vote in the Environment Council of 28 February 1983 came only months before the UK general election of 9 June 1983.

In the run-up to polling day, Ian MacPhail, who served as the coordinator of the Seal Protection Group, received a letter from the Conservative candidate for the Finchley constituency. MacPhail had written to all of the candidates asking for their views on the future of the temporary ban the Council had just adopted.

The letter was dated 31 May 1983 and read as follows:

Dear Sir,

Thank you for your letter of the 25th May on behalf of the Seal Protection Group (UK).

If returned to power on 9th June, I will support the implementation and continuation of the EEC-wide ban on the import of products coming from young harp and hooded seals which was agreed by EEC environment ministers on 28th February 1983.

Yours faithfully,

Margaret Thatcher

I congratulated MacPhail on a tremendous coup. For the cost of a first-class stamp he had elicited a clear commitment from Mrs Thatcher, who would be re-elected Prime Minister in June 1983 with a massive post-Falklands majority, not only to endorse the ban just agreed by the EC's Environment Council, but to support its 'implementation and continuation'.

The effect of the ban was immediate and dramatic. That year, 1983, the harp seal catch dropped to fewer than 60,000 animals. By 1985, it was down to fewer than 20,000.

In March 1985 (after I had left Parliament to return to the Commission), the Parliament debated a report by Hemmo Muntingh on the implementation of the seal ban, due to end that month, and requested the Commission to come forward with an indefinite extension.

There were, once again, some hesitations on the part of the UK.

Back in Brussels as adviser to the director general of the Commission's Environment Directorate-General, I found myself arguing the case for an extension.

The UK representative in the working group demurred.

'My government is not convinced,' he argued.

I immediately held up my hand. 'Might I ask, through you, Mr Chairman, whether the distinguished representative of the United Kingdom is aware of the position of the UK's Prime Minister on this issue? I refer in particular to her letter of 29 May 1983, to one Mr Ian MacPhail of the UK Seal Protection Group.'

It was fun to see the UK delegate scrabbling among his papers. A look of alarm crossed his face. He clearly hadn't read the letter, which was not surprising, since it had been sent by Mrs Thatcher as a parliamentary candidate in a forthcoming general election and not in her capacity as prime minister.

I put the poor man out of his misery, fossicking dramatically among my papers and then reading out Mrs Thatcher's unambiguous message, which was immediately copied and circulated among the delegates.

The fact that Mrs Thatcher's address was shown at the top of the letter not as 10 Downing Street but as the Finchley Constituency Office, 212 Ballards Lane, Finchley, London N3 2LX did not appear to deter other members of the Council Environment Working Group from taking it very seriously.

In the event, the Council agreed in September 1985 not on an indefinite extension of the seal ban, as we had hoped, but on a four-year extension (1985–89). It wasn't till May 1989, at the EU Environment Council's meeting in Luxembourg, that the ban was prolonged indefinitely, becoming in effect a permanent ban.

That particular meeting, as I shall explain later, was indeed memorable, and not just because of the seals.

In recognition of our efforts on behalf of the seals and those who campaigned to end the seal hunt, Mrs Maij-Weggen and I were also honoured to receive, at a ceremony in Luxembourg, certificates of appreciation from the World Society for the Protection of Animals (WSPA).

And I was especially pleased to be presented with the Greenpeace Award for Outstanding Services to the Environment. Peter Melchett, then director of Greenpeace, welcomed me to Greenpeace's Islington office, and the broadcaster Trevor Philpott handed me a large, framed pen-and-ink drawing of Planet Earth bobbing on a troubled ocean, supported by a lifebelt on which the word 'Greenpeace' is inscribed.

William Waldegrave, then Minister for the Environment, sent a delightful telegram of congratulations to the Greenpeace offices, regretting that he was unable to attend in person but saying he couldn't think of a worthier recipient.

It was good to know that there were no hard feelings at the UK's Department of the Environment.

In a year-end review of developments in the European Community, *The Economist* reported that the 'seal issue' showed that the Parliament did, after all, count for something.

Pride, of course, comes before a fall. Given Brigitte Bardot's own involvement in the great seal campaign from very early days, and given our common interest in the successful outcome, I thought it might be fun to meet her, so I sent a message to her 'chief of staff' in Paris, suggesting that BB and I might perhaps find a moment to celebrate an outstanding victory. *Un petit pot, peut-être?*

In due course, I received a less than enthusiastic response.

'*Madame Bardot ne voit pas la nécessité.*' Mrs Bardot doesn't see any need for a meeting.

Chapter Five

The Crocodile Club

With hindsight, the most significant figure to be elected to the European Parliament in 1979 was undoubtedly Altiero Spinelli, the former Italian Communist who, at the ripe old age of seventy-two, arrived in Strasbourg to sit as a 'non-aligned' member.

It was entirely thanks to Spinelli that I became a founder member of the Crocodile Club.

At the beginning of the July 1980 plenary session, I emptied my pigeonhole on arrival at the Parliament and carried the mail to my office. There were the usual reams of paper about the forthcoming debates and briefings from our highly efficient secretariat at the European Democratic Group (EDG). Among all the bumf, I found a somewhat different communication.

'Altiero Spinelli invites you to join him for dinner on Tuesday 8 July 1980 at the Restaurant Au Crocodile at 8 p.m. *Tenue: informelle.*'

I assumed that I was not the only MEP to receive this communication. It seemed likely that Spinelli's invitation had been distributed to most, if not all, MEPs. Still, I was intrigued.

It wasn't just the venue that attracted me.

Au Crocodile was probably the most famous restaurant in Strasbourg at the time, having been accorded two stars in the Michelin guide. (It owed its name to the full-sized stuffed Nile crocodile brought back by one of Napoleon's generals from Egypt and displayed in the foyer.) Of course, I was keen to try its culinary delights. But there was more to it than that. What was Spinelli up to?

There were nine MEPs altogether in the Crocodile restaurant that evening, including Spinelli himself. For the record, the other eight were Hans Lücker, Karl von Wogau, Paola Gaiotti de Biase, Bruno Visentini, Silvio Leonardi, Richard Balfe, Brian Key and myself.

Over a four-course meal, Spinelli told us about his own plan for improving on Jean Monnet's work and 'rebuilding the architecture of Europe'.

Christopher Booker and Richard North in their well-researched and fascinating book *The Great Deception*, published in 2003, describe me as the 'lone Conservative' member of the Crocodile Club. That seems to me to be a fair description, given that Richard Balfe, like Brian Key, was then a Labour MEP. (In 2002, he subsequently defected to the Conservatives and, indeed, was elevated to the House of Lords as a Conservative peer in August 2013.)

Sitting next to Spinelli at the table was Pier-Virgilio Dastoli, Spinelli's chief of staff and the man who would help keep Spinelli's ideas alive long after the man himself had passed on. At the time of writing, Dastoli is living in Rome and, *inter alia*, serves as the acting president of the Italian European Movement.

Collectively, those who attended Spinelli's dinner at the Crocodile are considered 'founder members' of the club.

That night, in a private upstairs dining room, Spinelli outlined his thinking. He believed that there should be a new treaty of the European Union, one that set out more clearly the objectives and the powers of the European institutions. He also believed that the Parliament itself, rather than the European Commission, should prepare the draft of such a new treaty and that in due course that new treaty should be endorsed by the member states of the Community.

Spinelli's plan to reform the Treaty of Rome did not go unopposed. My own political group, the European Democratic Group, which consisted of the sixty-one British Conservatives in alliance with two Danish Conservatives (a 'slice of Danish blue'), was less than enthusiastic, as can be deduced perhaps from the fact that – as noted above – I was the only Conservative MEP to accept that initial invitation to dinner at Au Crocodile.

Spinelli was naturally worried about the EDG's apparent lack of enthusiasm for his ideas. Given the arithmetic of the Parliament, EDG support was vital. The EDG was the third largest group in the Parliament, certainly too large to be ignored. A vote by the Parliament as a whole would be needed to set up a new committee. If the EDG with its sixty-three members voted against it, or even if we abstained, Spinelli's grand project might be stillborn.

Before that crucial vote, Spinelli buttonholed me in one of the Parliament's long corridors. Next time the political groups were meeting in Brussels, please could I arrange a lunch between him and James Scott-Hopkins, the EDG's leader?

Two weeks later, four of us, Spinelli, Scott-Hopkins, Dastoli and myself, met in a restaurant in the Rue Franklin, a stone's throw from the Berlaymont.

It was a friendly lunch. I think Scott-Hopkins, though politically they were poles apart, had considerable respect for Spinelli. He may have taken the view that a man who had served ten years in a Fascist jail and a further six in confinement at the very least deserved a hearing.

And he proved as good as his word. I don't think Scott-Hopkins was entirely persuaded of the merits of Spinelli's proposal to set up an 'institutional' committee to draft a new treaty, but he certainly didn't oppose it outright.

The formal proposal to establish an Institutional Committee came before a plenary session of the Parliament on 9 July 1981, precisely one year after the dinner in the Au Crocodile restaurant.

Given my own involvement with the Spinelli project, I took the floor in the course of the debate.

'Madame President,' I began, 'I want to welcome the resolution by Mr Abens and others on the institutional question. I want to congratulate Mr Spinelli for the work he has put in, and I want to do that on behalf of the European Democratic Group.

'The European Democratic Group welcomes this initiative,' I continued, 'and a few moments from now, we shall be supporting it with our votes. We think it is timely.'

I argued that that one of the reason we needed a new treaty was because the old treaties were no longer fit for purpose.

'The treaties', I continued, 'were conceived twenty or thirty years ago, at a time when there were six, not ten or eleven or twelve, member states of the Community. They were conceived at a time when the world was very different and when preoccupations were very different. So much has changed. Today, the challenges are to do with industry, energy, trade, political cooperation, the environment. We are taking a new look at agriculture.'

I went on to say, 'Don't let anybody take this exercise as a grab for power by the Parliament. It is nothing of the sort. It has to do with relevance. It is to do with trying to see whether or not we are moving in the right direction. We are talking here first of all about a mechanism, a quite straightforward mechanism. That is what this motion is all about. Nothing is prejudged in one sense or another by the fact that we establish a constitutional committee. But it will give us the chance to go forward into the next European election on some kind of manifesto, which has been adopted and approved by the European Parliament, a manifesto, I believe, for change which we should all be able to support.'

A mechanism! A quite straightforward mechanism! In practice, the Institutional Committee turned out to be far more than that.

That day, the Parliament approved the proposal to establish the Institutional Committee by 164 votes in favour, 24 against and 2 abstentions. An Italian MEP, Mauro Ferri, was elected chairman, while Spinelli himself took on the key role of rapporteur-general.

The Committee worked hard and it came up with some far-reaching ideas. I was, of course, delighted that the draft treaty on the European Union eventually included the environment as one of the areas where the Union should be active. And I was particularly pleased that Spinelli, as rapporteur-general, had proposed the inclusion of specific language calling for the protection of animals. The precise words to be found at the end of Article 59 in the draft treaty provide that *the Union shall take measures designed to provide for animal protection.*

As a member of the Institutional Committee, I had stressed the need for such language in the course of several interventions. I had actually proposed a more comprehensive text than the one finally retained. At the last meeting of the Committee before the debate in plenary, Spinelli presented his own final draft, going through the paragraphs and provisions of the proposed draft treaty one by one. He paused when he came to that one short line on animal protection.

'Some proposals for this particular text', he nodded in my direction, 'were somewhat longer, but I hope I have retained the essence of the idea.'

I gave Spinelli all credit for that. I hadn't let him down. I had helped deliver sixty-one votes for his grand project, as Christopher Booker and Richard North pointed out. But he hadn't let me down either.

Years later, when the Amsterdam Treaty was adopted in 1997, it contained a specific protocol on animal welfare.

On 14 February 1984, the European Parliament approved the draft treaty on European Union by 237 votes to 31 with 43 abstentions, thereby giving the whole 'European project' an immense push, as Spinelli had all along intended.

The intergovernmental negotiations that followed the adoption of the draft treaty led not only to the Single European Act, which was ratified in 1986 and aimed at the completion of the Common Market. It also led, via the Milan European Summit, where Mrs Thatcher was famously ambushed, and the intergovernmental conference that Milan agreed to under QMV (Qualified Majority Voting), to the Maastricht Treaty on European Union, signed on 7 February 1992.

In September of that year, a referendum in France only narrowly supported ratification. In Denmark the ratification process had to be repeated before the Danish government got the necessary approval from the Danish people. In the UK, Conservative 'Maastricht' rebels (the 'bastards') almost brought down Conservative Prime Minister John Major's government.

Nonetheless, the Maastricht Treaty, establishing *inter alia* the common currency and the Eurozone, entered into force on May 1993.

There have been since then a succession of further treaties – Amsterdam (1997), Nice (2001) and Lisbon (2007). All of these treaties are, to a greater or lesser extent, the lineal descendants of the European Parliament's own draft treaty on European Union.

From tiny acorns – in this case, nine MEPs having a meal together one summer night in Strasbourg – mighty oak trees have grown!

There may, of course, be a strong case today for pruning some of the branches of those trees. In Britain at least, and probably in other countries too, there is an ongoing debate about the powers and relevance of the European Union. That debate is inevitable and from my point of view, welcome.

If the Conservatives win the next election, they are committed to a 'renegotiation' and an 'in or out' referendum. David Cameron, as Conservative leader and Prime Minister, has laid out a series of objectives to be achieved in a renegotiation. Some of them may require a full intergovernmental negotiation; others may be dealt with more simply.

By the time of the promised referendum in 2017, it will be more than forty years since the British people last expressed themselves on whether or not they wished to be or to remain (the precise wording of the question is not yet clear) members of the European Union.

I am sure the British people, with all their wisdom and experience, will make the right decision!

Chapter Six

Wooing the Greeks

As I have already mentioned, MEPs didn't see a great deal of Mrs Thatcher, Prime Minister and leader of the Conservative Party. We didn't have passes into the Palace of Westminster. I don't think I ever sat in the Strangers' Gallery of the House of Commons and listened to a debate. Of course we received briefings about issues of importance to the UK that were liable to be discussed and voted on in Strasbourg or Brussels. But there was no day-to-day contact with the Conservative Party hierarchy.

That said, whatever her personal feelings might have been about the European Parliament and its members, the first direct European elections had happened on Mrs Thatcher's watch, as it were. In those days the Conservatives were seen as the 'pro-European' party, in contrast to Labour, who had won only seventeen seats in the 1979 European election. I don't know whether the Foreign Office put her up to it, or whether the Prime Minister thought of the idea all by herself. In any case, quite soon after the election, all sixty-one Conservative MEPs received an invitation to 10 Downing Street.

No. 10 Downing Street! I thought of all the men who had, in theory at least, run the country from that building. And now there was a first female prime minister to be added to the long list of chaps.

We were ushered into the famous building at the appointed hour to sit on rows of gilded chairs. I imagined that there would be a question-and-answer session. Or at least a dialogue of some kind. I was wrong. The Prime Minister in due course swept in, harangued us for about an hour, mainly about the need for a British rebate, and swept out again.

We met the Prime Minister again later on. This was a much less formal occasion. The venue was, again, No. 10. But this time we were invited to drinks in a reception room on the first floor. I walked up the stairs past the photos of former prime ministers. I gawped like a grouper fish.

That evening Mrs Thatcher had more time for us. She progressed around the room, talking to small groups of MEPs.

At one point I found myself being interrogated on a one-to-one basis. 'And what did you do before you were elected?' she asked, leaning towards me with her impeccably coiffed blonde hair.

I panicked. What on earth could I say? I didn't think the Prime Minister needed to know that I had most recently been employed by the European Commission in Brussels, not when she was going on about 'getting our money back'.

Before that I had spent years promoting population and family planning around the world, working for the United Nations and the International Planned Parenthood Federation.

I imagined her finger jabbing me fiercely in the chest: 'And how many children do *you* have, Mr Johnson?'

I cast my mind even further back. To my first job, as a trainee spy, with MI6. No, that wouldn't do either. In those days, MI6 didn't exist officially. You weren't allowed to talk to anyone about it. I probably wasn't even allowed to talk to the Prime Minister.

Inspiration dawned.

'I used to work for the World Bank, in Washington,' I said.

I had caught her attention. She paused in mid-stride to plant her handbag behind a potted plant.

'And what did you do in the World Bank?'

'Well, actually,' I replied, 'I worked on the Mangla Dam hydroelectric project on the Jhelum River in Pakistan. It's almost finished now.'

Mrs Thatcher's mood brightened. 'The Mangla Dam is a great *British* project. *British* engineers have played a key role there.'

I still don't know what came over me. I think I was suddenly affected by the 'rabbit-caught-in-headlights' syndrome.

Only that morning I had read an article in the *Financial Times* about a recent untoward event out there in west Pakistan.

'I am afraid the chief British engineer just committed suicide by throwing himself off the top of the spillway.'

Mrs Thatcher looked at me as though I was a raving lunatic.

I think I redeemed myself in her eyes later. The Prime Minister was about to leave the party (was she going upstairs to cook supper for her family?) when she realised she was missing something.

'Has anyone seen my handbag?' she asked.

The word quickly went round the room. The Prime Minister was looking for her handbag.

Aides scurried by. My old friend Tim Lankester whizzed past.

Tim had been in the World Bank in Washington at the same time as me. He had joined the Treasury on leaving the World Bank, and was now on secondment to No. 10.

'Don't know why you had to mention the Mangla Dam,' he hissed. 'Quite upset her. Have you seen her handbag?'

'Look behind the potted plant in the far corner of the room, where the Prime Minister and I were standing,' I hissed back.

The Prime Minister was soon reunited with her handbag. She flashed a smile in my direction. Phew!

A year or two later, we were invited to another reception at No. 10. Once again I found myself tête-à-tête with the Iron Lady.

Keep it light, keep it cheerful, I urged myself. Don't talk about dams in Pakistan.

As it happened, the press had reported that day that the Prime Minister had returned from a brief holiday in Cornwall. I knew about Cornish holidays. As I have already recounted, only a year or two earlier, I had had an epic journey from Exmoor to Penzance.

'You look very well, Prime Minister,' I said. 'I hope you found the sea warm enough for swimming.'

The timbre of her voice had changed since our last brief exchange. It was lower, less abrasive. Apparently she had had elocution lessons.

'I'm afraid I didn't have time for that. I had work to do.'

At least she didn't look at me as though I was bonkers.

Years later, when I was the Conservative candidate for Teignbridge in the run-up to the 2005 general election, Archie and Anne Hamilton invited us over to their house in Devon to meet Mrs Thatcher. Archie (now Lord) Hamilton had been Mrs Thatcher's PPS. The Hamiltons stayed close friends with the Prime Minister after she had been forcibly retired, though perhaps 'retired' is too gentle a term. 'Defenestrated' might be a better one.

Mrs Thatcher's yearly visit to the Hamiltons on Exmoor usually took place in September. In theory, for security reasons, no one was meant to be in the know. But the locals had their suspicions, as police cars buzzed along the country lanes checking for IRA booby traps.

The Hamiltons very kindly sat me next to Lady T at dinner. I felt strangely protective. Mrs Thatcher, at the beginning of her long, gentle decline, reminded me of my mother.

I can't remember what the two of us talked about that evening. I'm pretty sure we didn't mention the Mangla Dam in Pakistan or the temperature of the sea at Polzeath.

In the drawing room after dinner, Lady T signed a bottle of Laphroaig single-malt whisky for me.

'You can auction it for your campaign fighting fund,' she advised.

Even when she was not physically present, Mrs Thatcher was a powerful influence on the life of the sixty-one Conservative Euro MPs. Indeed, she was a major influence on the deliberations of the European Parliament throughout the whole of that first five-year term.

She was determined to sort out the problem of the 'British rebate', and to rebalance the Community budget so that Britain was not constantly paying in far more than it got out. At successive summits she banged the table and demanded that Britain should be 'reimbursed'. She antagonised almost everyone along the way. At one point, Chancellor Schmidt actually fell asleep (or pretended to) when the British Prime Minister was in the middle of a long diatribe.

Finally, at the Fontainebleau summit of June 1984, she got her way and a 'solution' to the British problem was found that has more or less endured to this day.

If the 'British rebate' took up a lot of our attention, so did the issue of 'enlargement'.

The European Community began in 1957 under the Treaty of Rome as a grouping of six nations: France, Germany, Italy, Belgium, Luxembourg and the Netherlands. In 1973, Britain, Ireland and Denmark joined. When I was elected as an MEP in 1979, the Community still consisted of nine nations.

But a tenth, Greece, was already waiting in the wings. Now that the colonels had finally been turned out and democracy had been restored in the land where the very concept of democracy had first been invented, a firm date had been set for Greek 'accession'.

Jim Scott-Hopkins, now Sir James, spelled out the importance of the upcoming event in party political terms at our EDG meeting in Strasbourg one evening.

'We haven't had much success so far, ladies and gentlemen,' he told us, 'in enlarging our group to include other nationalities apart from our Danish colleagues.' And here he gave a friendly nod to the two Danes, Paul Møller and Kent Kirk, who still loyally provided the 'multinational' tinge to our political group.

'The Italian Christian Democrats still look at us with some suspicion, in spite of the overtures we made in Rome and elsewhere. In point of fact, the accession of Greece may give us the best opportunity we are going to have in the foreseeable future to build an alliance with a political group from another country.'

Soon after, it was decided that the EDG should have an 'away day' in Greece in the hope of wooing some future Greek MEPs.

Since it was half-term and my turn to look after the children, or at least some of them, on their exeats from school, I flew with Rachel and Jo, then seventeen and eleven, to Athens to get in a few days' holiday with them before the official meetings began. We took a taxi from the airport to Piraeus, then boarded the ferry to Paros.

Paros is one of the Cycladic Islands – bright white houses, sun and wind. We found a guest house in a little village on the north coast and spent the weekend swimming, eating and walking.

Boris Kiddell, a friend from my Washington days, had a house on Paros. When he was in America, he worked for the *Daily Mail* but he decided to change careers and write novels instead. Windswept Paros was the place he had chosen to settle, at least in the summer months.

'My house is on the north-east corner of the island,' he had told me years earlier. 'You can't miss it.'

The paper tablecloths in the nearest taverna were printed with a blue and white map of the island.

'This must be the north-east corner,' I said to Rachel and Jo while we polished off the *keftedes*. 'Let's walk over there after lunch. Can't be more than 10 kilometres away.'

Kiddell was right when he said we couldn't miss his house. The coast tapered to a promontory where half a dozen whitewashed little houses were perched at the cliff's edge, looking out over the blue Aegean Sea.

From one of the houses, we could hear a distinct tapping sound. The front door was open.

Boris Kiddell was sitting at his desk, on the other side of the room, in front of an open window, facing the Aegean. In front of him was an old-fashioned, much-used, clackety-clack typewriter on which he was hammering away as though his life depended upon it. Maybe his publisher had set a deadline.

We walked in and, as we did so, I called out, 'Hello, Boris. I hope we are not disturbing you. We just thought we would look in. There don't seem to be any phones on the island.'

Kiddell jumped to his feet. He was smoking a cigarette but otherwise totally naked.

'Sorry, I prefer not to wear any clothes when I'm working out here. Too hot. I don't have a phone, anyway.'

The European Democratic Group meeting took place in the famous Hotel Grande Bretagne on Syntagma Square. In December 1944, after British troops had liberated Athens, Winston Churchill had addressed the jubilant crowd from the hotel's balcony.

At the end of the first day, we all went down to the harbour for a grand reception laid on by the new Greek MEPs from the Nea Demokratia party.

We arrived in our bus at the Piraeus Yacht Club, a grand waterside establishment much frequented by Greek ship owners and their playboy sons.

White-coated waiters were lined up to greet us.

The party was soon in full swing. Greek MEPs and British MEPs were exchanging warm embraces, and toasting future cooperation. Rachel and Jo helped to pass the *dolmades* around.

At the side of the room, a long table was laden with food and drink. The table was covered by a long white cloth, which stretched down to the ground on both sides.

At one point, having returned to base in search of a refill, I found myself talking to Dr Alex Sherlock, the MEP for Suffolk. He was a large, heavy man, well into his sixties, with a booming voice that he used to considerable effect in the European Parliament's debating hemicycle in Strasbourg. At that particular moment he was engaged in tackling an enormous pile of grilled prawns.

'What a splendid show, Alex, don't you think?' I said.

Sherlock was a real doctor, an MD rather than a PhD. 'Not so good for the cholesterol.' He speared some huge grilled prawns onto his plate.

An elderly Greek MEP, with a glass of wine in his left hand and his right hand outstretched in greeting, walked over to join us. The old fellow looked at Dr Sherlock; he looked at me.

'I want to tell you, gentlemen,' he said, 'we Greeks have so much admiration for you British. If it hadn't been for Churchill and the help Britain gave us after the war, the Communists would have taken over. MEPs from the Nea Demokratia party are dying to join your group.'

At that very moment, just as he was assuring us that he and his colleagues were 'dying' to join us, he clutched his hand to his chest and fell to the floor.

Even today, in my mind's eye, I sometimes see a vast Dr Sherlock lying, literally, on top of that poor expended Greek, giving him mouth-to-mouth resuscitation.

Alas, Dr Sherlock's efforts were to no avail. Our Greek hosts went into a huddle. One of them suggested that their unfortunate colleague might be temporarily 'parked' out of sight under the table.

'It is what Mr Theodorakapopoulos would have wanted,' he suggested, nudging the corpse beneath the tablecloth with his foot.

Later that evening, Rachel, Jo and I had dinner with Tim Bainbridge in a little tavern on the harbour. Tim was on the staff of our group. He and his fellow staffers basically did the hard slog as far as research was concerned. They prepared the position papers for the group and, after taking soundings, worked out which proposals we should support and which we should oppose. Basically, they told us what to think. It was much easier that way.

We sat there, studying the menu. We weren't very hungry. We had already had a lot of canapés.

'It was Dr Sherlock's "kiss of life" that did it for him,' Tim reflected. 'Would *you* want to find Dr Sherlock on top of you, giving you the kiss of life with a mouthful of giant prawns? The poor man probably died of shock.'

Chapter Seven

How to Write Off a Volvo

In May 1982, when Julia was five months old, Jenny and I decided to drive out to Strasbourg in the Volvo. We rented a *gite* for the week on the outskirts of town. It was Rachel's half-term and she had been able to join is. Rachel was seventeen at the time and had recently switched from Bryanston to St Paul's Girls School. I wouldn't say that the change of school had been entirely voluntary. As I recall, she had been caught drinking Cinzano at a midnight party on the playing field. I had received a couple of letters from Bryanston's headmaster wondering 'if I had had any luck finding Rachel a new school'.

I can take a hint as well as the next man. I didn't tell St Paul's about the Cinzano.

We brought our Swiss au pair girl, Marie-Claude, with us as well.

One afternoon, when parliamentary business was light, we left Julia with Marie-Claude and drove down to Colmar, a pretty Alsatian town about 60 miles south of Strasbourg.

I had told my mother, last time we were at Nethercote, that we planned to visit the home of her ancestors and she had been delighted. 'There's a de Pfeffel statue in the main square in Colmar,' she informed us. 'Do try to find it.' My mother's mother was a de Pfeffel, as was her maternal grandfather, and she was proud of her French heritage.

I am glad to say we discovered the statue that afternoon. We also discovered the Brasserie de Pfeffel. So we toasted our ancestor with some fine Gewurztraminer and, with time to spare, decided to return to Strasbourg not via the autoroute but via the country road known as the *route des vins d'Alsace*, which winds among the vineyards in the foothills of the Vosges.

If I look back on those years in the European Parliament, one of the abiding images I have is the sheer beauty of the country-side and of the still-medieval villages that lie between Colmar and Strasbourg. Ribeauvillé, Riquewihr, Molsheim – those evoca-tive names stay with me long after the memory of parliamentary debates about trading standards has faded.

We bought a hundred bottles of wine that afternoon, filling the back of the Volvo. Too many Gewurztraminers perhaps, but on the whole a fair selection, I thought.

Next morning, we set off on the long drive back to England. It was a hot day. I drove with the windows wound down and one of Julia's tapes in the tape deck. If the engine sounded odd, I didn't notice it.

As we neared Metz, the engine made an extraordinary grinding and shuddering sound and we came to an abrupt halt on the hard shoulder of the motorway.

When, eventually, a roadside patrol came to our aid, the patrolman swiftly diagnosed the problem. '*C'est foutu, le moteur,*' he explained.

Basically, I had wrecked the engine by driving for a long distance at high speed in second gear!

'Didn't you hear the noise of the revolution?' the patrolman asked. I imagined Tsar Nicholas II asking his prime minister something along those lines as the crowds gathered outside the Winter Palace in 1917.

The patrolman pointed to the gearbox. Where the gear lever of our Volvo automatic should have been in D, I had put it in 2 instead. And left it there! Mile after flipping mile!

A breakdown van arrived in due course and we were towed to a garage in Metz. Since there was no chance of the car being repaired until a new engine could be obtained and fitted, we decided to catch the train. We unloaded the carry-cot and the packs of nappies and tins of baby food. We piled ourselves, our suitcases and other paraphernalia into a taxi to catch the train from Metz to the Gare St Lazare in Paris.

Once back home, I got in touch with the garage in Metz.

'Tell me the bad news first,' I urged.

The bad news, as I had already suspected, was that they would have to install a whole new engine if the car was to be put back on the road.

'And the good news?'

'*Ah, oui, monsieur. En ce qui concerne le vin, vous avez très bien choisi. C'est une bonne selection!*' At least he approved of the choice of wine!

The *garagiste* indicated that he had removed the wine from the car for safe-keeping. It wouldn't do, he said, to store it in the car, not in the heat of the summer. And he wasn't sure that the journey home would be good for it. These Alsatian wines were all very good, but did they travel well?

We struck a deal, of course, in the end. I traded over 100 bottles of fine Alsatian wine against a new Volvo engine but had to throw in several thousand francs as well.

Some weeks later I made my way back to Metz to pick up the car with its new engine.

The *garagiste* seemed pleased to see me. He had been working his way steadily through the cases of wine we had left behind.

When I drove back that evening to London, I kept checking the gear lever, just to make sure I was in D for Drive. Even today I make a habit of glancing down at the gearbox whenever I move off, to make sure that the gear lever is in the right position.

There are always lessons to be learned in life.

One of the most crucial moments in my political career, such as it was, came a few months later, not in Strasbourg or Brussels, but in Brighton. I had been attending the Conservative Party annual conference, which was being held there that year, 1982.

In those days the party's grandees sat on the dais, providing a loyal backdrop to the speaker. Mrs Thatcher herself, resplendent in blue and gold, walked confidently to the speaker's lectern and held her audience transfixed. Behind, a huge banner proclaimed 'THE RESOLUTE APPROACH'.

As a lowly MEP, I sat in the body of the hall. The room was totally packed. The Prime Minister's speech, punctuated by frequent applause, recalled the victory in the Falklands. This successful campaign had transformed the Conservative Party's prospects.

Afterwards, I went for a walk along the seafront. It was a bright, sunny morning. Delegates were already heading to their hotels for lunch or 'fringe' events. The Conservative MEPs present in Brighton that morning (quite a few had turned up) were holding their own gathering with drinks and canapés in one of the smaller reception rooms in the Grand Hotel.

There are times in life when chance encounters prove totally providential. Halfway along the Brighton seafront between the conference centre and the Grand Hotel, I met Olly Webb, a large, amiable man, then in his fifties, who was the chairman of my Euro constituency council, coming from the opposite direction.

I wouldn't say I knew Olly well. My Euro constituency was a large one, covering nine parliamentary seats, including the Isle of Wight. Olly himself lived and worked on the Isle of Wight, not an easy place to reach at the best of times. You didn't just drop in on your way home after work.

Of course, we stopped in our tracks and greeted each other.

An MP may be the servant of his constituents but he is above all the servant of his constituency association, that small band of party loyalists who have been largely responsible for selecting him in the first place. (If you don't get selected, you don't get elected. In the Conservative Party, at least, it's as simple as that.)

'Hello, Olly,' I said.

'Hello, Stanley,' Olly replied. Then he continued, ominously, 'I'm glad to see you. I thought that we ought to talk about fundraising for the next Euro election.'

I have often tried to analyse why I reacted at that moment the way I did. Was it the mention of fundraising? Was I shirking those endless raffles and after-dinner speeches, the never-ending series of Conservative fêtes ('fêtes' worse than death)? Or was I simply reacting to the dose of political Viagra that Mrs Thatcher had delivered that morning in the conference centre?

On balance, I think it was the latter more than the former. I realised that morning as I listened to the Prime Minister spelling out a new direction for Britain ('rolling back the frontiers of socialism') that being an MEP would never be more than a sideshow in political terms. If I truly wanted to have a career in politics (and I thought I did), then I would have to throw my hat in the ring for a Westminster seat.

'I don't think I'm going to stand again, Olly,' I said. 'I'm going to look for a seat in the Westminster Parliament.'

Olly Webb looked surprised. Less than three years earlier I had landed the Isle of Wight & Hants East Euro seat with a majority of over 95,000. Why on earth, he seemed to be thinking, would I want to throw aside lightly the second safest Euro seat in the UK?

In practical terms, that meant he would have to preside over a whole new candidate selection process, with all the expense and hassle that involved.

But Olly was a kindly man. He effectively disguised whatever anger or irritation he might have felt. Instead, he put his hand on my shoulder.

'Don't you want to think about it?'

'I have thought about it,' I replied. 'If I announce my intention to stand down now, you will have plenty of time to get a new candidate in place before the next Euro election in May 1984.'

As a West Countryman, I was keen to find a seat in, say, Devon, Somerset or Cornwall. As it happened, the Westminster parliamentary seat of Wells started looking for a candidate soon after I told Olly Webb of my intention to stand down from my Euro seat at the next election.

I made it through the preliminary rounds and in due course found myself in the 'final'. Early one evening, Jenny and I drove over from Nethercote to the beautiful cathedral town where the selectors had gathered in force.

When we had all made our speeches and the selectors were deliberating, some of the candidates and their wives gathered in the local pub. We met that evening, for the first time, David Heathcoat-Amory and his wife Linda. David came from a well-known West Country family. While we waited for news, I whispered to Jenny, 'David's definitely the front-runner here.'

I wasn't wrong. We were on our second round of drinks when the agent came to find us. I couldn't help thinking of the line at the end of *Hamlet* when the messenger announces: 'The election lights on Fortinbras.'

Well, David Heathcoat-Amory was invited back in to the meeting as the newly elected Conservative candidate for Wells that night, while the rest of us 'hopefuls' headed out into the night. He was elected the following year in the general election of May 1983 and faithfully served the people of Wells until he lost his seat in 2010.

My next serious attempt to catch the selectors' eye was in South West Surrey, where a by-election was pending. When the boundaries were being drawn up for the European constituencies, the Westminster parliamentary constituency of South West Surrey (or Farnham, as it was then known) was included as one of the constituencies in the Isle of Wight & Hampshire East Euro-constituency, which I now had the honour to represent.

In the spring of 1984, with the end of my time as a Euro MP only months away (the next European elections were scheduled in June that year), I found myself on the final shortlist with an invitation to attend the candidate selection meeting at Charterhouse School.

Peter Brewer, the chairman of the Farnham Conservative Association, had added a friendly postscript to the letter.

'Wanda and I much hope you will stay the night with us after the meeting,' he wrote.

I passed the letter over to Jenny. 'This is very promising, isn't it? Peter and Wanda couldn't be inviting *all* the shortlisted candidates to stay the night.'

In the event I decided to decline Peter Brewer's kind offer of hospitality. Farnham was just a short hop down the A3 from London. And however optimistic I was, things might go wrong on the night.

Well, things certainly did go wrong on the night.

I don't know whether I was the runner-up in Farnham, but I certainly wasn't the winner. Virginia Bottomley, tall, blonde and graceful, by all accounts turned in a stunning performance in Charterhouse's huge school hall, whereas I comprehensively blew it. I thought I could wing it with a series of one-liners and flippant or facetious answers to perfectly good questions. ('Mr Johnson, what are your views on education?' 'I don't really have any views on education. I sent all my children to boarding school at the age of eight. I just let the schools get on with it.' 'Mr Johnson, have you any experience of business?' 'No, but if anyone wants to offer me a job…')

Basically, I misjudged my audience completely. Jenny and I walked out into the night as Virginia Bottomley, accompanied by her husband Peter (already an MP), stepped forward to make her acceptance speech.

I didn't hear that speech, but I heard the applause as we wandered around the car park looking for the Volvo. So much applause. Prolonged bursts of clapping. So many Volvos, too. Row after row of them. We couldn't find our car. When we arrived at the school, there had been only a handful of cars outside. But while we were in the anteroom, waiting our turn to perform with the other shortlisted candidates, the car park had filled up. Nowadays, the Conservative Party on the ground is pretty thin, as least in terms of fully paid-up members. Not so in 1984. Three or four hundred Conservative loyalists in South West Surrey turned out that night to witness the start of Virginia Bottomley's dazzling political career.

'What a shambles,' I said to Jenny, as we walked in the dark up and down the rows of vehicles. 'Listen to that! Virginia is obviously wowing them completely.'

I felt a bit like Grendel, lurking on the outside, while all the Spear Danes wassailed away in Heorot.

We found the car at last and drove away.

'Well, at least we didn't accept Wanda and Peter Brewer's kind invitation to stay the night!' I said. 'That would have been embarrassing on all sides.'

Chapter Eight

First Trip to Antarctica

One day, early in October 1981, towards the end of Mrs Simone Veil's term of office as President of the European Parliament (as noted earlier, she was succeeded by Piet Dankert in January 1982), I was invited to go to see her in her office in Strasbourg. Since I was a vice chairman of the European Parliament's Environment Committee, she wondered if I would like to make a speech on her behalf, at the triennial meeting of the International Union for Conservation of Nature (IUCN), which was to take place in Christchurch, New Zealand.

I was more than delighted. I was thrilled. I had never been to New Zealand.

The Parliament's travel agents agreed that it was perfectly possible to 'stop off' in Australia en route to New Zealand without incurring any penalties, so this is what I did, spending a long weekend with my older sister Hilary and her growing family, then living near Newcastle in New South Wales. Hilary and her husband, Peter Heanly, had emigrated with their four boys to Australia in 1969, soon after I returned from America. I had not seen them since, so it was a happy reunion.

At the IUCN meeting in Christchurch, I made my formal speech on behalf of Mrs Veil, explaining what the European Community was doing and hoping the Community and the IUCN could work constructively together. I stayed on to participate in some of the scheduled sessions.

One thing that struck me forcefully was that the future of Antarctica was very much the 'hot' topic among the delegates to the conference. In the halls and meeting rooms, people were busy drafting and redrafting position papers and resolutions, all of them designed to reconcile potentially irreconcilable positions. As a fully fledged world issue, Antarctica had come of age. The question in a nutshell was this: could Antarctica be 'saved' or was it to be 'ruined'? Could it be 'exploited' without losing its apparently unique character – its wildlife, its wilderness, its advantages for scientific research?

I sketched an outline for a book: *Antarctica: The Last Great Wilderness*. In due course, I heard back from my agent. Weidenfeld & Nicolson were keen to publish, but unfortunately not in a position to sponsor an Antarctic expedition!

Time was of the essence. The Antarctic summer had already begun and quite soon it would be over. Once the pack ice began to harden over the surrounding seas, I could say goodbye to the idea of visiting the deep south.

I dialled directory enquiries that Friday and asked for the number of the British Antarctic Survey in Cambridge. I learned that BAS's director, Dr Laws, had already 'gone south', by which was meant that he had left for the Antarctic, but Dr Raymond Adie, BAS's deputy director, would be in his office on Monday and why didn't I ring back then?

I didn't ring back on Monday. Instead, I drove to Cambridge at the crack of dawn.

Ray Adie, a burly, soft-spoken man who had wintered in the Antarctic a good many times himself, enduring several months of 24-hour darkness, was politely sceptical. It would be very difficult, he thought, to find space on board a BAS vessel bound for

Antarctica. There were only two ships – the *Bransfield* and the *John Biscoe*. Even if their itineraries happened to coincide with the timing of my projected visit, it would be very unlikely that there would be room for me.

'Frankly,' – Dr Adie spoke kindly but there was no mistaking his meaning – 'BAS is not running a tourist operation. This is science. Our ships are there to service BAS bases in Antarctica and to carry out their own scientific programmes.'

In the event, Dr Adie changed his mind. Or someone changed it for him.

He rang me a couple of days after my visit to Cambridge.

'We've been looking at the schedule of our ships,' he said, 'and we think we may be able to help you. The *John Biscoe* will be leaving Punta Arenas in southern Chile on 12 January for Antarctica. It will be visiting two BAS bases on the Antarctic Peninsula. Those are Rothera and Faraday. Then it will be coming up to take supplies in the Falklands before going south again to our base at Signy in the South Orkneys. From Signy, the *Biscoe* will go to Bird Island, which is just off South Georgia, and then steam on to Rio de Janeiro. You can fly home from Rio if you like. Or else you can stay on board the *Biscoe* until it returns to the UK in the middle of March.'

The journey I made to Antarctica with the British Antarctic Survey on board the *John Biscoe* covered over 5,000 miles. Apart from the spectacular scenery – iceberg and cliff, mountain and sky – which no one who has seen it could ever forget, that voyage through the Antarctic revealed to me a world of unbelievable biological abundance. There were, so I learned, probably 1 million Weddell seals, 200,000 leopard and Ross seals, 600,000 southern elephant seals and over 500,000 fur seals. I have never seen such a profusion of birds as I did as the *Biscoe* swung across to the Falklands from the tip of the

Antarctic Peninsula, or again when we visited South Georgia and Bird Island.

When we visited the South Orkneys and South Georgia we saw the sad relics of the whaling industry: beach after beach strewn with whalebone; giant skulls on the foreshore; industrial artefacts that were the tools of this trade.

This was the 'journey of a lifetime'. Indeed, that was the excuse I offered Jenny when I explained that I planned, like the man in T. S. Eliot's poem, to 'go south in the winter'.

I am not sure she was wholly convinced but she didn't make a fuss. 'Try not to fall down any crevasses,' she advised.

While the *Biscoe* refuelled in Port Stanley, Adrian Berry – the *Daily Telegraph*'s science correspondent and a fellow guest of BAS on board the ship – and I had a chance to meet Sir Rex Hunt, at Governor's Mansion. Hunt showed us round.

This is what I wrote at the time in my notebook:

A splendid dining room looks out onto the lawn where a Union Jack flies from the flagpole. There is a glass-fronted mahogany sideboard in which place mats and other table furnishings are stored. Some of the items have been damaged by rifle or machine-gun fire.

'They fired from outside into the room,' Hunt tells us. 'You can see the holes in the walls too. When Menendez occupied the house, they had dinner parties in here.' He points to a splendid life-size portrait of the Queen above the sideboard. 'They kept that portrait in place all the time they were here – illuminated, too, when they dined.'

I posted cards to England from Port Stanley. 'From Stanley in Stanley.'

Jenny had warned me to look out for crevasses. She didn't mention minefields. One afternoon, during my brief stay in the

Falklands, I hired a motorcycle with a view to driving across the island to visit Goose Green, where 2 Para had fought a tough battle.

I followed some sheep tracks across soggy ground for a few miles. It began to rain. Then it poured. After a while, the track petered out. I found myself confronting a large sign. The legend on the sign was written in bold red letters. It said: 'MINEFIELD RED AREA.' Then underneath, just because the world is full of idiots on hired motorcycles who think they are cleverer than they really are, the message was spelled out in detail: 'This is a Minefield Area Situation Map as at 20 December 1983. It supersedes the previously produced Minefield Area Situation Map dated 12 November 1983.'

My advice, if you find yourself in the middle of a minefield on a motorcycle, is to turn the bike round and go back the way you have come, sticking exactly to the track you made on the outward journey.

Disappointingly, the publisher decided not to include any of my photographs in my book, *Antarctica: The Last Great Wilderness*. In fact, they decided not to include any photographs at all. John Curtis, my editor at Weidenfeld & Nicolson, wrote: 'Your descriptions are so vivid that we felt photographs might be a distraction.'

Jenny and I were having breakfast in the kitchen of 'my flat' in Maida Avenue when that letter arrived. From where we sat, we could see the ducks and the houseboats on the canal. The sun shone and Julia was happily smiling in her high chair.

But John Curtis's letter annoyed me. 'Huh!' I exclaimed. 'They're just trying to save money!'

In the event, Weidenfeld did use one of my photographs, an evocative icescape that they made into a splendid wraparound book jacket. But I was disappointed they didn't use more of them.

I went back to Antarctica a few years ago to write an article for *The Independent*. I took some photos of a leopard seal grabbing a passing penguin, which, I am glad to say, the paper was happy to use. If you take out a magnifying glass, and squint at the bottom left-hand corner of the picture, you can see that they even gave me a photo credit.

Chapter Nine

Channel Tunnel Thriller

Roger Smith, an editor at Heinemann, who had overseen the publication of my first five novels for the publisher, acted as midwife for the sixth as well.

Actually, he did more than that.

We were having lunch together one day at the Savile Club in Upper Brook Street in the spring of 1983.

'How is Bartholomew getting on?' I asked. Bartholomew Smith was my godson.

'Oh, quite well. He's just had exams. They had to write an essay about the Channel Tunnel.'

Roger pulled a crumpled exam paper from his pocket. 'Describe a situation,' he read out the exact phrasing of the question, 'where a train going through the Channel Tunnel is taken over by terrorists.'

I was intrigued. Though a century earlier some preliminary digging had taken place near the cliffs of Dover with a view to building a 'fixed link' between Britain and France, the idea had soon been abandoned. The Duke of Wellington and other grandees had apparently been worried by the idea of French cuirassiers emerging armed to the teeth amid the fields of Kent. But the idea was being seriously canvassed once again.

Even Mrs Thatcher was coming round. She had apparently let

it be known that she was not opposed as long as 'not a penny of public money was involved'.

The precise route such a tunnel might take had not been sorted out. Nor was there clarity about whether there would be one tunnel or two. Would people be able to drive from England to France or would cars have to be loaded onto trains?

Three weeks later, Tom Rosenthal, who had succeeded Charles Pick at the head of Heinemann, offered the princely sum of £7,500 for the UK rights to *Tunnel*. (I had submitted an 'outline' a few days after that lunch with Roger Smith.)

From my point of view, £7,500 was – in the early 1980s – a very decent advance. Charles Pick had offered £5,000 for *The Doomsday Deposit* only a few years earlier. Even allowing for inflation, this was real progress.

I bought a pocket Dictaphone and spouted away in taxis or airport lounges. After I had accumulated a number of tapes, I posted them off to a firm in north London, All-Hours Word Processing, where a good lady called Sharon Livingstone converted the spoken word into text and mailed great wedges of paper back to me.

As far as I was concerned, it was a perfectly efficient system.

The only drawback was that it would sometimes be weeks before the typed-up draft of the latest chapter or two dropped through the mailbox. It was easy to forget who was doing what to whom.

Of course, I tried to keep track of the key elements. Sometimes I jotted down the salient features of the main characters, e.g. bald/balding, spectacles/no specs, high-pitched voice versus deeply seductive voice, big bosom/no bosom etc. The only problem with that system, in those pre-computer days, was that you had to keep track of the jottings.

Once I even forgot what sex one of the key protagonists was and had to wing it with some ambiguous drafting until Sharon posted the typed-out text back to me. She was kind enough to point out that Jack had become Jill in mid-stream or vice versa.

There were also some unsuspected hazards in using a Dictaphone. I am sure there are some more streamlined models now, but the one I bought – back in the early '80s – was rather chunky.

I remember once, lying on my back in the garden at Nethercote during the summer break. I was dictating into the Dictaphone, holding the machine more or less at arm's length directly above my head. As I dozed off – wine at lunch, I fear – the Dictaphone fell from my grasp, hitting me full in the face and chipping one of my front teeth.

It wasn't a life-threatening injury, but the tooth had to be repaired.

'Next time,' Declan the Dentist tut-tutted, as he peered into my wide-open mouth, 'if you're dictating a "thriller", at least try to stay awake!'

Tunnel presented me with some other more technical problems.

In due course, when they had sorted the various options out, the Channel Tunnel, or Chunnel, would be built with two tracks so that two trains, travelling in opposite directions, could use it at the same time. But for the purposes of my book, I envisaged a one-track-only formula. That, it seemed to me, would make the dénouement far more dramatic.

The principal character in *Tunnel* is an ex-SAS officer called Oliver Grantham (I named him after Mrs Thatcher's birthplace as a subliminal tribute to the Iron Lady). Grantham is the man whose single-minded energy and determination drives the project forward. He has all sorts of obstacles to contend with, not least a Greek ship owner, Dimitri Karapolitis, who owns a rival sea ferry company likely to be put out of business by the tunnel.

Grantham careers triumphantly through all dangers and difficulties. The climax comes, naturally, on the day of the tunnel's official opening. The train carrying the Queen, the Prime Minister and other high officials, including Grantham himself, of course, heads off to France at high speed for a grand rendezvous on the other side of the Channel with the President of France, Mr Mitterrand, and his party.

According to the official programme, the two trains are to meet up in Calais. The dignitaries would disembark, luncheon would be served, speeches would be made and a new era of Franco-British cooperation would be inaugurated.

Of course, things go wrong. Terribly wrong. President Mitterrand's train is hijacked by terrorists soon after it leaves Paris. Instead of stopping at Calais, where the grand banquet is already prepared, Mitterrand and co. shoot on at over 200 miles an hour into the tunnel and under the Channel.

Meanwhile, the Queen and Mrs Thatcher are being propelled at a similar speed along the single-track line in the opposite direction.

I had explained all this in person one day to Tom Rosenthal in the course of an elegant little lunch à deux in his office, surrounded by Lowry originals. (Tom had been collecting L. S. Lowry's paintings and drawings long before most people had heard of him.)

'You have a problem, Stanley.' Tom poured me another generous glass of claret. (Those were the days when everyone drank wine at lunch.) 'If you absolutely must, you could sacrifice Mrs Thatcher and President Mitterrand. But the Queen must come to no harm. I insist on that.'

Tom's office was in Great Russell Street. When lunch was over, I mounted my bike and wobbled my way back to Little Venice.

I outlined my dilemma to Jenny later that day. 'Basically,' I told her, 'the two trains are going to collide in the tunnel under the Channel at a combined speed of over 400 miles an hour. There is going to be an almighty pile-up. The dignitaries, including the Queen, are bound to be hurt.'

By coincidence, I had been invited later that week to visit a research establishment at Farnborough where a vast wind tunnel had been constructed. Though aviation was its main concern, the Farnborough laboratory was also examining aerodynamic issues that might arise in the context of the Channel Tunnel, were such a project ever to get off the ground, or, more accurately, under the ground.

My guide, a Mr Duckworth, flipped a switch inside the vast chamber. There was a sound, as of a rushing mighty wind.

'Basically,' Mr Duckworth had to raise his voice to make himself heard above the noise, 'if you compress it enough, air can be as solid and as resistant as a brick wall.'

Inspiration struck! I thought I saw a way of avoiding a mega-pile-up in the Chunnel with certain danger to royal life and limb, not to speak of Mrs T and President M.

But I needed to pin it down.

'What if you had a train pushing the air in front of it at high speed in the tunnel, but there's a blockage the other end caused by another train pushing its own wall of air in front of it?'

Mr Duckworth decided to humour me. It was a quiet afternoon in Surrey. There wasn't much else going on. He switched the wind machine off so we could hear each other better.

'If the blockage was solid, and if there was no seepage, the compressed air itself would force both trains to a halt before the point of actual collision. Of course, there could be seepage at both ends. In that case, both trains would experience a rapid decelera-tion. But they wouldn't actually crash. Hopefully not, anyway. We could run some calculations.'

I still have the press release that the European Democratic Group in the European Parliament put out on 14 April 1984.

It says:

> *Tunnel* is an action-packed, high-powered adventure containing elements of high technology and political infighting. Mrs Thatcher, along with other members of the Cabinet, has received an advance copy of the book. She has written to Mr Johnson to say 'she hopes to find the time to read *Tunnel* during the Easter recess'.

The press release went on to say: '*Tunnel* has been written by Mr Johnson, author of *The Doomsday Deposit* and *The Marburg Virus*, with the intention of arousing more public interest in the Channel Tunnel project, which banks are due to report on within the next month.'

The press release also announced that on 25 April, a special train would leave Victoria at 10.53 a.m. and arrive at Dover at 12.30 p.m. where it would be met by local MEP Christopher Jackson. 'There will be light snacks and a press briefing at the Holiday Inn with MEPs, British Rail and the Channel Tunnel consortia.'

Well, we didn't exactly fill a train, but we were certainly more than a quorum that fine end-of-April morning when *Tunnel* was launched in Dover.

Ian MacPhail, who – as IFAW's European representative – had given me so much help with the seal campaign, arrived with a large bottle of Glenmorangie. Tim Heald, who had overlapped with me at Sherborne, was going to cover the event for the *Daily Express*, which he duly did.

The high point of the day was to be a visit to the site of the 'old' Channel Tunnel. Back in 1975, they had actually started digging under the sea at Dover. When Harold Wilson's Labour government ran out of money, the project had been scrapped. (So had the third London airport, to be built at Maplin. Wilson would have scrapped

Concorde too, except he couldn't because the UK was tied by an Anglo-French treaty.)

After the 'light lunch', and the press briefing, we piled into buses for the short journey to the gates of the 'old' tunnel. Exceptionally, the authorities had agreed that we could drive on down using the old access road to see just how far the previous tunnelling had progressed.

Was it Carl von Clausewitz or Helmuth von Moltke who famously said 'no plan of battle survives contact with the enemy'?

Whichever it was, he was spot on.

The British Rail people had *naturellement* forgotten to bring the keys to the gates, so we had to wait in the buses while someone went to Maidstone to fetch them.

One or two of the journalists phoned their offices to say, rather tetchily, that their copy might be late.

In the end the key was located, the gates to the old tunnel workings were unlocked, and we transferred to a minibus that drove down into the bowels of the earth.

We actually made our way in the minibus several hundred yards under the sea that day, before walking the last bit. We could still see some of the abandoned tunnelling equipment.

Whatever the press release might have said, I don't suppose the publication of my novel *Tunnel* influenced the outcome of that debate one way or the other. But we had a wonderful day in Dover, though the champagne ran out on the return journey to London.

Next day, I read Tim Heald's account in the *Daily Express*. Loyal to his schoolmates as ever, he began his article with the phrase: 'Another superb Johnson cock-up!'

Before *Tunnel* was published, I wrote to my old friend Alastair Morton. Alastair had been working for the International Finance Corporation (IFC) in Washington when I arrived there in 1966 to join the staff of the World Bank. (The IFC was part of the World Bank Group.) We had stayed in touch. Sara Morton, Alastair's wife, is godmother to my second son, Leo.

Alastair was also the newly appointed chief executive of the Channel Tunnel project and the man who more than anyone else would be responsible for seeing the largest civil engineering project of the twentieth century through to a successful conclusion.

'Dear Alastair,' I wrote. 'My publishers would much appreciate it if you could send them an endorsement of my new novel: *Tunnel*.'

I was actually very pleased with the book and I thought Alastair would be too.

I was particularly keen on the dramatic climax. The two trains are rushing towards each other at a combined speed approaching 400 miles an hour. But the wall of air, as correctly predicted by Farnborough's estimable Mr Duckworth, builds up into a solid mass as the gap between the two trains rapidly closes. As the engines come to a halt, nose-to-nose within yards of each other, Grantham, my ex-SAS superhero, jumps onto the track, boards the French train and quickly eliminates the hijacker terrorists with some quick, well-aimed bursts of his machine-pistol. In due course, the President of France awards Grantham the Légion d'Honneur and a grateful Queen of England offers him a knighthood.

Alastair clearly wasn't as keen as I was on the dramatic dénouement.

'Dear Stanley,' he wrote. 'Neither I nor Eurotunnel can endorse a book that encourages terrorism as a means of achieving regime change.'

Alastair was a brilliant man. Nor for nothing was he one of Britain's top businessmen. He must have realised that he had just given me a totally quotable quote because he went on to say: 'No part of this letter may be quoted on the book jacket or elsewhere used as an endorsement of the book.'

I really enjoyed working on *Tunnel*.

In the spring of 1983, for example, I joined William and Caroline Waldegrave on a two-week skiing holiday in the French Alps. William was MP for South West Bristol and Caroline ran Leiths School of Food and Wine.

I had been a bit hesitant at first when Caroline rang. 'There's a plenary session of the Parliament bang in the middle,' I said.

'Can't you miss it?'

'There might be a three-line whip.'

'Well, couldn't you pop over to Strasbourg for the day from the mountains?'

The Waldegraves had rented a chalet in Méribel for the first week and another chalet in Courchevel for the second. William's elder brother, Jamie, was part of the group too. Chalet girls would be in attendance to make sure we had hot chocolate and scrambled eggs etc.

It was the Easter holidays. Rachel and Jo came out with me for the first week's skiing in Méribel and Boris and Leo came for the second week in Courchevel.

They were all – the Waldegraves and the younger Johnsons – so much better at skiing than I was. They stayed on the slopes till it grew dark, whereas I tended to totter back to the chalet, exhausted, after lunch.

But I still had plenty of time to get on with my writing.

A quick shower, a quick glass of *glühwein*, and I would soon be sitting in front of the plate-glass window of the chalet with my tape recorder in hand, watching the skiers on the mountain face opposite and the 'eggs' of the bubble cars and cable cars criss-crossing the valley.

Here is a sample as typed out by Sharon Livingstone of All-Hours Word Processing from the tape I posted to her from Méribel:

The German watched the bubbles swinging up the mountain towards him. He played a little game with himself. Was Grantham's 'egg' red, or orange, or green, or yellow? He decided it would be yellow; and he was right. Even without his field glasses, he could distinguish the three occupants clearly. He wondered idly, as he raised the rifle to his shoulder, whether he should take out Grantham first, and then Karapolitis or should it be the other way round? Two virtually simultaneous shots rang out...

I am not sure, at this distance in time, why Grantham is in the 'egg' with his arch-rival, Dimitri Karapolitis, or why the 'German' (who he?) has it in for them both.

I missed a day's skiing during the second week, because – as Caroline had suggested – I decided to go to Strasbourg for a vote in the plenary. There was indeed a three-line whip on one of the votes that week (the British rebate question, as ever).

'Popping over to Strasbourg' from Les Trois Vallées is not as easy as it sounds. I arrived back in a taxi at the chalet well after midnight and rang the bell. No reply. The temperature was sub-zero. It was beginning to snow. I was wearing just a light jacket and a business suit. Feeling the cold and a slight sense of panic, I rang the bell again. Then I banged on the door. Still no response.

I walked round the side of the chalet, my shoes sinking deep into the snow. I saw the light still on in the room where Boris and Leo were sleeping.

My spirits rose. 'Good!' I thought. 'The boys are still awake. They just didn't hear the door.'

I looked in through the window. I banged on the glass. Both boys were clearly dead to the world.

In the end, one the chalet girls heard my plaintive cries.

Chapter Ten

Rafael Salas

Strictly speaking, I was due to resume my career as an international civil servant working for the European Commission as soon as my mandate as a MEP ended. In practice, the Commission more or less shuts down in the summer, so – at the invitation of Rafael Salas – I spent the first ten days of August 1984 in Mexico City attending the International Conference on Population.

Rafael Salas was one of my heroes. If I was asked to list the people I have known who have made a difference to the world – and to me personally – I would put Salas near or at the very top. We had been friends ever since he was appointed as the first head of the United Nations Population Fund (UNFPA) in 1969. I had met up with him many times since, in New York and elsewhere.

In June 1981, while I was still an MEP, and Mrs Simone Veil was still President, Salas came to Strasbourg. Mrs Veil was keen to meet him, and she kindly invited me too. Given Mrs Veil's own crucial role in her time as Health Minister in liberalising France's abortion law, it is not surprising that the two of them found much to talk about. Salas's political antennae were particularly acute. Very early on during his time at the UN Population Fund he had realised that the Fund couldn't just bang on about birth control. Women's rights, women's health and education, better nutrition – all of these had an impact on fertility, and the Population Fund had to be ready to expand its efforts in that direction.

As it happened, I had to be in the chamber later that afternoon for a debate on the Commission's proposal 'relating to the harmonisation of the labelling of fruit juices'.

For some reason, I had been invited by my group to present our point of view on this weighty matter.

I met Salas in the lobby afterwards. I think Salas was rather puzzled by the minutiae of European legislation as evidenced by the debate in the chamber that afternoon.

We headed for the European Parliament's restaurant.

'Restaurant!' I pointed out. 'That's one word you don't have to harmonise. Everyone understands restaurant. It's the same in every language!'

I owe a lot to Salas. He suggested to me, in the course of the meal we had that day in Strasbourg, that I might like to write a book about the United Nations' efforts to tackle the world population problem.

In due course I contacted Robin Pellew at Cambridge University Press. (I knew Pellew, or rather knew of him, because of the research he had done on elephants before he became a publisher, a subject I had also been closely involved with.) The CUP signed me up.

I wrote to Salas, telling him the good news. He phoned me as soon as he got the letter, suggesting that I include a chapter on the next World Population Conference, which would take place in Mexico City in August 1984.

'You can be part of the UNFPA delegation,' he told me. 'It will be like Bucharest ten years ago. Remember?'

Remember Bucharest in the summer of 1974? How could I forget it? Romania then was still under the iron control of President Ceauşescu. I had listened to Ceauşescu's speech at the opening session of the conference, held in Bucharest's Great Hall

After the count for the first directly elected European Parliament, Portsmouth Town Hall, June 1979. I am elected MEP for the Isle of Wight & Hampshire East by over 95,000 votes, the second largest majority in the country.

Jenny, 1982.

My parents at Nethercote, c. 1982.

Being received by Pope John Paul II, 1980. Sir James Scott-Hopkins, leader of the Conservative MEPs, is on the right, Jenny on the left.

With my third son, Jo, then aged nine, in Corfu, Greece, 1981.

On the ice, with a harp seal pup, in the Gulf of St Lawrence, Canada, 1982.

Addressing the crowd at a Save the Seals rally, Trafalgar Square, London, 1983.

With Joanna Lumley, Trafalgar Square, London, 1983.

The Save the Seals rally, Trafalgar Square, London, 1983. Ian MacPhail, the seal campaign coordinator, is on my right.

Receiving the Greenpeace Award, 1984, for outstanding services to the environment.

From the left: Boris, Jo, Rachel and Leo, March 1990.

With former Prime Minister Margaret Thatcher, 2005.

With Jenny and Harry, our Jack Russell terrier, 2005.

Genk, Belgium. Commemorating the twentieth anniversary of the EU's habitats directive and the establishment of NATURA 2000. Ignace Schops, a leading Belgian environmentalist, is on the left. The EU Environment Commissioner, Jan Potočnik, is standing between me and former Dutch MEP Hemmo Muntingh, March 2014.

Laurens Jan Brinkhorst, the Commission's director general for the environment, comes to my office. The Commission is overwhelmed by letters from the public about animal welfare. Most of these are sent on to me! Brussels, Belgium, 1988.

The film of my seventh novel, *The Commissioner*, starring John Hurt, is premiered at the Berlin film festival, 1998.

The EU Environment Council meets in Luxembourg in May 1989. I am standing next to EU Environment Commissioner Carlo Ripa di Meana. Laurens Jan Brinkhorst, the EU Commission's director general for the environment, is in the foreground on the left.

With President George H. W. Bush, at the White House Global Change Conference, 1990.

On holiday in Portugal, 1991.

Protesting against the World Trade Organization, Seattle, December 1999.

David Cameron MP very kindly came down to Devon to campaign for me in the 2005 general election when I stood as the Conservative candidate for Teignbridge.

ABOVE: Julia, Jenny and Max on the terrace of our house in Pelion, Greece, 2012.

LEFT: Boris and I play a squash match for charity in Newton Abbot, Devon, in the course of the 2005 general election campaign. Boris wins.

Climbing Mount Kilimanjaro
for the first time, 2011.

At Gilman's Point, Mount
Kilimanjaro, 2011.

The quick way down! Mount
Kilimanjaro, 2011.

With my guide, on the summit of Mount
Kilimanjaro, October 2013.

of the Republic (*Sala Palatuloi Republicii*). He took an unrepentantly Marxist view of the population issue. 'The problem of the population is, therefore, primarily linked to the multilateral, progressive development of human society, to a correct distribution of a national product and to equitable social relations, both on a national and international plane.'

This was gloomy stuff. Bucharest, at the time, was a fairly gloomy city. The restaurants were terrible. There wasn't much meat on the menu and most of the fish was *crap* (Romanian for 'carp').

For want of anywhere better to go, in the evening delegates tended to congregate in the Hanul Manuk Hotel, an old-fashioned establishment in the heart of the city with a halfway decent bar.

I was enjoying a pint or two of slivovitz there quite late one Friday evening at the end of the first week of the conference when I encountered Germaine Greer, internationally renowned feminist and author of the recently published bestseller *The Female Eunuch*.

Germaine, it turned out, was living in Italy at the time and had actually driven to Bucharest in her own car. She told me she was thinking of heading north at the weekend, to visit Transylvania and Dracula's castle.

'Care to come along, mate?' she said. 'I hope you can map-read.'

Naturally enough, Germaine, as an alpha female, took control of the wheel when we headed out next morning for Transylvania. Besides, it was her car.

I was just the bloody map-reader, as Germaine had made clear. So I looked at the map, which is what map-readers do. It was a bright, colourful affair, showing a veritable network of routes: motorways, A roads, B roads and so on. It reminded me a bit of the map I had found at a wayside fuel station in the Dasht-i-Lut desert in Iran a decade or so earlier when I was attempting to ride a motorcycle along Marco Polo's route from Oxford to China.

'I wonder if all these roads actually exist,' I said. I traced a possible route with my finger. 'We ought to aim for Brasoff first.'

Germaine looked at me sharply. 'I think it's pronounced Brashov, not *Bras-off*!'

'We should get to Pantsov just before Dracula's Castle!' I added, being careful to say 'Pantshoff', not '*Pants-Off*'. I didn't want to irritate Germaine. Not more than I had already. 'As far as I can see, Pantsov comes after Brasov.' I decided it was better not to mention that the map showed a village, apparently called Bëd, lying about 20 miles further on!

In the event, we didn't get much further than Snagov, an hour or two north of Bucharest.

We stopped to swim in the lake there. Germaine disappeared from view under the water, only to emerge spluttering and distressed.

'Weeds, man! There are weeds at the bottom!'

Once we were back on the road, she told me there had been an unhappy incident in her childhood, when she was growing up in Australia. Someone close to her had been caught up in weeds while swimming and had actually drowned.

'My God, I'm so sorry.'

I was indeed sorry but maybe I didn't make it clear enough. I really was having trouble with the map by then. As I had feared, roads that seemed to be clear enough on the map didn't seem to exist in real life.

I realised I wasn't scoring a lot of points. I hoped she wasn't going to start shouting at me. 'Jeez, man, can't you read the bloody map?'

Germaine had to slow to walking speed to negotiate a particularly vicious hairpin bend. It was now or never. I opened the door.

I next met the ever more famous Germaine Greer about three decades later. Jenny and I were staying for the weekend at Thriplow, near Cambridge, with our friends Oliver and Anne Walston.

Germaine, now a leading academic at nearby Cambridge University as well as an international celebrity, had been invited for lunch.

Seeing me must have rung a bell. 'Whatever happened to you?' she asked.

It is a question I frequently ask myself.

That aborted trip to Dracula's Castle, back in 1974, had another strange consequence. Somewhere along the way, I must have lost the front-door key to our Brussels house. We were living at the time in a fin-de-siècle *maison de maître* house in Square Marie-Louise. In the old days, before oil-fired central heating arrived, the house's supply of coal for stoking the furnace would be replenished via a long chute that led from the manhole in the street to the coal bunkers in the cellar.

As it happened, only the previous month, having gone out without my keys, I had been forced to gain entry via the coal chute, to emerge in due course in the kitchen, blackened but unbowed.

I tapped the taxi driver on the shoulder. 'Just hold on a moment. I think I'm going to have to climb in.'

The man regarded me quizzically. 'But the door to your house is open, sir.'

The door was indeed open. Not wide open, but definitely ajar.

'By Jove, so it is!' I exclaimed.

To this day, I do not know whether I failed to shut the door of the house properly on leaving for Bucharest, or whether it had been forced open by someone else who had then failed to shut it. I rather suspect the fault lay with me.

The good news was that I didn't have to go down through the coal chute after all. The bad news was that the house had clearly received an unauthorised visitor in my absence. Some long-playing records were strewn about in the sitting room overlooking the lake with its famous fountain. I spent a few minutes putting them back into the correct sleeves and replacing them on the shelf.

As I did so, I noticed to my chagrin that all of my Beatles records had been taken, as well as my treasured double album of Churchill's wartime speeches.

I never replaced that double album, but I can still hear the cadences, the characteristic lisp, as I write these words. 'If the British Empire, and its commonwealth, last for a thousand years, men will still say "thish" was their finest hour.'

Not my finest hour, perhaps.

Anyway, fast forward to 1984, ten years after Bucharest. From my point of view, the timing of Rafael Salas's invitation to the World Population Conference in Mexico City could not have been better timed. My last session in Strasbourg as an MEP was in July 1984. I would not be returning to the European Commission in Brussels until September. A week or two in Mexico was totally doable.

I made sure, as I set out for Mexico, that I had the right documentation. The last time I had visited Mexico had been when I was researching my book about world agriculture, *The Green Revolution*, and had arranged to meet Dr Norman Borlaug, Nobel Prize winner, then doing pioneering work in Mexico's Sonora State, way up north.

Unfortunately, when I arrived at the immigration controls at Mexico City's international airport, I was told that I needed a visa and I didn't have one.

I thought of slipping the immigration official a couple of $20 notes inside my passport but then decided against it. What if, by some mischance, I had stumbled across an honest man who wouldn't think twice about turning me in?

'So how can I get a visa?' I asked.

'You must go to the Mexican embassy in some other country.'

Easier said than done. Most of the other countries in striking distance with Mexican embassies themselves required an entry visa. This had the makings of a Catch-22 situation.

Eventually I had to fly all the way to Colombia before being allowed back into Mexico.

This time, happily, I was equipped with a nice blue UN passport. An official car met me at the airport and whisked me to my hotel, a modern skyscraper.

My room was on the twenty-fifth floor. When the conference wasn't in session, I sometimes sat at a desk by the window, looking down at the smog below. It was a strange sensation. A bit like being in an aeroplane above the clouds. In those days, Mexico City was one of the most polluted cities on the planet.

Officially, as Salas had promised, I was part of the UNFPA delegation for the duration of the conference. If the Bucharest gathering ten years earlier had been a politically fraught occasion, the Mexico City meeting was even more so. It witnessed a bizarre reversal of roles between the United States and China. Whereas in the past the USA had been one of the most vigorous proponents of population control, it now took a much more cautious stance. With the arrival of a Republican administration and the growing influence of right-wing fundamentalists, the USA had announced that it 'rejected compulsion or coercion in family planning programmes'. The administration would no longer 'contribute directly or indirectly to family planning programmes funded by governments which advocate abortion as an instrument of population control'.

Writing in the *Sunday Times* on 5 August 1984, Rosemary Righter clearly took the view that internal political considerations were a determining factor.

As she put it:

The Reagan administration's team, headed by the conservative ex-Senator James Buckley, a Roman Catholic, will arrive with speeches and policies which pander to the phobias of the anti-abortion Moral Majority and the arch-conservative lobbies in the US and which also plainly have an eye on the Republican Party convention the following week.

While James L. Buckley sat on his hands, Mr Wang Wei, China's delegate, stressed that China had been making unremitting efforts to develop her economy while controlling rapid population growth. China's national population growth rate had dropped to 1.154 per cent in 1983 from 2.089 per cent in 1973. 'All this has proved,' said Mr Wang Wei, 'that the policy decision of promoting family planning along with planned economic development is the correct one.'

For me, the conference's high point was when Rafael Salas came to the podium. By then, he had been executive director of the UN Population Fund for fourteen years. He had earned his spurs.

Salas didn't mince his words. The previous month the World Bank's World Development Report had urged intensified population control activities by governments, calling such efforts vital for successful development efforts. Now Rafael Salas stated unambiguously, 'Our goal is the stabilisation of global population within the shortest possible period before the end of the next century.'

One morning in the course of that 1984 UN World Population Conference, I took time off to visit Teotihuacan, one of the Aztec pyramids outside Mexico City. I found myself in the company of Lord Glenarthur, leader of the UK delegation and parliamentary secretary to the Ministry of Health and Social Security. As we climbed the steps to the summit of the pyramid, Glenarthur confirmed that the UK government's position on population was, from my point of view at least, totally sound. Next day he assured the plenary that the

British government was 'committed to continuing our development efforts and, within them, our support for population-related activities'. He announced a 50 per cent increase in funding for multilateral organisations working in the population field.

But the United Nations proceeds by consensus. Salas's appeal for an international commitment to 'global population stabilisation within the shortest possible period before the end of the next century' was never actually incorporated in the Mexico City Declaration on Population and Development that was adopted at the twelfth and last plenary meeting on 14 August 1974.

If the conference as a whole had been ready to endorse Salas's call for an international commitment to global population stabilisation, that would indeed have been a superb achievement. He had plenty of supporters. If I look back at my notes, I can't help noticing how much more forthright some countries were about the need to bring down birth rates and population growth rates than they are today.

It's almost as though we've given up on the population question. Just too hard to tackle. Like global warming.

I said goodbye to Salas as the meeting ended. He did not seem too downhearted. He might not have got everything he wanted, but he had avoided a major defeat, which, in the run-up to the conference, had seemed possible.

'I'm looking forward to reading the book,' he told me.

Though Rafael Salas read the final draft before my book, *World Population and the United Nations*, published by Cambridge University Press, he never saw the printed version. On 4 March 1987, he was found dead in his hotel room in Washington, DC, having apparently suffered a heart attack.

There was much speculation at the time about the real cause of death. Having once been President Marcos's right-hand man,

Salas had in recent years distanced himself from the Philippine President. Some people thought that he might himself one day run for his country's highest office. Maybe there was more to his death than a 'simple' heart attack.

As far as I know, none of the rumours was ever substantiated. Salas's widow left New York to live in California. When my book was published, which I dedicated 'to the memory of Rafael M. Salas, executive director of the United Nations Fund for Population Activities, 1969–87', she sent me a charming note.

Chapter Eleven

Back to Brussels

Jenny and I bought a house on the border of Uccle and Rhode St-Genèse of Brussels in the summer of 1984.

I won't say we bought it 'sight unseen' but we came quite close to it. One day, during my very last session in Strasbourg, I picked up a copy of *Le Soir*, a Belgian daily newspaper, from the newsstand in the European Parliament's building.

Knowing that within months we would be returning *en famille* to Belgium, I flipped idly through the *Petits Annonces* in the property section. One advertisement, in the 'property for sale' column, in particular, caught my eye. It was only a few words long. '*Villa à refraichir. 40 ares. Terrain de tennis. Limite Uccle-Rhode St-Genèse. 12 million francs.*' And it gave the vendor's contact details.

Forty ares! 0.4 of a hectare! By my calculations, that was about an acre of land. And a tennis court too! I could imagine popping back for lunch at home and a quick game of tennis after a morning's work, before returning to my desk for the afternoon stint.

I rang up Kathleen Lippens, an old friend who herself lived in the leafy and salubrious Brussels suburb of Rhode St-Genèse.

'Kathleen,' I pleaded, 'I'm in Strasbourg and not planning to come to Brussels any time soon. Could you go and see a house for me? I'm coming back to the Commission after the summer and Jenny and I need somewhere to live.'

Two days later Kathleen rang back.

'I went round on my bicycle,' she said. 'The house is in Avenue Boesdael, very close to me, actually. I met the owners. A charming couple, quite elderly. The garden is fantastic. More of a park, really.'

I noticed that Kathleen hadn't said much about the house.

'What's the house like?'

'Well,' she said, '*à refraichir* is *le mot juste*. It's a large house, eight bedrooms, but it will need a lot of work. And the tennis court will probably need resurfacing. Do you want me to make them an offer? Twelve million seems a bit high, but I'm sure they would come down.'

I was already certain 3 Avenue Boesdael was exactly the house we needed. I could visualise it as Kathleen spoke. One of those turn-of-the-century Belgian mansions, surrounded by a mature garden.

'Of course you can make an offer, Kathleen,' I replied.

'Don't you want to see the house first?' she asked.

Personally, I would have been quite happy to have let Kathleen Lippens conclude the deal there and then. She was a woman whose judgement I trusted. But some sixth sense told me it would be a good idea to consult Jenny first.

'The place sounds absolutely brilliant to me,' I told Jenny over the phone from Strasbourg. 'Do you think we ought to see it or shall we just let Kathleen make an offer?'

In the event, Jenny met me in Brussels and we called on the owners, an elderly couple called Mr and Mrs Ullens de Schooten. Strictly speaking, as we learned from Kathleen, they were *Monsieur le Baron et Madame la Baronne*. Whereas France abolished the use of titles after the French Revolution, the Belgians hung onto theirs. Almost everyone in Belgium seems to have a title. The Boëls, the de Lannoys, the de Spoelberchs, the Lippens, the de Borchgraves, the d'Oultrements, the d'Ursels, the de Wouters – you could go out to a dinner and find yourself totally surrounded by the Belgian aristocracy. Charming, intelligent, sophisticated people. For the most part, stinking rich, too, though it didn't do to enquire too deeply into the source of their wealth.

I am not sure whether the Ullens de Schootens had fallen on hard times, or whether they just wanted to downsize, now that they had reached a certain age.

Jenny and I sat in the sitting room, which, if all went to plan, would soon be ours. French windows opened out onto a terrace. The lawn stretched into the distance. There was a veritable orchard of fruit trees. Beyond the trees, I could see the tennis court. It was a clay court with a wonderful warm brick-coloured surface.

Oh God, I said to myself, I can't believe this. This is too good to be true. We could be happy here, I thought.

Admittedly, there wasn't much of a kitchen and upstairs, though there were eight bedrooms in varying states of disrepair, there was only one bathroom, and there were holes in some of the walls.

'What about 8 million?' I said. 'We're ready to offer 8 million.'

The baron seemed rather taken aback. Eight million was some way short of the asking price. Four million francs short to be precise.

He looked at his wife, sitting quite prim and upright in her chair by the fireplace.

I saw her give a little reluctant nod of her head. Kathleen Lippens had found out that the house had actually been on the market for some time. Maybe 8 million was not a totally unrealistic offer.

The baron wasn't happy. But he wasn't going to go without a fight.

'*Et le mazout?*' he asked. '*Qu'est-ce qu'on va faire avec le mazout?*'

'*Le mazout?*' I enquired, puzzled. Why was the Baron talking about heating oil?

'*Oui, le mazout. Il y a encore presque deux milles litres dans la citerne.*'

The baron's point of view was we should pay separately for the heating oil that was left in the tank. The oil fed the boiler deep in the cellar, and the boiler – in theory at least – fed the radiators with hot water.

I didn't at the time share the baron's opinion, though I later learned that it is common practice in real-estate transactions in Belgium for people who are buying a house to offer to pay for the oil separately.

'Non, monsieur,' I said firmly. '*Nous offrons 8 millions, c'est tout.*'

I could see that this was a crucial moment. The baron looked at Madame la Baronne. Then he gave a little sigh, a faint exhalation. Even if I wasn't going to pay extra for the *mazout*, they had decided that this would not be a deal-breaker.

'*Nous acceptons votre offre, monsieur.*'

We shook hands and I wrote the Ullens de Scootens a cheque on the spot for a million francs on a Brussels bank by way of deposit.

A few days later the bank rang me, pointing out that I didn't have a million francs in my account.

Apparently unauthorised overdrafts are not as normal in Belgium as they are in Britain, so it took a while to sort things out but the Ullens de Schootens soon got their money.

I have to hand it to the Ullens de Schootens. We got our comeuppance in due course over the business of the fuel oil.

My term as an MEP having come to a self-inflicted end, Jenny and I moved to Belgium, lock, stock and barrel, in September 1984. We rented a house in Woluwe, a suburb of Brussels quite near the Commission, while our 'villa' in Rhode St-Genèse was being 'refreshed'. We found a wonderful Polish worker called Joseph (probably an illegal immigrant), who masterminded a small team of other Polish workers as they worked through the winter months, even when there was snow on the ground.

Each week Jenny drove across town and into the leafy suburbs off the Chaussée de Waterloo with armfuls of cash to pay the workers.

It was, in some ways, a race against time. Our second child was due in March and we hoped, obviously, that we would be able to move from our rented accommodation into a house of our own before the baby arrived.

We made it with a few weeks to spare. Joseph and his team, used to sub-zero temperatures in Warsaw and the Polish steppes, had worked through the winter in an unheated house.

When Jenny and I finally installed ourselves in our newly refurbished villa in the spring of 1985, I went down to the cellar to start the boiler.

The boiler refused to fire. I consulted Joseph. Though his fellow workers had gone on to other jobs, Joseph remained our loyal supporter, not just then but throughout our time in Brussels. I think he even became a 'legal' as opposed to an 'illegal' worker, though I'm not sure about this. Joseph's dealings with the authorities were, as I saw it, his problem not mine.

'*Ça ne marche pas*, Joseph,' I complained, taking him down to the cellar with me and showing him the switches I had pressed on the boiler to get it to work.

Joseph tried to get it started himself. He peered at the fuse box with a torch. All the fuses seemed to be in good order.

Finally he climbed into the dark recesses of the cellar to inspect the fuel tank.

'*C'est vide, monsieur*,' he said, on his return. '*Pas de mazout.*'

Empty! Not a drop!

'Could the fuel have leaked out?' I asked.

Joseph shook his head. '*Non, monsieur.* The tank has been emptied.'

Of course, I was cross at the time. Jenny was cross too. With me.

'Why didn't you just pay the Ullens de Schootens for the oil when they asked?' she said. 'If you had, they wouldn't have had someone pump it out so they could take it away with them.'

Never underestimate the Belgians. They are nobody's fool. Even the oldies, like the Ullens de Schootens, had their wits about them. Particularly the oldies. They have had more time to learn the ways of the world.

When I first joined the European Commission, in early 1973, it had already sent its very first proposal for an Environmental Action Programme to the Council. The draft programme of action covered the years 1973–76 and it was actually being negotiated by the environmental attachés of the nine member states in the Environment Working Group of the Council when I arrived.

One of my first jobs, as the newly appointed head of the Commission's Prevention of Pollution and Nuisances Division, was to accompany Michel Carpentier, the brilliant, pugnacious Frenchman who headed what was then known as the Commission's Environment and Consumer Protection Service (ECPS), as he headed off to defend the vital chapters of the European Environmental Action Programme.

Ten years later, it was déjà vu all over again. My new job was that of adviser to the ECPS. Almost as soon as I arrived in Brussels to re-join the ECPS in this new capacity, Mr Athanase Andreopoulos, a charming Greek who had succeeded Michel Carpentier as the head of the EPCS, asked me to take overall responsibility for the drafting and presentation of the European Community's Fourth Environmental Action Programme (to cover the years 1987–92) and for negotiating it through the European Parliament and the Council.

Of course, I wasn't faced with a blank sheet of paper when I settled down to work. I sent a note around the department, inviting colleagues to send in their ideas and proposals.

Some of my colleagues were a bit surprised when I returned to Brussels and saw my renewed stint in the Commission as just another way of continuing an environmental campaign, but this time from within, not outside, the citadel of power.

I know some of them thought my methods unorthodox, to say the least. Claus Stuffman, in charge of 'nature protection', certainly did. I went to see him in his office. He looked gloomy. I don't think he was looking for new ideas. Not at that point. The Commission was finding it difficult to implement some of the measures that had already been agreed in earlier environmental action programmes.

'We've got an EC birds directive already, Claus,' I said. 'But that's not enough. We need a directive covering *all* species and *all* habitats.'

Claus didn't really like the idea of an all-encompassing EU-wide habitat and species directive, which was what I was proposing. Or, even if he did, he didn't see how the member states would ever agree to such a measure.

But I pushed hard and it worked. In the section dealing with the 'Conservation of Nature and Natural Resources', the EU's Fourth Environmental Action Programme, adopted by the Council on 7 December 1987, repeats word for word the draft text I had typed out at home in Brussels. It says:

More than six years have elapsed since the Council adopted its directive and resolution on the conservation of wild birds ... What essentially is needed is a Community instrument aimed at protecting not just birds but all species of fauna and flora; and not just the habitat of birds, but the habitat of wildlife – animals and plants – more generally. Such a comprehensive framework should ensure that, throughout the Community, positive measures are taken to protect all forms of wildlife and their habitat.

Today, around 18 per cent of the territory of the EU's member states is designated as conservation areas. And these are not just paper parks. The directive provides for strict measures of protection. If the member states don't live up to their obligations, they can be – and are – taken to the European Court of Justice in Luxembourg.

I know that in these Eurosceptic days, some people – including senior politicians – look askance at EU directives, and wonder why we have to have them at all. My answer to that is that member states, acting individually on their own, would never have managed to achieve the coherent network of protected areas that we now have under the habitats directive and which is known as Natura 2000. Either they wouldn't have thought of it at all, or they would have failed to drive the measure through *chez eux* against the combined forces of inertia on the one hand and vested interests on the other.

In October 2013, an organisation known as the EUROPARC Federation, representing protected areas in thirty-six countries, invited Hemmo Muntingh and me to come to Genk in Belgium to receive an award for being 'joint founders' of Natura 2000.

There is a third 'founder' mentioned in the citation: Claus Stuffman. After I left the Commission in 1990, Claus negotiated the final text of the habitats directive through the European Parliament and the Council. Unfortunately, he was not able to come to Genk that day but he was honoured *in absentia* and properly so.

Actually, I almost didn't get to Genk in time to receive the award. I took the Eurostar from St Pancras International through the Channel Tunnel to Brussels, then made my way from the Gare du Midi to the Gare Central.

I thought I heard an announcement for the train for Genk, some 60 miles south of Brussels, only to find that I had boarded the train for Ghent, 40 miles to the north.

It took a while to sort things out. I arrived in the huge hall at Genk where the EUROPARC Conference was being held just in time to join Hemmo Muntingh and Europarc's director, Ignace Schops, as they cut a huge celebratory cake. EU Environment Commissioner Janez Potočnik made a speech celebrating the achievements of Natura 2000 and presented us both with a commemorative certificate.

Apart from the small unprogrammed detour at the start, this was a totally satisfying outing, and made all the more so by the long interview I had the following morning in my hotel with a young Irishman called Andrew Jackson who was, amazing as it sounds, writing a PhD thesis on 'the origins of the habitats directive'.

We sat on the terrace having an early breakfast (I was heading back to Brussels that morning to catch the Eurostar home) while Andrew posed some key questions.

'There's no way,' he began, 'the European Commission would be ready to propose such a comprehensive measure today. Today, you simply couldn't get that kind of proposal through the Commission, could you? OK, you might have your colleagues in your own department on side, but what about the other departments of the Commission, the industry people, the agriculture people. Didn't the President's cabinet, Delors's people, want to throw it out? Why didn't they succeed?'

The tape recorder was whirring away, but I didn't let that deter me. Andrew Jackson had come all the way from Dublin for this interview. He had obviously done his homework. A lot of homework. You don't get to the final stages of a PhD by sitting on your hands. He deserved an honest answer.

'I agree with you,' I replied. 'I don't think we would get a proposal like the habitats directive out of the Commission today. But twenty-five or thirty years ago it was a different story. The Commission was very much in the driving seat. It wasn't always looking over its shoulder. Even so, I was lucky. Very lucky.'

'What do you mean?' Andrew asked.

'I had one of those old-fashioned Amstrads,' I explained, 'the kind Alan Sugar invented, with a dot-matrix printer. If you look out the original text of the habitats directive, the one in the archives, not the one they printed in the official journal, you'll find that the English version – and that was the version I circulated to the other departments of the Commission – is clearly photocopied from my Amstrad original.'

Andrew didn't quite follow the thread. 'You had better explain.'

'We didn't have emails in those days,' I said. 'We didn't have electronic means of sending texts from one Commission department to another. If you sent them a directive typed out on a machine that was quite incompatible with the machines they were using in their own departments, they'd have to retype the whole thing if they wanted to change it. The odds were they would simply wave it through. That's what they did.'

Jackson laughed. I don't think he believed me.

'What about the President's Cabinet? Wasn't Delors terrified the French, who love shooting small birds whenever they get a chance, were going to have a pop at him instead, next time he visited the French *paysage*?'

Jackson had a good point there.

I told him I remembered being rung up one day by André Jacquot, the member of Delors's Cabinet who had particular responsibility for agriculture. Jacquot was apoplectic with rage. I could feel the spray even over the phone.

The President was going to block the habitats and species directive, he said. They had had enough trouble in France with the birds directive. French hunters had rioted when they were told they were no longer allowed to shoot their beloved ortolan, or bunting.

'Your habitats directive is ten times worse,' he fumed. 'You've got forty pages of different animals to be protected. Ten pages of different habitats. *Ça ne va pas. Ça ne vas pas du tout. Nous allons le bloquer.*'

Jacquot was clearly about to hang up. Inspiration struck.

'Okay,' I said, 'we'll leave all of the annexes blank, including the lists of habitats and species to be protected. They can be filled in later by a technical committee. *Un comité technique.*'

I could hear the pause at the other end. Basically, I was proposing that the Commission should just send the Parliament and Council a skeleton framework.

From my point of view, that was better than nothing. Once the draft was on the table, once the text – any text – of a habitat and species directive had been sent to Parliament and Council, battle would at least have been joined. We could build up the pressure in the press and the media, and above all with the NGO community, to make sure that in due course meat was put on the skeleton. Lots of meat.

Organisations such as the Royal Society for the Protection of Birds (RSPB) had already devoted resources to helping us produce a good draft. Alastair Gammell, for example, an RSPB official, was actually living in Brussels full time. Then there was Simon Lyster, who was working for WWF. Friends of the Earth fielded a strong team too, with Tony Juniper very much to the fore.

And it wasn't just a question of profiting from the technical proficiency of such men (and women). By involving them and their organisations at the drafting stage, we were – we hoped – helping to ensure the more formal support of their organisations at a later date.

A few days later, the skeleton directive, stripped of its vital annexes, was adopted by the Commission. I don't think Delors's

Cabinet were at all pleased. I don't think Delors himself was pleased. But they let it go through.

The ensuing game of ping-pong between the Community institutions went on for years.

The Parliament threw the directive back at the Commission, calling for the detail that we had been forced to leave out. The Commission in the end did what the Parliament asked. The Parliament, delighted to have had its way, with Hemmo Muntingh as the rapporteur, did a magnificent job of improving the text and actually tightening the provisions. Some five years after the habitats directive was first proposed, it was finally adopted by the Council. Natura 2000 was at last officially born.

A car drew up outside the terrace where Jackson and I were having breakfast. My good friend Hemmo Muntingh, who had had another breakfast meeting elsewhere, was in time to join us. Half an hour later, I got into a taxi and headed for the station.

I haven't seen Hemmo since that day in Genk but we keep in touch. He's a great man and he made a huge difference to Europe's environment.

Chapter Twelve

Working for Animals

During my time as an MEP, I was the founder-chairman of the all-party group on animal welfare. The group met in Strasbourg most months when the Parliament was in session. Like most all-party groups, attendance varied. Sometimes we had as many as twenty MEPs attending; sometimes as few as three or four.

Madron Seligman, MEP for West Sussex (and the only person in the June 1979 European election to achieve a larger majority than I did in the Isle of Wight & Hampshire East) was a regular attender, usually accompanied by his wife, Nancy-Joan.

Madron had been at Balliol with Edward Heath. They had both been President of the Oxford Union. They had been travelling around Germany together just before the outbreak of the Second World War and had only just managed to get back to Britain before the opening of hostilities. Madron remained close friends with Edward Heath, who was not the most clubbable of men.

Madron (we called him 'Mad Ron'), like Ted Heath, was keen on music. He used to play the piano at our group's Christmas parties.

Another stalwart of the Parliament's animal welfare 'intergroup' was Otto von Habsburg. Otto had been the heir apparent to the Austria-Hungary Empire but unfortunately (from his point of view) the Austria-Hungary Empire disappeared before he could take over.

Otto, when told that an Austria–Hungary football match was being televised that evening, once famously asked, 'Oh, who are they playing?'

One day, Otto and I were despatched on an official visit to Turkey on behalf of the European Parliament's Turkey delegation. We were coming in to land when Otto, who was sitting in a seat across the aisle, leant over and showed me a photo of himself as a child of three, sitting on an embroidered cushion, being presented to the Sultan.

John Taylor, then an MEP and now Baron Kilclooney, was also a Member of the European Parliament's delegation on that occasion. He recently reminded me that, when asked at a press conference what our view was of the military regime in Turkey, I replied that on the whole we preferred generals to colonels.

'That went down well, as you can imagine,' John said, 'given the way the Turks felt about the Greeks.'

'Good of you to remember my *bon mots*, John. I should have kept a diary.'

As a matter of fact, I did keep a diary for those first few years in the European Parliament, writing almost daily entries in a very posh leather-bound Smythson notebook. It was lying on the chair in our place in Maida Avenue with some newspapers on top of it when our cleaning lady arrived.

She was in fact quite a mature woman, well over seventy I would say. She was slow but she was thorough. In the course of cleaning up one morning, she scooped up the pile of papers, as well as the notebook, and threw the whole lot into the bin.

Nowadays, of course, we 'back things up' on our computers, which is fine until the computer crashes, when you lose it all anyway. Recently, I have been sending documents into something called 'The Cloud'. It is good to know that they are all safely there, snuggling up to each other in 'The Cloud'. I have not yet found a way of retrieving them.

I gave up keeping a diary after that minor disaster, though I did, during the course of the 2005 general election campaign, write a daily 'blog' for Channel 4. I was not, as it happened, elected to Parliament in 2005, though, as we shall see in a subsequent chapter, my Channel 4 blog helped earn me a brief but highly enjoyable stint as a *Guardian* columnist.

But back to the European Parliament's animal welfare group. Officially known as the Intergroup for Animal Welfare, the European Parliament's all-party animal welfare group owed a lot to the RSPCA. The RSPCA gave the group its strong moral support. Even more important, it provided practical support as well.

Mike Seymour Rouse, the RSPCA's man in Brussels, came down to Strasbourg each month to act as the secretary of our group.

I once asked him why he was called Mike when his real name was Edward.

He pointed to his guardsman's tie. 'I wasn't really tall enough for a guardsman. Nowhere near 6 ft. First day on parade, the sergeant-major comes along. Sticks his face about an inch from mine and shouts, "What's your name?"

'So I shout back, "Seymour-Rouse!"

'He shouts even louder. "What did you say?"

'"Seymour-Rouse, *sir*!"

'"Seymour bloody Rouse!" the sergeant-major roars. "Mickey bloody Mouse if you ask me."'

The name stuck. From that day on, except perhaps to his mother and childhood friends, Edward Seymour-Rouse was Mike or Mickey.

When he wasn't campaigning for the welfare of animals, Mike's passion was vintage cars. He was also a great linguist. He had perfected his German in a prisoner-of-war camp. His French was of a high standard too. Held in respect by MEPs of all parties and nationalities, he succeeded in making sure that EU regulations regarding noise levels, exhaust emissions and fuel efficiency contained all the necessary exemptions to allow him and others to continue to drive their lovingly tendered 4-litre behemoths on Europe's roadways without let or hindrance.

He had been married more than once and was still on good terms with his last but one mother-in-law, whom he referred to as 'the Ayatollah'.

For technical and scientific details, as opposed to active lobbying, the RSPCA lent us their chief vet, David Wilkins. Where animal welfare is concerned, the devil is always in the detail. The Parliament's animal welfare intergroup didn't limit itself to the welfare of wild animals, even though achieving the ban of seal imports had been our proudest achievement. We were also concerned with the welfare of farm animals and that issue went to the heart of the Community's agricultural policy. How could there be a level playing field if one country imposed strict animal welfare standards (e.g. banning battery hens and calves reared in veal crates) while other countries had much laxer standards or no standards at all?

David Wilkins, and the scientists to whom he had access, could be relied upon to come up with the numbers. If sheep are being transported from the Scottish Highlands to Bari in the heel of Italy, how many breaks in the journey should there be? What about food and water en route? The book David Wilkins in due course published about EU animal welfare policy is several hundred pages long and is still seen as an authoritative text.

Under the prodding of the intergroup, the Parliament adopted several resolutions calling on the Commission to propose measures to improve animal welfare.

As always, of course, the real power to change things lay (in those days at least) with the Commission, not the Parliament. The Parliament could flex its muscles and pass resolutions asking the Commission to do this or that, but there was no legal obligation on the Commission to respond.

It was a bit like that passage in Shakespeare when Glendower says, 'I can call spirits from the vasty deep' and Hotspur replies, 'But will they come when you do call for them?'

I didn't forget Mike Seymour-Rouse and David Wilkins when I returned to Brussels. I didn't forget the sterling efforts of the Parliament's animal welfare intergroup, which I had chaired for five years and which was still flourishing under Madron. Nor did I forget the organisations with which I had worked so closely when I was an MEP.

When you get to my age (seventy-three at the time of writing) you start looking back at your CV. In terms of my professional career, I consider the three most important achievements of my life to have been: (a) helping to set up the United Nations population agency, (b) being one of the 'founders' of Natura 2000, Europe's great network of protected areas, and (c) the work for animal welfare that I did both in the European Parliament and in the Commission.

Of course, it could be argued that conservation of wild animals is itself a form of animal welfare, but I use the term here in its more traditional sense of action taken to avoid suffering and improve the welfare of individual animals or groups of animals.

At the end of 1984, soon after I returned to Brussels, I managed to insert under the Environment chapter of the Commission's Programme for 1985, which President Delors duly presented to the European Parliament in January of that year, the following paragraph:

> An improvement in the quality of life also entails respect for animals in the member states and in the member states dealing with the rest of the world. The regular debates concerning the hunting of seal pups should not conceal the many questions raised by the exploitation of animals in Europe: the use of animals for experiments, factory farming, trade in animals and the processing of animals for consumption purposes. The Commission will examine all possible steps which can be taken in this connection.

I have already mentioned that I was responsible for drafting the European Community's Fourth Environmental Action Programme (4EAP). Given that the Commission had already approved this paragraph in the context of its 1985 work programme, I felt the best thing to do was to simply repeat it word for word in the draft. There is a sound bureaucratic principle: wherever an agreed text will serve the purpose, stick to that text, however clunky it may sound.

Anyway, I didn't think it sounded at all clunky. *An improvement in the quality of life also entails respect for animals in the member states and in the member states dealing with the rest of the world.* That sentence, to my mind, is as valid today as it ever was.

The crucial thing, having established the rationale, as it were, was now to provide some legislative impetus by including some specific priorities for EU action.

That is precisely, I am glad to say, what the Fourth Environmental Action Programme did. The 4EAP goes on to say:

> It will be important in the context of the Fourth Environment Programme to put some flesh on this brief statement. Priorities will

include the better enforcement of existing Community Directives relating to animal protection and the proposal of new Community measures, where this is appropriate, e.g. for the protection of laboratory animals and the welfare of farm animals.

I don't want to give the impression that it was all plain sailing from then on. It wasn't.

As far as the issue of animal experimentation was concerned, I soon ran into opposition from within the Commission itself.

The Commission's Directorate-General V (DG V), which looked after the Community's then fairly limited interest in health and social affairs, was not at all keen on having an EC directive on animal experimentation. The responsible director was a former British doctor, Dr William Bennett, who had joined the Commission not long after I had. DG V was based in Luxembourg, and I made a couple of trips to Luxembourg with a view to talking him round, but was not successful. The problem was twofold. Number one, I think he genuinely believed that clamping down on vivisection might hold back important medical research. Number two, he thought that DG V, which dealt with health, not DG XI, which dealt with the environment, should be the competent service.

I might have agreed with him on the latter point if I had been convinced that Bennett's claim of 'competence' for DG V wasn't simply a blocking tactic, the oldest trick in the book. Simply say, 'sorry, that's my job', and once people have agreed it's your job, just do nothing.

Bennett certainly knew how to sit on his hands. It was immensely frustrating. The Council of Europe had produced a very good Convention on the Use of Animals for Scientific Purposes. As I saw it, it was just a matter of transposing the provisions of the Convention into a Community directive.

Bennett said, 'Why do we need an EU directive on animal experimentation if the member states are already ready to sign up to a Council of Europe Convention on the same subject?'

I replied, 'Signing up to a Council of Europe Convention and applying an EU directive are two different things. With an EU directive, you can rely on the whole force of EU law. You can go to the European Court of Justice if you have to.'

To keep DG V happy, I agreed with Dr Bennett that they could 'share' the responsibility for the directive. In bureaucratic terms, this was incredibly naive of me. Given the amount of work the Council of Europe had done by now, I already had a very good draft to put before other departments of the Commission, such as the Industrial Affairs department, which wanted to be sure that we didn't hold up major pharmaceutical and medical breakthroughs with our insistence on regulating animal experimentation.

Bennett still procrastinated. I pointed to the commitment that was to be found in the Fourth Environment Programme regarding a Commission proposal 'for the protection of laboratory animals'. Bennett countered by saying the text included the condition 'where this is appropriate'. He refused to join me in convening an interservice meeting to discuss the draft text of the directive we had prepared.

Days passed; weeks passed. In the end I asked my secretary, Anne Crossley, to send out a telex anyway.

'What about Dr Bennett?' Anne asked. 'Shouldn't he sign too?'

'There's no need to sign a telex,' I said. 'Just print Dr Bennett's name at the end of the telex, next to mine.'

Bennett arrived in our Rue Guimard building half an hour before the meeting was due to begin. He was spitting fire. He had never signed the telex convening the interservice meeting. He was not at all happy.

Well, I wasn't happy either. As I saw it, this was a wonderful opportunity to do something for animals. Not just thousands of animals, but hundreds of thousands of animals, who suffered daily in the name of 'progress'.

I wouldn't say Bennett gave in with good grace, but he gave in. Stanley Clinton-Davis (now Lord Clinton-Davis) was the Commissioner for the Environment when I re-joined the Commission. He made it clear very early on that he was 100 per cent behind my efforts to make progress at Community level on animal welfare efforts and he approved wholeheartedly of the draft directive on animal experimentation, which he now was able to present to the Commission for adoption.

We had some powerful allies too, outside the Commission. Once the Commission had formally approved the text of the animal experimentation directive, the Euro-Group helped to ensure that the Parliament approved it in the shortest possible time.

The story didn't end there. By some stroke of good fortune, the Dutch, who took over the Presidency of the Council in January 1986 (the Presidency rotated among the member states every six months), decided that they would make the adoption of the animal experimentation directive one of the key objectives of their term of office.

Willem Hoogendoorn, a tall man with a luxuriant moustache, was the Dutch environmental attaché. He scheduled meeting after meeting of the Council Working Group to discuss the long and detailed text we had prepared. Barely six months after the proposal had left the Commission, the Dutch decided to put it on the agenda of the Environment Council. I don't remember now what key issues, if any, were still left for the ministers to decide. I was optimistic that agreement would be reached.

The Council didn't always meet in Brussels. As a result of some complex inter-institutional negotiations that I do not need to go into here, Council meetings which fall in May are held in Luxembourg.

I drove up from Brussels through the Ardennes, checked into the Holiday Inn on Luxembourg's Kirchberg Plateau, and got to the Council meeting in good time the next morning. It was good to see a handful of demonstrators outside. I stood for a moment, reading the placards and listening to the chanting. The environment was becoming an increasingly hot topic. In Germany, for example, the 'death of the forests' – *waldsterben* – had become a major political issue. Once, when I was an MEP, I had accompanied a German MEP, Siegbert Alber, on a tour of the Black Forest, where his constituency was situated.

To see the tall fir trees stripped bare was a truly tragic sight. My German leaves something to be desired, but I knew enough to sing the famous song as Siegbert and I held hands around the table after dinner.

'*O Tannenbaum, O Tannenbaum, Wie treu sind deine Blätter!*'

The trouble was the leaves weren't verdant (*treu*) at all. They had fallen off the trees altogether.

Acid rain, caused by air pollution, had been identified as the culprit. You could deal with air pollution only by cracking down on the polluters. And that had an EU dimension too. If Country A cracked down on the polluters, but Country B didn't, then industry in Country B could enjoy a free ride.

The demonstrators who gathered that morning in front of the Council building in Luxembourg were vocal, if not numerous. One by one the ministers arrived in their cars. Some of them seemed surprised by the demonstrators. In those days, environment ministers were not often the centre of attention. But they seemed pleased too. Maybe, after all, they were doing something that mattered.

Because animal experimentation issues in Britain have always been handled by the Home Office, David Mellor, then a Minister of State in that department, accompanied William Waldegrave, then Environment Minister, to Brussels. While Waldegrave took the strictly environmental items on the agenda, including in particular the acid rain problem, on which the Commission had proposed a directive to regulate emissions from large power plants, David Mellor dealt with the vivisection issue.

I have to say, Mellor played a blinder. It was perfectly clear that the UK had decided this was a directive they were ready to support. Indeed, UK legislation to regulate the use of animals in experiments was in the final stage of the legislative process. In less than two hours, the complete text of the directive with its accompanying annexes had been agreed.

At the end of 1986, the EU established a special centre in Italy devoted to studying and validating alternative test methods, not involving animals. Dr Michael Balls, director of the Fund for the Replacement of Animals in Medical Experiments (FRAME) was appointed the first director.

A couple of years ago, I was invited by my third son, Jo (now MP for Orpington), to go to Lord's to watch the Lords and Commons XI take on the MCC. I got there soon after the start of play to see that Jo was bowling and Ed Balls was keeping wicket. Both of them, as far as I could see, were turning in superb performances. Jo was fairly hurling them down. But, if the balls beat the batsman, they did not beat the wicket-keeper. Ed Balls threw himself this way and that and even narrowly missed a stumping.

Unfortunately, rain intervened before the match had progressed very far.

The players retired to the pavilion. Amid the splendour of the Long Room, I had a chance to talk to Ed Balls, the shadow Chancellor of the Exchequer, while the teams waited for play to resume.

'Your dad's a hero of mine,' I said. 'FRAME led the way in the fight against vivisection.'

My personal view is that any man who has Professor Michael Balls as a father deserves our respect, for that if for no other reason. And I am still hoping, even at this late hour, that Ed Balls is going to drop Labour's commitment to the HS2 – high-speed train – project.

On 10 February 1987, with the EU's directive on animal experimentation in force in all the member states, I was authorised to go to the Council of Europe's headquarters in Strasbourg to sign the Council's own 'Convention for the Protection of Vertebrate Animals used for Experimental and Other Scientific Purposes' on behalf of the European Community.

This was the first time I have ever officially signed an international treaty. I suspect it will be the last time too.

Chapter Thirteen

The Zoos Directive

The directive on animal experimentation was not the only legislative text to see the light of day as a direct result of the inclusion of that key paragraph about 'animal welfare' in the text of the European Community's Fourth Environmental Action Programme. 'The Commission will examine all possible steps that can be taken in this connection,' was what the text said.

All possible steps! If that wasn't carte blanche, I was colour-blind!

When I re-joined the staff of the Commission in Brussels in September 1984, I was a trustee of an organisation called Zoo Check. It had originally been set up by the actress Virginia McKenna and her husband, Bill Travers. Virginia and Bill had famously starred, along with Elsa the Lioness, in the film *Born Free*. Each directorate-general in the Commission, including my own DG (we were now DG XI – Environment) had a modest budget to fund research. When Zoo Check approached me to suggest the Commission should support a survey of Europe's zoos, focusing on animal welfare, I was delighted.

A few months later, we received the report. It revealed a horrendous state of affairs. More than half the zoos in Europe were simply not up to scratch as far as basic animal welfare standards were concerned. The report included distressing photographs of animals demonstrating 'stereotypical behaviour': gnawing at the bars of their far-too-small cages, bashing their heads from side to side, sometimes starving and crippled.

Kersten Sundseth, working in Claus Stuffman's division but passionate about animal welfare issues, made time to help me draw up the text of the directive.

Of course, we weren't the experts. The people who knew what needed to be done to improve the welfare of animals in zoos were above all the people who worked with the animals, in the zoos, on a day-to-day basis.

One day in my office I held a meeting with a delegation from the European Association of Zoos and Aquaria (EAZA). These far-seeing people realised only too clearly that the reputation of the whole industry was at stake and that urgent action had to be taken. EAZA had already drawn up some standards for basic animal welfare in zoos, but the trouble was that these EAZA standards were purely voluntary. They were simply recommendations. And, like many recommendations put out by well-meaning international bodies, they were more often honoured in the breach than the observance. If we managed to incorporate them somehow in a European directive, then they could be enforced through the European Court.

We made progress. We circulated a text within the DG. After that, we circulated it to a few trusted colleagues in other DGs. I wouldn't say the text was received with enthusiasm but no black-balls were cast. That meant, crucially, that the text could go forward as an A Point on the agenda on the Commission itself. If one or more other services had objected (the Legal Service, for example), the draft directive would have had to go to a meeting of the chefs de cabinet.

The chefs de cabinet (each one of them looked after the interests of a different Commissioner) were very busy men. I knew that if they took one look at the 'draft directive on zoos', they would start asking questions. And that meant trouble. They would probably kill it on the spot. Another possibility was that the chefs de cabinet, failing to agree on the text themselves, would leave the matter for the Commission itself to decide at one of its weekly formal sessions.

My heart quailed at the thought. The Commission was talking more and more about the importance of 'subsidiarity'. They were committed, in other words, to leaving to 'the appropriate level' whatever decisions needed to be taken; in other words they wanted to show, to restive people like the Brits, for example, that they weren't wedded to EU-level action at all costs.

I simply couldn't imagine that the honourable members of the Commission, sitting around that famous round table on the thirteenth floor of the Berlaymont, would conceivably allow my little directive on zoos to go forward to the Council and the Parliament on the next stage of what would undoubtedly be a long and hazardous journey.

I could imagine one of the commissioners intervening in protest: '*Monsieur President, je ne vois pas la nécessité*', as Brigitte Bardot had said when I suggested meeting her after the successful seal campaign.

Would Jacques Delors, the President of the Commission, intervene on behalf of the animals? I very much doubted it. Delors – as I have already mentioned – was regularly barracked by his countrymen in rural France, *la France profonde*, because, as a result of the birds directive, the hunting of birds such as the bunting had been banned.

Was there a way forward? Yes, there was.

If you were a *fonctionnaire*, as I was, the best possible way of ensuring that the Commission as a whole approved a contentious text without discussion was to use something known as *procedure écrite*, or 'written procedure'. This meant that though a particular item was formally listed for approval on the Commission's agenda, it would go through without discussion.

Of course, the rules had to be respected. The Commission's weekly agenda was prepared by the Commission's Secretary-General and his secretariat. To get an item in front of the Commission under 'written procedure' you had to take a pink form to the Secretary-General's office. That pink form had to indicate that, at service level, all the necessary agreements had been sought and received. And, crucially, the pink form needed the signature of the 'Cabinet' of the responsible Commissioner himself.

Late one night I walked up from my office on the Rue Guimard to the Berlaymont.

I took the lift up to the twelfth floor, where Carlo Ripa di Meana, the Italian Commissioner now responsible for the environment, had his offices.

His deputy chef de cabinet, Marco Santo Pinto, was at work, surrounded by papers. He looked harassed.

Marco Santo Pinto and I always talked French together.

Johnson: Ah, bonsoir, Marco!

Santo Pinto: Bonsoir, Stanley.

Johnson: Excusez-moi de vous interrompre aussi tard. J'ai besoin d'un petit paraph [signature] *(I put pink form on Santo Pinto's desk)*

Santo Pinto *(takes out pen, ready to sign the pink form, but pauses)*: De quoi s'agit-il?

Johnson: C'est un projet de directive sur *les zoos*.

Santo Pinto: Ah oui, *les eaux*! C'est tres important! Le Commissaire veut faire beaucoup de progrès pour combattre la pollution des eaux! *(signs the pink slip)* Voilà, c'est fait. Bonsoir, Stanley.

Johnson: Bonsoir, Marco!

Thus is history made. Maybe a Frenchman or Frenchwoman can distinguish a subtle difference in the pronunciation of '*les zoos*' and '*les eaux*'. But here was an Italian talking to an Englishman and the nuances, at least as far as Marco Santo Pinto was concerned, were lost. To all intents and purposes, these were total homophones.

Should I have told Santo Pinto that the 'draft directive' was actually about the protection of animals in zoos, rather than water pollution, as he imagined?

The idea crossed my mind but I firmly rejected it.

As will emerge later in this narrative, I was very fond of the Environment Commissioner, Carlo Ripa di Meana. He and I had been elected to the European Parliament at precisely the same time. He was famous for being the husband of Marina, who in her turn was famous for being famous. If any man was going to fight for animals, Carlo was that man.

On the other hand, I said to myself in that split-second of reflection, why rock the boat? If I had told Marco that this was a directive about zoos, when he thought it was a directive about water pollution, his hand might have paused in mid-signature. He might have asked about the whys and the wherefores. The pink form might have remained unsigned.

Thus it was – I kid you not – that the Commission's famous draft directive on the protection of animals in zoos was officially adopted by the European Commission under 'written procedure'.

I would like to report that everything afterwards went swimmingly but, alas, I fear that was not the case.

By the time the European Parliament had approved the 'zoos directive', which it did in June 1993, the European Commission had got cold feet. Anxious to appease member states who increasingly seemed to be clamouring for the Commission to demonstrate that it had 'got the message' as far as 'subsidiarity' was concerned, the

Commission set in motion a major trawl through the statute book. Individual directorate-generals were ordered to come up with pieces of legislation, actual or proposed, that could be publicly 'sacrificed' to make it clear that the Commission was indeed sensitive to the concerns of the member states and had no wish to stick its nose into matters that were none of its business.

Like so many exercises of this nature, the results of the trawl proved to be disappointing. DG after DG reported that (surprise, surprise!) they couldn't really think of anything that was clearly inappropriate for action at EU level and which should therefore be repealed or not proceeded with.

The word got out that Jacques Delors, and his henchman, Pascal Lamy, were exceedingly disappointed with the failure to find a single sacrificial lamb. The trawl was to continue!

But then, lo and behold, someone remembered the zoos directive, which, having been approved by the Parliament, now lay on the table of the Council for consideration and adoption.

Sighs of relief all round. The Commission announced to considerable fanfare that as a result of a comprehensive examination of Community legislation by way of implementing the 'principle of subsidiarity', it proposed to withdraw the zoos directive. The cry had gone up: 'Who speaks for animals?' and the Commission had answered: 'Not us, mate!'

Well, the Commission got it wrong. The Commission's legal department is known as the *Service Juridique*. The SJ, collectively, had forgotten one thing. Under the treaty, the Commission, as I have already mentioned, has the exclusive right to propose legislation and other EU measures. The Commission, under the treaty, also has the right to withdraw its proposals. But what the distinguished men and women of the *Service Juridique* appeared to ignore, when they advised the Commission, as a result of the trawl, to withdraw the zoos directive, was that, in a situation where all the member states are unanimous in opposing the Commission's decision to withdraw a particular legislative proposal, the Commission's decision to withdraw a proposal can itself be overturned.

And that its precisely what happened with the 'zoos directive'. By then I had left the Commission, having – as I shall explain later – decided to move on to other tasks. But I followed the growing campaign in the various countries of the European Community to build support for the directive and gave what help I could.

The European Parliament played a crucial role, giving its enthusiastic approval to the directive. One after another, the member states followed suit.

Britain, alas, always keen on the 'subsidiarity principle' ('we don't like being bossed around by Brussels'), was not convinced. Though Michael Heseltine, as Secretary of State for the Environment, had signalled his interest in and support for, the proposed zoos directive, he had famously walked out of the Cabinet to announce his resignation to the assembled press corps. He was no longer calling the shots.

The intricacies of the Westland Affair that led to Heseltine's resignation need not concern us here. Suffice it to say that Michael Howard, who took over as Secretary of State for the Environment, seemed ready to support the Commission in its decision to ditch its own proposal.

This was massively worrying. If the Commission's proposal to withdraw the directive was to be defeated in the Council, total unanimity was required. It wasn't a question of QMV, qualified majority voting. If just one member state supported the Commission, the Commission's decision to withdraw the zoos proposal would be upheld.

I wrote to Michael Howard, suggesting that he might like to discuss the zoos issue with me and with Virginia McKenna and her son, Will Travers, who was now running Born Free (the successor in title to Zoo Check).

I soon received a very polite reply. Michael Howard suggested we might like to see his Minister of State, Lord Strathclyde.

In due course, Virginia, Will and I went up to London, to the Department of the Environment building in Horseferry Road, possibly the ugliest building in London (it has since been demolished). Tom Strathclyde was perfectly courteous, as were the senior civil servants who were present at the interview. But he gave us no assurance that the government would change its mind.

In the end, however, the government did change its mind. As I understand it, at the crucial Council meeting, minister after minister opposed the Commission's proposal to withdraw the zoos directive. When Britain finally came off the fence and decided, after all, that it would vote for the adoption, not the withdrawal, of the zoos directive, the Commission knew that the game was up and it officially withdrew its 'proposal to withdraw'.

All this may seem good clean fun as far as constitutional historians are concerned. And the chequered history of the zoos directive is certainly a fascinating story, demonstrating – as the Seals Campaign a decade earlier had also demonstrated – how the force of public opinion is never to be underestimated and can even achieve, as it did in the case of the zoos directive, sudden and surprising victories.

But there is more to it than this. The zoos directive was actually an important instrument in achieving improvements in animal welfare in zoos throughout Europe. It also laid a requirement on zoos to work for conservation abroad and to demonstrate that they were just as interested in protecting animals in the world as they were in keeping them – in appropriate conditions – in zoos.

I am not arguing, of course, that all this has flowed from the zoos directive. I am just making the point that if you are looking for sacrificial lambs, be sure to pick the right one. The zoos directive was the wrong choice. But it was a close-run thing and it's a bit of a miracle that the directive lived to tell the tale.

Kerstin Sundseth, whose assistance had been invaluable as far as the protection of animals in zoos was concerned, proved equally indispensable when it came to drafting the 'fur-trap' directive.

The genesis of this directive was unusual. I was flying back from Washington one day (the Commission's environment staff had regular meetings with the United States' Environment Protection Agency) when I read an intriguing item in the paper.

'The Prime Minister, Mrs Thatcher,' the report indicated, 'has rejected a proposal by Trade Minister, Alan Clark, that furs imported into the UK coming from animals caught in leg-hold traps should be labelled.'

Leg-hold traps! They were really grim! Britain had banned those years ago. In the barn at Nethercote there was still a rusty pile of gin-traps, left over from the days when we trapped rabbits by the score. (Later, of course, myxomatosis kept the rabbit population under control.)

When I got back to Brussels, I wrote to Alan Clark. I was very keen on animal welfare, I said. I was delighted that he had taken the initiative on leg-hold traps. I was sorry that the Prime Minister had turned him down. I wondered whether it might help if I pursued this at the European level.

This is where things became a little murky. I received a myste-rious message from Alan Clark. He couldn't, he said, contact me officially because his officials watched him like hawks. He said he was going to be in Luxembourg the following week for a meeting of trade ministers and he suggested that I should meet him in the gentlemen's lavatory of the Holiday Inn at 7 p.m. on the Tuesday.

Having, as I explained in the first volume of this memoir, been exposed to 'the most intensive training in clandestine techniques known to man' during my brief time in MI6, I was not disconcerted by the cloak-and-dagger nature of the rendezvous.

Clark would go on to be famous for his diaries and his 'coven' of women. But all that lay ahead. I saw at that moment only a tall, elegant man, facing the urinal with his back to me.

He turned round when he heard me enter, buttoned himself up and checked there was no one else in the cubicles, before explaining: 'The Prime Minister just said "no" to my proposal for labelling products coming from animals caught in leg-hold traps. She looked at my shoes. "I see you wear leather shoes, Mr Clark. Where do you suppose the leather comes from?" And that was that! Of course, the real reason was the submarines. She was just about to go to Canada and she wanted to sell two of our surplus nuclear submarines to the Canadians. She had word that if Britain proceeded with the fur-labelling measure, the Canadians would cancel the order.'

As his diaries would make clear, Clark was a fan of the Prime Minister. And Mrs Thatcher clearly liked him. There was a hint of flirtatiousness in their relationship. But Clark was an ambitious man too.

He took his time drying his hands. 'Of course, an EU-labelling measure would be a different thing. It wouldn't have the UK's fingerprints all over it. It wouldn't have *my* fingerprints on it.'

'I think we'll do better than a labelling measure,' I assured him. 'We'll propose a total ban on the import of furs into the European Community if the furs come from animals caught in leg-hold traps.'

Clark made for the door. 'Officially we never met,' he said.

Well, that's what he thought. Years later Roger Beetham, a Foreign Office friend of mine, told me that officials had been quite worried by Clark's Luxembourg gambit.

'We knew he met you. We weren't sure what he was up to.'

The Commission's proposal for a directive banning the import of furs coming from animals caught in leg-hold traps was approved by the Council on 4 November 1991. In order to give the exporting countries (mainly Canada and, as it then was, the Soviet Union) time to change their trapping methods for more humane alternatives, it was agreed that the directive wouldn't actually come into force before 1 January 1995.

I suppose I should have smelt a rat then, but I didn't. By then, I had left the Commission (for the second time), as I shall explain later, and was back in England working as an environmental consultant.

We were all down at Nethercote for Christmas that year, 1994, and were planning to stay on till early January.

On New Year's Eve I received a call from one of my colleagues in the animal welfare world. Was I aware that two days earlier the director general of the Commission's External Affairs Directorate-General, Mr Horst Krenzler, together with the head of the Commission's Customs DG, a fellow Brit called Peter Wilmott, had written a letter to the heads of all the custom services in all the member states requesting – in fact, ordering – them not to put into effect the fur import ban? The letter stated that the Commission was worried about a possible WTO challenge!

My interlocutor was totally stunned. So was I. The situation, as far as I knew, was quite unprecedented. Here was the Commission, the guardian of the treaty, sneakily waiting till the very last minute (there were literally only hours to go before the import ban was due to take effect) before firing its very own Exocet missile.

'Trust Krenzler and co. to wait till everyone's on holiday,' I exploded to Jenny, as I put down the phone. 'Nobody works between Christmas and the New Year. They probably thought they could get away with it.'

IFAW sought an injunction from the High Court, arguing that the Commission was acting *ultra vires* and that it had no right to try to strike down a directive that had been properly agreed by the Council four years earlier. Ergo, the British government was wrong not to implement fully a directive that had been properly adopted by the Council.

Well, the law is a law unto itself. We engaged an expensive barrister from a Brussels law firm. We went to the High Court. Counsel pleaded the case for us. I couldn't imagine that we could possibly lose. I looked at the Treasury solicitor who would be defending the British government's actions. You're on a hiding to nothing, I thought.

How wrong I was!

The presiding judge that day was Lord MacPherson, who would later become even more famous as the author of the MacPherson Report, which was set up following the murder of the schoolboy Stephen Lawrence and which, famously, accused the police of 'institutional racism'.

It was, as it happened, MacPherson's last day in office. He was already in 'demob' mode.

Arriving at the law courts in the Strand well before the allotted time, I sat in on a couple of the preceding cases. Both the cases I listened to involved appeals against deportation. MacPherson was having none of it.

'Back you go, Mr Dasgupta,' he pronounced.

He spoke in similar terms to a gentleman named Aggarwal. 'I'm afraid this is the end of the road, Mr Aggarwal.'

The only thing that was missing, as far as I could tell, was the black cap.

I could see that Lord MacPherson was on a roll.

In due course, it was our turn to be called. Our expensive QC from Brussels made, I thought, a very good case. And the Treasury solicitor, as far as I could see, made a very feeble riposte.

It was time for the bench to pronounce. We all held our breath.

Rummaging among his papers, Lord MacPherson found the Krenzler–Wilmott letter. He held it up so that the court, and his two fellow judges of appeal, had a clear view of the document. Then he turned to our Counsel.

'You are asking us, Mr Bentley, to ignore this letter, this official document, to conclude that it is without validity.'

MacPherson peered at the two signatures. 'For example, underneath Mr Krenzler's signature it says "Director General for External Relations". Would I be correct, Mr Bentley, in thinking a director general is a very eminent personage in the European Commission? There is no higher rank, as I understand it, except the rank of Commissioner itself?'

I think Bentley knew where His Honour was heading but he appeared to have no way of diverting him.

'That is so, your honour.'

MacPherson peered over his spectacles in my general direction. Various friends from the animal welfare movement had accompanied me to court. Though I myself had put on a suit for the occasion, some of my colleagues looked fairly scruffy.

'I have to say,' MacPherson continued, 'that I am minded to take the letter which Messrs Krenzler and Wilmott have written very seriously. Very seriously indeed.'

I knew the game was up when MacPherson turned to his two fellow appeal justices and asked them, 'Do we need to confer?'

MacPherson's two colleagues didn't need to say anything. They just shook their bewigged heads sadly to signify that they too saw no need to confer.

The humiliation I felt at that moment was intense. Not even a need to confer! Wow, how badly we must have done!

Out of the corner of my eye, I noticed that Bentley had already packed up his papers and was half out of his seat as MacPherson said, 'Case dismissed.'

One thing lawyers apparently learn early on in a career at the bar is that you don't hang around when you've lost.

We didn't actually give up at this point. A few weeks later I went to Strasbourg and called on Leon Brittan, who was answering questions that day in the European Parliament. Leon had been appointed one of the British commissioners (in those days the larger EU member states, like Britain, had two commissioners) after his famous falling-out with Mrs Thatcher over the Westland affair, and was responsible for the External Relations portfolio. In other words, he was Krenzler's boss.

Leon was, as always, tremendously friendly and polite. I am sure he was and is as keen on animal welfare as the next man. He seemed to be genuinely surprised at the level of indignation caused by the Commission's request to the member states to ignore a properly adopted Council directive.

'The application of the directive has not been cancelled,' Leon explained to me patiently, when I caught up with him after the session had ended. 'The directive has just been suspended while alternative intergovernmental arrangements, compatible with the WTO, are agreed.'

Pigs might fly, I muttered!

We had been comprehensively outplayed. That was the truth of the matter.

Over in Canada, animal welfare activists, who hoped European action would solve an animal welfare issue that they had not been able to solve for themselves, hadn't given up hope. The Fur-Bearers of Canada invited me to Vancouver to put the case. Maybe if I was eloquent enough, the Canadians themselves would ban the use of leg-hold traps anyway.

I duly obliged, shunting in the course of one long afternoon between several different TV stations.

Later that night, having had an early dinner with my Canadian hosts, I went back to my hotel room and turned on the TV. As I flipped from one channel to another, I was surprised to see how much interest there seemed to be in the trapping issue.

It was, I have to say, a one-sided affair. I had had a tough interview that afternoon with a Mr Dubois, a representative of the Canadian Trappers Association, who was beamed in from Yellowknife. The channel played the clip in full.

'Why are you sticking you noses into our business?' was the general gist of my interlocutor's remarks.

The presenter clearly thought the man had a point, letting him run on at considerable length.

Vancouver urbanites might be on our side, I thought. But what would it be like out in there in the wide white world of the Arctic or near-Arctic North?

I remembered the time, years earlier, when I had flown out to the Magdalen Island in the Gulf of St Lawrence and had met a group of sealers. They didn't have hakapiks, but they had some nasty clubs in their hands and they looked as if they were ready to use them. As my friends put it, I'm a very clubbable kind of fellow.

I was still watching TV when the telephone rang. It was the man from the Trappers Association, speaking from Canada's far north, the very man I'd just been watching on the screen.

'We'd very much like to fly you up to Yellowknife,' Mr Dubois said, 'so you can meet some trappers and "walk the lines". Things aren't the way you say they are.'

Mr Dubois didn't go so far as to say the animals actually enjoyed being trapped, but he did maintain that the lines were inspected regularly and that it was wrong to say an animal could be held in a trap for days before dying.

He talked about the trappers too. 'Maybe you people don't understand what it's like, trying to earn a living up here.'

Guilty as charged!

Looking back, I know I should have accepted Mr Dubois's invitation. But, unusually (normally I say 'yes' to everything), a sense of caution held me back. How difficult would it be to arrange a convenient skidoo 'accident' up there in the icy Arctic wastes? Might I myself step clumsily onto some cunningly placed leg-hold trap and be held for hours in those grim steel jaws? How quickly do you freeze to death in sub-zero temperatures?

The TV was still on in the background and I looked at it as I talked to the man from Yellowknife.

'Up in Yellowknife,' the cheerful weather lady informed us, 'it's minus forty and falling.'

'Thanks, but no thanks,' I said firmly. 'I just don't have the gear.'

If the leg-hold trap directive was, as I have explained, effectively throttled at birth by the European Commission, the animal welfare movement had some striking successes elsewhere.

Though we lost the legal battle to persuade the UK's Ministry of Agriculture (as it then was) to ban live exports of calves to the Continent, where they were going to be reared in crates (a practice banned in England), a campaign of direct action was nonetheless effective.

I have spent days in Brussels or Dover waving placards and chanting, 'BAN LIVE EXPORTS.'

In the end, the outbreak of mad-cow disease, and the need to avoid movement of animals between Britain and the Continent, achieved the objective we all sought, and the lorries loaded with live calves were stopped in their tracks overnight.

The introduction of EU measures relating to the welfare of farm animals owed much to the tireless efforts of a wonderful organisation, then based in Petersfield, Hampshire, known as Compassion in World Farming (CIWF). Headed first by Joyce d'Silva, and now by Philip Lymbery, CIWF has led the way in seeking to improve the sometimes horrendous conditions under which farm animals are reared, transported and finally slaughtered. Battery hens, tethered sows, veal crates, stunning before slaughter, long-distance transport – all these are issues where CIWF, in alliance with organisations such as the RSPCA, has really made a difference.

Yes, progress has been slow. But it has been sure. In Brussels, organisations like the Eurogroup for Animal Welfare have helped to coordinate national as well as EU-wide campaigns.

The most stunning success, in which CIWF played a major part, came when the EU heads of state and government actually agreed to add a new Protocol on Animal Welfare to the EU treaty.

That particular EU summit was held in Dublin. Early one morning, just as the sun was rising, I joined Joyce d'Silva and her team outside Dublin Castle, where the summit was being held.

Don't let anyone tell you that ministers, prime ministers, heads of state don't take any notice of demonstrations. Of course they do. You may not be able to see them through those tinted windows, but they can certainly see you.

The Garda being very cooperative, we positioned ourselves at the entrance to the long drive that leads up to the castle. We waved our banners, we hollered, we shouted.

'ANIMALS ARE SENTIENT BEINGS! ANIMALS ARE SENTIENT BEINGS! ANIMALS ARE SENTIENT BEINGS!'

As a classicist, I was thrilled with CIWF's choice of the word 'sentient'. It had such a Latin ring about it.

And 'sentient' was precisely the word the heads of state and heads of government retained when the Protocol on Animal Welfare was eventually agreed.

CIWF and its allies scored an even more spectacular victory when the Animal Welfare Protocol was upgraded from Business Class to First Class. The Lisbon Treaty itself now contains a substantive article on animal welfare.

Sometimes you win battles when you least expect to.

Chapter Fourteen

The Commissioner

Max was born in Brussels in March 1985. I believe that technically he is entitled to a Belgian passport. This may be useful if (a) the Conservatives win the next election, (b) the promised in/out referendum happens, and (c) Britain decides to leave the European Union.

Our house in Brussels was ideally suited for small children, with eight bedrooms split equally between the two upper floors. (I shudder to think how much we would have paid each month if the Belgians had applied the dreaded 'bedroom tax'.)

Having had a great deal of experience of such matters (Max was my sixth child and Jenny's second), I have long since concluded that there is absolutely no need to be within earshot of young children.

In fact, the house offered so much space that Julia and Max were not only out of earshot as far as Jenny and I were concerned, they were also out of earshot of each other, an added advantage.

That ancient villa was perfect in so many other ways. The house was set in the middle of a veritable 'park'. Julia, almost thirty years later, recalls that there were six different lawns as well as the tennis court on which she learned to ride a bicycle.

To a young child the house and garden must have seemed unimaginably vast. I loved it. The sitting room opened up onto the terrace and the terrace looked out over a vast array of fruit trees.

The first year there were so many cherries – rich, fat, dark red cherries – that we couldn't pick them all. Mowing all those lawns was quite a performance. I dutifully carted the grass to the far corner of the garden, well hidden behind the trees, known as the *sale coin*, the 'nasty corner', where in due course it turned into compost.

I think Jenny found the house a bit cold and draughty, at least in winter. We had central heating in the sense that several of the rooms had radiators, but I don't think it made a great deal of difference.

The fuel tank itself was in the basement. Sometimes I walked down the rickety stairs to check how much fuel was left. There were some rats in the basement when we first arrived but I put warfarin down for them. The next time I went down, I found their corpses lying around, like soldiers on the field of battle.

My mother would not have approved of this warfarin warfare. She had a high regard for rats. She had a favourite party trick that involved demonstrating how a rat steals a hen's egg. She would lie on the floor and clasp her arms around her chest.

'One rat clutches the egg like this,' she would explain, 'while a second rat pulls the first rat, plus the egg, to wherever it wants to go. Rats are very clever animals.'

About once a year, we summoned a man with a lorry to empty the septic tank. His tanker, which he drove right into the garden and parked in front of the terrace, was labelled 'Daniel Vergin – Vidange'. We called him Monsieur Le Vidange. I could see he took pride in his job, which involved unreeling a large, thick hose across the lawn to the tank, then pumping out the contents.

One of the good things (and there were many good things) about working in Belgium in those days was that you could come home for lunch. I got to see Jenny and the children (if they were not at school); there was often time for a quick game of tennis. Even a snooze on the grass.

Julia went to the Brussels English Primary School, on the far side of the Bois de la Cambre. I often dropped her off on the way to work. On those dropping-off days, cycling to work was out of the question. But even in a car, and even with the morning traffic, which had certainly increased since the last time I had lived in Brussels, the daily commute (twice daily if you came home at lunchtime) was not at all painful. In fact, it was often a positive joy. You went down the Chaussée de Waterloo, cut through into the Forêt de Soignes, where Wellington's troops camped the night before Waterloo, then segued into the Bois de la Cambre.

There was another advantage. When we arrived in Brussels, I bought an old Toyota with automatic transmission. I was able to get at least half an hour's 'writing' in each day since I didn't have to change gear and could therefore hold my dictating machine in my spare hand.

As before, I sent the tapes off to All-Hours Word Processing in Hendon, and Sharon Livingstone sent the typed-up version back to me in Brussels.

Soon *The Commissioner* was ready for the printers. This was probably the most successful of my (so far) nine published novels.

Unlike my previous novels, the book was published by Century Hutchinson, where Christopher Bland – a friend of long standing – had taken over as chairman. Christopher and Gillon Aitken had dinner together in London. As I understand it, Christopher (never a man to mince words) told my agent that I was perfectly capable of writing a respectable novel if I put my mind to it.

The Commissioner was certainly one of my better books, possibly because a lot of it was based on real-life experience.

Roy Jenkins, former President of the Commission and then back in the UK Parliament as leader of the newly formed Social Democratic Party, very kindly sent the publishers a quote for use on the jacket: 'Strong on authentic detail.'

Hayden Phillips, then Roy's deputy chef de cabinet, once asked me to add a bit of colour to a speech Roy was due to make in London so I produced some paragraphs about cycling. The *Evening Standard* printed a photo of Roy arriving at the Dorchester in a large chauffeur-driven car with the caption: 'Roy Jenkins, Europe's boss, urges more cycling in London.'

Roy was still President of the Commission when I was elected to the European Parliament. I can see him now, rising to his feet from the Commission bench in the vast chamber, to address honourable members with that famously judicious gesture. 'Swilling claret gently in the glass' was the kind description. 'The seigneur cupping the breast of a peasant woman' was perhaps less kind, though just as funny.

The Commissioner was made into a film with the support of Canal Plus, the French media giant. By a stroke of luck, John Hurt, veteran of stage and screen, agreed to play the title role.

An author doesn't usually have much say in the way his or her book is adapted for the screen, and that was certainly true in my case. The film script went through several drafts, the last being written by the producer herself, Christina Callas. Though her English was perfectly serviceable (Christina was Greek and lived in Berlin), I couldn't help feeling the text was lacking in nuance.

But John Hurt is a consummate professional and did his best to make up for deficiencies in the script through some fine acting. I visited the set one day when they were filming a scene set in a café in Brussels. I was given a chair by the bar. All seemed to be going well when Hurt suddenly held up his hand in mid-take.

'Stop,' he shouted. 'Stanley is in my eye-line!'

The Commissioner was selected for the competition section of the Berlin Film Festival in February 1998. That was quite an honour. No one expected it to win but just to be in contention was no mean achievement.

As the author, I was invited to attend the festival. Jo, who by then had graduated with a First in history from Oxford and was working for the *Financial Times*, arrived from London. Jenny, Julia and Max flew in with me from Brussels. Leo, my second son, then working for the World Bank, came over from Washington. He checked into the hotel ahead of us and somehow had time to get hold of the official posters advertising the film and post them in the hotel lifts and corridors.

I remember Julia exclaiming, 'Leo must be here already!'

If I look back and try to make a shortlist of my life's 'highlights', I would say that sitting with my loyal wife and family, watching the credits roll ('Based on the novel by Stanley Johnson'!) and then walking up onto the stage to cries of 'author, author!' ranks fairly high.

As it happened, most of the events I predicted in *The Commissioner* soon came to pass. The first female Commissioner was appointed; the whole Commission was sacked; and there was a major pollution incident on the Rhine.

But the box office doesn't reward prescience. The film was shown on the big screen in Europe, but in the UK it appeared only on television. You can still buy the video on Amazon.

Carlo Ripa di Meana, and his wife, the gorgeous Marina, came to Berlin for the showing of *The Commissioner*. People in Brussels, and in the national capitals, sometimes criticised Carlo for being 'capricious' and 'lightweight'. They were wrong.

When he was Environment Commissioner in Brussels, for example, at the beginning of the '90s, Ripa di Meana realised that one way to deal with global warming is to have a carbon tax. When the Commission refused to support him, he in turn refused to go to the United Nations Earth Summit held in Rio de Janeiro, Brazil, in June 1992. (The Commission's President, Jacques Delors, had to be drafted in at the last moment.)

Carlo Ripa di Meana also did a lot for elephants. Every six months the presidency of the EU Council changes. In the first half of 1989, it was the United Kingdom's turn to be President. I flew with Carlo one day in early May to London to discuss key items on the agenda of the forthcoming Environment Council.

A Commission car met us at Heathrow. On the way in to London I mentioned to Carlo that the elephants were taking a hammering. Poaching was rampant. There had been drastic declines in elephant populations throughout much of Africa.

'Can't we do something?' Carlo asked. 'Can't we have a pro-elephant demonstration? What is Brigitte Bardot doing nowadays?' He looked wistful.

We met Lord (Malcolm) Caithness, the UK's Environment Minister, in his office at the Department of the Environment. Though his civil servants looked doubtful, Caithness seemed sympathetic when we raised the elephant issue.

'We'll try to help,' he said.

When I was running the 'save the seals' campaign, I had tremendous support from organisations such as IFAW, Greenpeace, the RSPCA etc. On the way back to Heathrow, I called Richard Moore, the director of IFAW, then based in Crowborough.

'Hello, Richard. This is Stanley,' I said, 'I'm in the car with the EU Environment Commissioner, Carlo Ripa di Meana. The Environment Council is meeting in Luxembourg in ten days' time. Could IFAW lay on a demonstration? You know, people chanting outside. Placards. That kind of thing. I know it's short notice.'

As it happened, IFAW was already planning to send bus-loads of supporters to Luxembourg to encourage ministers to make the 'seal ban' permanent. As I have explained earlier, the EU seal ban was still a fixed-term ban, subject to renewal. By now ministers were fed up with having to talk about seals and they had in fact already decided to make it apply *sine die*. The item was on the agenda in Luxembourg, purely as an A Point, i.e. it would be formally adopted, without discussion, at the beginning of the meeting.

'The permanent seal ban is already in the bag,' I said. 'Let's use your crowd for the elephants instead.'

Carlo was mouthing something as I spoke.

'Can you get Brigitte Bardot to come to the demonstration in Luxembourg, Richard?' I asked.

Well, we didn't manage to get Brigitte Bardot to come to Luxembourg but we got Loretta Swit, who played Margaret 'Hot Lips' Houlihan in the American sitcom *M*A*S*H*.

And the placards were rapidly reprinted and in some cases redrawn to feature elephants instead of seals!

Around 9 a.m. on a bright, sunny May morning a stream of environment ministers got out of their cars in front of the Council building on Luxembourg's Plateau Kirchberg, straightened their ties or patted their hair (there were one or two female environment ministers by then), and prepared to work their way through the day's agenda.

I still have that agenda. There is nothing, absolutely nothing, about elephants on it. There is an item on exhaust emissions from motor vehicles and another on pollution from large industrial installations. But nothing about large pachyderms.

The environment ministers (or at least those of them who had studied the agenda before the meeting) were undoubtedly surprised to be confronted by 'Hot Lips' and a sizeable banner-carrying crowd.

'SAVE THE ELEPHANTS!' shouted Hot Lips. 'SAVE THE ELEPHANTS NOW!' the crowd responded.

Some ministers scuttled on past. Others stopped to have their photos taken with Hot Lips. They were, after all, politicians. Such opportunities don't happen often.

During the coffee break, Carlo gave me the nod.

I quickly whisked around the room, placing next to each minister's seat a document headed 'Elephants: Draft Council Resolution'.

The text was very simple. The resolution called on the Commission 'to ban with immediate effect the import of ivory into the European Community'.

The draft resolution also called on the European Community 'to support an international, worldwide ban on trade in elephant ivory'.

This latter request was very timely since the Convention on International Trade in Endangered Species of Fauna and Flora (CITES) was scheduled to have one of its regular meetings in October 1989, in Lausanne, Switzerland, only a few months ahead.

From a procedural point of view, Carlo's actions were extremely naughty. There was no official paper from the Commission about elephants on the table, let alone a highly contentious proposal for an ivory trade ban.

But Malcolm Sinclair, twentieth Earl of Caithness and chief of the Sinclair Clan, rose to the challenge. When the meeting reconvened after the break, he immediately drew his fellow ministers' attention to the paper, which had suddenly emerged on the table.

'I would like to congratulate the Commission,' he said, 'on their very timely response to the crisis facing the African elephant.'

Carlo Ripa di Meana, scion of an ancient line of Italian aristocrats, gave a little self-deprecatory nod.

'*Grazie, Signor Presidente. Molte grazie!*'

We could hear the chanting outside. 'SAVE THE ELEPHANTS! SAVE THE ELEPHANTS NOW!'

Caithness looked around the room. 'I take it no one has any objections to the draft we have before us.'

Seconds later, he gavelled the resolution through. The European Community ban on the import of elephant ivory came into force a few days later.

The fact that the EC had already put a trade ban in place was of crucial importance in achieving the worldwide ban that was agreed in at the Lausanne CITES meeting a few months later.

The decisions taken in 1989, at EU and international level, were also of crucial importance in stemming the illegal killing of elephants. Today, alas, we are seeing a horrendous resurgence of the slaughter. Elephants are being massacred all over Africa. It has become clear that trade measures by themselves are not enough. We have to deal with the demand side as well.

In February 2014, HRH Prince Charles, Prince of Wales hosted a meeting at Lancaster House to see what further action may be taken to save elephants, rhinos, tigers and other threatened species from extinction. I was lucky enough to be invited to that meeting as part of the Clarence House delegation.

'The slaughter of elephants in both forests and savannahs,' Prince Charles said, 'has created frighteningly silent and sterile places. And without the elephants, some of whose populations are no longer viable and yet are often irreplaceable agents in seed germination, the long-term ecology or many forests is fatally disrupted. No elephants, no forests.

'This tragedy, of course, is not confined to Africa alone. It is crucial to understand that Asia's, specifically India's, wildlife is also being decimated and if the world's focus remains solely on Africa, we risk losing south-east Asia's wildlife, which includes 20 per cent of the world's species.'

And, the Prince of Wales added, 'As vital as strong enforcement is, we can – indeed we must – attack demand.'

It had been done before, successfully, he said, citing a campaign against shark fin soup. The result was that '80–85 per cent of those in major cities in China had reduced consumption – or completely stopped consuming – shark fin soup'.

Back in 1989, when the trade bans on elephant ivory were agreed, it seemed that a massive step forward had been taken, as far as the protection of the species was concerned. A vast pile of ivory was torched in the Nairobi National Park. Other countries followed suit. Elephant populations, having in many countries been in precipitous decline, began to stabilise.

But we have learned the hard way. In the long run, there are no permanent victories where the environment is concerned. The best we can hope for is stop things deteriorating as fast as they otherwise would.

Chapter Fifteen

Dragon River

My second stint in Brussels, working for the European Commission, lasted six years, from 1984 to 1990.

It was an astonishingly invigorating time. First, as I have attempted to explain, there was the real freedom that one had, as a senior-level *fonctionnaire* or civil servant, to actually promote new laws and regulations to deal with the outstanding environmental issues of the day in so far as they fell within the competence of the European Community and sometimes even when they didn't but you felt it was worth a try. The Commission, under the treaty, as I have already explained, had the sole right of initiative and, boy, did we make use of it! It was quite clear to me in those days that the Commission really was the driver here. Without the EU's dominant (some might say domineering) role in pushing policy forward, many basic environmental tools (such as environmental impact assessment, access to environmental information, pollution control legislation in a large number of fields and, increasingly, nature protection measures) simply wouldn't have been adopted at the national level.

So, yes, I spent a lot of time shuttling between the Commission, Council and Parliament buildings, defending the Commission's proposals. But there were many forays further afield as well.

Each year we had formal meetings with the United States Environmental Protection Agency (established by President Richard

Nixon in 1969). We didn't always agree on a common approach, but at least we discovered what our differences were. We learned from them. Maybe they learned from us too.

We also went to Japan. Here our principal interlocutor was the Ministry of International Trade and Investment, the mighty MITI.

These EU–Japan meetings also took place fairly regularly. En route to one of them, I decided I would to call in on Tom Mori, my Japanese literary agent. Two of my early novels, viz. *The Doomsday Deposit* and *The Marburg Virus*, had, thanks to Tom, been translated into Japanese. *The Commissioner* was about to be launched upon the world and I hoped that Tuttle-Mori, Tom's firm, would engineer a lucrative sale of the Japanese rights for that book too.

I arranged the RV with Tom at 4 p.m. on the day of my arrival in Japan. He sent me a fax with the address of his agency and I printed it off.

Things began to go wrong as soon as I landed at Tokyo's Narita airport after the long flight from Europe. The traffic into the city was horrendous, and the taxi ride took over two hours and cost an arm and a leg. When we reached central Tokyo, the driver was totally at a loss. The avenues and cross-streets are not conveniently numbered. There was no discernible pattern. The meter mounted as the minutes past. Quite obviously, we were nowhere near our destination. I grew increasingly agitated. Tom Mori was still waiting for me to arrive. It was long past his going-home time.

Suddenly I had had enough. I had been travelling for more than twelve hours on the plane, and now another two or more in the taxi.

I waved the piece of paper with Tom Mori's address on it and shouted at the driver. 'Stop, I'm going to ask directions. Here's a place. I'll try here.'

We had pulled up in front of some kind of tea shop. I burst into the room and, raising my voice, cried, 'For heaven's sake, can't somebody tell me where the Tuttle-effing-Mori Literary Agency is? It's meant to be in Chobe-Shinjuku block 361 or something. Is that anywhere near here?'

The man behind the counter – he was wearing a tall white chef's hat – looked at me. I don't know if he understood everything I was saying but he realised perfectly that I was just another *gaijin* or 'foreigner' who didn't know how to behave.

He didn't raise his voice but, as far as I was concerned, he could have held a foghorn to his lips.

'You not king here,' he said. 'In Japan, politeness is all.'

I crawled back into the taxi, totally deflated and ashamed. *You not king here. Politeness is all.* I have never forgotten that quiet ticking off. It seared the soul.

I found Tom Mori in the end. Everyone else in his office had gone home – lots of people who worked in Tokyo commuted three hours each way from outlying regions – but Tom was still there waiting for me. *(Politeness is all!)* Tom was the man who had brought Jeffrey Archer, Frederick Forsyth and John Grisham to Japan, and the Japanese reading masses had been duly grateful. Of course, I wasn't in the Archer-Forsyth-Grisham league, not by a million miles. But I had been travelling about twenty hours and I felt I deserved a drink.

Happily, Mori was only too ready to oblige. He was a large, ebullient man. I had been told that at the Frankfurt Book Fair he gave legendary parties. He certainly didn't stint on the hospitality that evening. In Japan, even in those days, Johnny Walker Black Label whisky cost about £80 a bottle. He poured us both a generous glass, put a huge arm round my shoulder, and holding the other arm out in front of us, took a photo with a Polaroid camera. Nowadays that's called a 'selfie'.

I told Tom that evening that I was looking forward not only to a Japanese version of *The Commissioner* (which duly appeared) but also to the publication, in Tokyo, of *Dragon River*, another novel that I had planned.

'It's mainly set in China,' I explained. 'There's talk about building a giant dam on the Yangtze. It's another disaster novel.'

Tom Mori poured me another drink. 'Your books have not been disaster in Japan. They have done very well.'

'I mean it's *about* a disaster. The Chinese build the dam all right, but there's a fatal flaw. The dam's in an earthquake zone and the pressure of the water in the reservoir triggers a seismic shock. That happens on the very day the new dam is being opened by the Chinese Premier. A crack appears in the dam wall and the water begins to seep through. The trickle becomes a torrent! Three hundred million people live downstream in the Yangtze valley! The flood could wipe them out!'

Tom Mori's attention was fully engaged.

'And does the dam actually fail?' he asked hopefully. On the whole the Japanese are not very keen on the Chinese. The feeling is mutual.

'I'm afraid I had to leave the reader in suspense, Tom,' I replied.

'Pity!' He roared with laughter.

Researching *Dragon River* gave me an excuse to make a return visit to China. I hadn't been there since the summer of 1975, when Chairman Mao was still alive and the Gang of Four held sway. That had been during my first period in Brussels. I had joined a small group of Commission officials on an extensive but tightly controlled tour of the main cities. Once, when I jumped off the boat that was giving us a scenic tour of Lake Wuxi to enjoy an impromptu swim, both I and our group were severely reprimanded for a breach of discipline.

When I got back to Brussels after that trip, I wrote a novel about China. It started as a comedy, entitled variously *Sweet and Sour, Peking*

Tom or *Chink in the Armoire*. After a while, I realised that the basic plot was actually quite gripping. There was a good thriller struggling to escape from the morass of bad jokes. So I ditched the jokes and just concentrated on the action, rewriting the book entirely. When *The Doomsday Deposit* appeared, it was listed – in the USA at least – as an 'alternate Book of the Month Club selection'. Wow!

My mother proofread the galleys and sent me a letter with helpful comments. One of them was especially stinging.

'I cannot believe,' she wrote, 'that any son of mine could write "Golden Labrador"! As you should very well know, it's either Yellow Labrador or Golden Retriever.'

Of course, I tried to weasel out of it by blaming Sharon Livingstone and All-Hours Word-Processing of Hendon for the mistake but, deep down, I knew my mother was right. She was a stickler for good grammar. She abhorred sloppiness.

My mother died in 1987.

To say that I, and my brother and sisters, as well as her numerous grandchildren, were saddened by her death would be a colossal understatement. If today I retain a generally positive view of life, it is my mother I have to thank. She set us all a wonderful example. A few years ago, out of the blue, a letter came to Nethercote. It was from a Swiss au pair girl who had worked for my parents on the farm in 1961. She wrote that her year with us was 'the happiest time of her life' and enclosed a snapshot of my mother, surrounded by sheep in the meadow next to the house. My mother is carrying Tiddles, a Jack Russell terrier, under one arm, and a newborn lamb under the other.

As I sit here in the garden of our London house, on a sunny Sunday morning in mid-April 2014, typing these words (I have ditched the Dictaphone), I can hear the birds singing. Ironically, it is easier nowadays to hear birdsong in the cities than it is in the countryside.

When I hear birdsong, I sometimes think of my mother. She became increasingly deaf as she grew older. She once said to me, 'Darling, what I miss most of all is not being able to hear the birds.'

She had several hearing aids but none of them worked for long. The trouble was, if the hearing aid buzzed or emitted a high-pitched whine, as it sometimes did, she would snatch it off in exasperation and leave it on the sofa or somewhere. For some reason, my parents' Jack Russell terriers (they always had two or three on the go) were attracted by those small pink plastic contraptions and never hesitated to pounce if an opportunity presented itself.

Even though I will be seventy-four by the time this book is published, I still miss my mother deeply. I am sure my siblings do too. She had an unquenchable optimism, even though life was not easy for her on Exmoor.

She was half-French, had been educated at Oxford, and had an idea, at one point, of teaching at a local school. But it was hard to square that with being a farmer's wife. There was just too much to do at home.

What she did do – in spades – was give me the sense that basically everything was doable and that, as she would put it, 'there is no such word as *can't*'.

I went to boarding school in Devon at the age of eight, then to Sherborne and Oxford. My mother's weekly letters were often long and amusing, and always well written. I awaited them eagerly.

They would often end: 'Must dash now to catch the post.'

Catching the post was not as easy as it sounds. If my father was out doing something on the farm, my mother would have to get the car started and then drive 2 miles down our bumpy track to get to the postbox on the main road. She had a little blue-and-grey VW Beetle and in my mind's eye I can see her now shooing the hens and ducks out of the way as she drove through the yard.

She once told Jenny that she loved Nethercote but that it was a 'gilded cage'.

Sometimes she did escape. She went once with her sister Denise (Aunty Den to me) to the Caribbean. Den painted and my mother wrote a book about life of the farm. The book had several possible titles. They included: *From Cheltenham Ladies' College to Exmoor Farm*, *Pitchforked into Deep Litter* and *Alas, poor Johnny*. My sister, Birdie, has been working on it recently. We all have high hopes that it may soon be published. Birdie has apparently had to trim some of the longer sections about lambing on Exmoor but has, I am sure, retained the original liveliness and humour.

By the time she reached her late seventies, my mother was not as sharp as she had been, though she could still beat me at Scrabble with one hand tied behind her back. She came to stay with us in Brussels when I returned to the Commission after my stint with the European Parliament and she was quite disorientated. Every few hours, she would ask, 'Where's Johnny?'

In October 1986, we all celebrated 'Buster' and Johnny's fiftieth wedding anniversary with a party at West Nethercote. Jenny brilliantly commissioned a large cake, covered in icing and modelled in the shape of a Land Rover.

My mother, who had done such a good job on my first Chinese novel, *The Doomsday Deposit*, never had a chance to repeat the performance with *Dragon River*. At the time of her death, I hadn't as yet put pen to paper. In fact, I was still engaged on the basic research.

It was perfectly clear to me that, to make real progress with the plot I had outlined to Tom Mori that evening in Tokyo, I needed to revisit China. As I have noted, more than a decade had elapsed since our little group of keen Brussels-based Sinophiles had dutifully recorded in our notebooks all the pap and propaganda we were fed, in one city after another, about the glorious achievements of China under Chairman Mao. Now a different regime was in place under Deng Xiaoping. China was in the throes of the Four Modernisations. The construction of the Three Gorges Dam, as I had explained to Tom Mori that evening in Tokyo, was to be one of the centrepieces in the transformation of China, producing – so it was hoped – over 16 Gigawatts of electricity.

'Sixteen Gigawatts, Tom!' I had explained. 'That's equivalent to the output of sixteen normal-size nuclear power stations.'

At the time that I was working up the plot for *Dragon River*, the construction of the Three Gorges Dam on China's mighty Yangtze River was by no means a done deal. The basic financing, for example, was not in the bag, the World Bank having announced that it was not ready to support the project.

What interested me most of all were the engineering considerations. Was the dam really safe? Who had done the original research?

Digging around as best I could, I discovered that the US Army Corps of Engineers, with an amazing track record of building dams in America in the 1930s (including the great Hoover Dam in Colorado), had been based in Chungking, capital of China's Szechuan Province, during the Second World War and had produced the first proposals for a dam on the Yangtze.

In the London Library I found a copy of Madame Chiang Kai-shek's memoirs. Madame Chiang, aka Mayling Soong (one of the three famous Soong sisters), vividly describes the nightly Japanese bombing raids on Chungking. Since Chungking was situated at the junction of the Jialing and Yangtze Rivers, on moonlit nights the Japanese simply had to fly up through the Three Gorges from Yichang till they saw the silver gleam of the confluence.

I also discovered that 'Vinegar Jo' Stillwell, commander of the US forces in Chungking, hated Chiang Kai-shek, whom he called 'the Peanut', a slighting reference to the shape of the

Generalissimo's head. Meanwhile the wily Chou En-Lai, probably the cleverest Communist of them all, was lurking in the background, just waiting for the moment when the Nationalists and the Communists, with the war against Japan behind them, could concentrate on ripping each other apart.

As a setting, Chungking sounded irresistible. Location, location, location!

I found a little Sino-Belgian tourist agency in one of the grimmer parts of Brussels. Could they please organise my trip to Chungking, where I hoped to catch a boat down through the Three Gorges to Yichang, the most likely construction site for the Three Gorges Dam?

'*Vous serez combien de personnes dans votre groupe, monsieur? Seulement les groupes sont permis.*'

Only groups permitted! This was a cosh-blow. But then I had a brilliant idea.

'*Je suis un groupe d'une personne!*' A group of one!

So the nice young Belgo-Chinese travel agent, though hesitant at first, sent off a cable to Peking, now Beijing, and quite soon we received an answer that, with the favourable evolution of events under the Four Modernisations, groups of one were now being permitted to travel in China, as long as they were accompanied by a guide.

Well, I don't remember the guide. I don't think we ever met up. All I remember is getting on the boat in Chungking, finding a berth in a fairly primitive cabin more or less at water level (the river lapped at the porthole) and spending five days and nights cruising down the Yangtze to Wuhan.

It certainly wasn't the kind of luxury Three Gorges Cruise you can sign up for nowadays. The food basically consisted of a bucket of rice dumped on deck. As far as I could see I was the only foreigner on board, but that certainly didn't guarantee me any privileged treatment. I was issued with a spoon and I waited in line to scoop up a plateful of the glutinous substance. Occasionally, you could find a bit of fish lurking at the bottom of the bucket, an eyeball perhaps or a piece of gelatinous fin or a scaly yellow chicken claw.

But as a means of firing the imagination, that trip down the Yangtze was ideal. I worked out the plot of *Dragon River* in detail and when I disembarked at Wuhan, I found a fax machine at the airport and whizzed off the outline to Paul Sidey, my editor at Century Hutchinson.

As it turned out, I actually had a lot of time at the airport and could probably have tweaked the outline a bit.

I was standing in line waiting to check in for the flight to Hong Kong when the announcement was made: 'China Airways flight to Hong Kong is delayed for three days due to technical problems!'

On the whole, I am reassured when I hear that a flight is delayed for technical reasons. It means that someone somewhere is checking something. And that is all to the good. Wuhan airport at the end of the '80s was not particularly comfortable. The air conditioning didn't work and the city is one of the hottest places in China. But the alternatives, e.g. crashing on take-off or mid-air engine failure, seemed much less appealing.

The nuclear accident at Chernobyl in the Ukraine occurred on 26 April 1986. Thirty-one people lost their lives as a direct result of the event and the longer-term consequences for health and the environment of the spread of radioactive material were certainly severe.

A few weeks after the explosions, Boris, who was then in his final year at Oxford (doing Classics – 'Greats') and President of the Oxford Union, rang me in Brussels with an irresistible invitation.

'Hey, Dada! How are things? How's the tennis court? Would you like to give one of the speeches in my Farewell Debate?'

Of course I was delighted to be invited to make a speech at the Oxford Union, the cradle of so many aspiring politicians. When you walk up the stairs in that famous old building off the Cornmarket, you can see their photographs: Edward Heath, Anthony Wedgwood Benn, Michael Heseltine, William Waldegrave, Peter Jay, Robin Day, Benazir Bhutto, William Hague, Michael Gove. So many of them went on to become household names. So many still are household names!

The truth of the matter was I had never actually made a 'paper' speech at the Union in my life in the sense of having my name published on the order paper in advance as a listed speaker either 'for' or 'against' the motion. I had been a member of the Library Committee and had evolved what I thought was an excellent method of selecting books by plotting on a piece of graph paper the price (P) against the weight (W) of the book to be considered. On this basis, a book that didn't cost much but was quite heavy was a natural choice!

But I hadn't progressed further than the Library Committee. Even at Oxford, I had spent a good deal of time travelling, including making a trip across Europe and Asia on a BSA 500cc twin-cylinder Shooting Star motorcycle in the steps of Marco Polo, which I have described elsewhere.

I had, for example, still been in Calcutta when, at the beginning of the Michaelmas term 1961, the crucial elections for the Union Standing Committee (the next rung up the Union ladder) were held. In the Union, as in other walks of the political life, you need to win the voters over and I didn't even try.

Anyway, I was thrilled that Boris had thought of me. Some may call this a classic example of reverse nepotism. That this was far from being the case became clear as our conversation continued.

'That's brilliant!' I said. 'What's the wording of the motion?'

Boris read it out. *'This House believes that nuclear power is neither safe nor efficient.'*

'Piece of cake!' I said. 'I'll be happy to propose it. And I'm sure we'll win. People are bound to remember Chernobyl. It only just happened! Of course nuclear power isn't safe or efficient!'

'Well, actually, Dada, I'd like you to *oppose* the motion.'

'You mean you want me to argue that nuclear power *is* safe and efficient!'

'Exactly,' Boris replied. 'In the Union we like to argue both sides of the case.'

Well, I did my best. I dug out my dinner jacket and black tie and Jenny had her hair done and packed a long evening dress and we flew over to Oxford in good time for the debate.

The proponents of the motion had a very strong team that included Petra Kelly, the radical leader of the German Greens. Petra arrived with her partner, General Gert Bastian. She was a bit nonplussed to find everyone dressed to the nines. In the green room before the debate, she complained that no one had told her it was evening dress.

'I would have been quite happy to dress for the occasion,' she told me a little wistfully.

I had met Petra during my first Brussels stint when she turned up in my office one day on a lobbying mission. Young and extremely pretty, she was a leading environmentalist, an icon of the German radicals. She was rumoured to have had an affair with Sicco Mansholt when he was President of the European Commission. Her father had been an American soldier stationed in Germany.

She had only one kidney because, so she confided one day, she had given the other to her sister who had needed a transplant. That was the kind of person she was.

Of course, Petra spoke quite brilliantly for the motion, arguing that nuclear reactors, wherever they were, should be closed down.

The proponents of the motion didn't have it entirely their own way. Lord Marshall, chairman of the UK Energy Authority and the country's leading advocate of nuclear power, made a powerful speech for the opposition. By the time it was my turn, the hour was getting late. I thought a little light relief was in order.

'Statistically,' I began, 'even after Chernobyl, the chances of dying as a result of a nuclear accident are about as small as the chances of finding your bicycle if you leave it unlocked outside Balliol for an hour…'

Well, realistically, the opponents of the motion were never going to win that one. Not then. Not six weeks after Chernobyl. But in fact we got far more votes than I expected, the final tally being – as far as I remember – 160 for the motion and 65 against.

Petra Kelly was found dead with her partner, General Gert Bastian, less than two years after that Oxford Union debate. The precise cause of death – double suicide or murder followed by suicide? – was never clear.

On the literary front, I would like to be able to record that, besides writing novels and a number of non-fiction books, I had – by the end of the '80s – written some more poems. At one stage in my life I took poetry seriously. I am not sure I agreed with Percy Bysshe Shelley when he said that 'poets are the unacknowledged legislators of the world' but I certainly regarded poetry as a high calling. As I mentioned in the first volume of this memoir, *Stanley, I Presume*, in 1961 I won the Newdigate Prize for Poetry at Oxford with a poem entitled 'May Morning'. This was a 98-line effort in Chaucerian rhyme royal (seven lines per stanza), written one morning at Nethercote while we were waiting for my father to come back from the pub for Sunday lunch. And, on the back of the Newdigate, I had gone off to America in 1963 on a Harkness Fellowship to write poems in Iowa.

Of course, over the intervening decades, I did produce some occasional verse. I wrote a *Gelegenheitsgedichte* for Martin Jay's fiftieth birthday and another for Christopher Bland's sixtieth. These quite lively contributions to some quite lively celebrations were clearly not destined for publication.

I had better luck with my poem about St Francis of Assisi. I should explain that in September 1986 Jenny and I attended the twenty-fifth anniversary celebrations of the World Wildlife Fund, which were held in Assisi, Italy. The high point of the event came at a 'multifaith' service held in the marvellous Basilica of San Francesco of Assisi decorated with Giotto's famous frescoes, including, of course, that lovely rendering of St Francis preaching to the birds.

At the start of the service, six giant banners were borne in procession into the church. Five of them carried the symbols of the world's five great religions: the cross, the star and crescent, the prayer wheel, the menorah, and the (to me) opaque squiggle denoting Hinduism's om or aum. The sixth banner depicted the giant panda, WWF's well-known logo, first designed by Sir Peter Scott in 1960.

I had my reservations at the time about parading the giant panda alongside the cross, the menorah etc. Wasn't that pushing it a bit? I was also worried by the increasing talk among businessman and academics about the need to 'put a value' on nature. I wasn't sure I liked the direction in which the WWF seemed to be going.

Jenny and I had dinner one night with an old friend from Brussels, Marie Lippens, and the Maharaja of Baroda.

'Jacky' Baroda, who had probably shot more tigers than anyone else in Assisi that weekend, opined firmly over some roast wild boar, with mushrooms and garlic, 'Nature must pay its way.'

'Surely, Your Royal Highness,' I countered, '"Having value"' doesn't always or necessarily mean having value for human beings. Wildlife has value in its own right.'

The Maharaja of Baroda harrumphed and said he would be spending June in London – he always did. Such a busy time, June, what with Wimbledon, Ascot and the Henley Regatta.

I never met the Maharaja of Baroda again, though I did once sit next to the Maharaja of Bikaner on a plane from Delhi to Chandigarh. He told me he was the world's clay-pigeon shooting champion.

I still hear regularly from Marie Lippens, usually from some far-flung destination where she is fighting some environmental outrage.

Soon after we returned to Brussels, I received a letter from the novelist Angela Huth. We had been on holiday one year in Porto Ercole in Italy with Angela and her husband, James Howard-Johnston, a don at Corpus Christi, Oxford. Angela explained that she was frustrated by the dearth of good new poetry to give to her young daughter, Eugenie, and would I like to contribute to an anthology that she was now preparing for publication?

So I did. It expresses the mild scepticism I felt at the turn the conservation movement seemed to be taking. I liked David Pearce, the environmental economics 'guru' of the time, but I didn't think he was right about everything.

Here is the poem I sent off to Angela in the light of those reflections.

St Francis of Assisi
Who had never heard of ecology
Loved birds and beasts and flowers
All the same. He spent his hours
In prayer and contemplation
Believing that God's Creation
Covered all things, great and small.
St Francis knew that every animal
And plant has a right to life and space
And that each one has its certain place
Among the other million trillions.
Nowadays, clever people like Oxford dons
Explain that natural stability
Is linked to biological diversity
And that mankind's own future depends
On how we treat our feathered friends.
Ecology, they seem to say,
Is just self-interest put another way.
I wonder what St Francis would have thought
About arguments of that sort.

I explained in a covering letter that when I spoke about 'clever people like Oxford dons', I wasn't of course thinking about brilliant classicists like her husband James.

Angela Huth's *Anthology of New Poems* appeared in 1987, with my modest contribution included. Since my Newdigate poem, though deposited in the Bodleian Library at Oxford alongside all other prize-winning entries (authors: Matthew Arnold, Oscar Wilde,

James Fenton etc.), never actually appeared in print, I can truthfully say that 'St Francis of Assisi' was my first (and, so far, last) published poem. Thanks, Angela. You're a brick!

The great Basilica in Assisi was severely damaged by an earth-quake in 1997. I have sometimes wondered whether this could be seen as a kind of retribution for WWF's chutzpah with the Giant Panda banner. A banner too far? Was there some divine message here?

Chapter Sixteen

Mishap in Maseru

My formal speeches to gatherings in Africa have not always been trouble-free occasions. I was once called upon to address the First International Conference on Environment and Development in Lesotho. Because the conference was to be officially opened by the King of Lesotho, and because I was officially representing the Commission of the European Communities, I broke the habit of a lifetime and actually thought in advance about what I was going to say.

I checked with my loyal secretary, Anne, who was always cheerful and often full of ideas.

'Do you think it's the "First International Conference on Environment and Development in Lesotho", meaning it's all about Lesotho?' I asked her. 'Or is it just the First International Conference on Environment and Development to actually be held in Lesotho in which case I could range widely, as it were.'

'You decide,' Anne said. 'I'll do the typing.'

I was already on the dais, waiting for the King to arrive and take his seat next to me, when an official darted up. The interpreters, he said, needed a text of my speech. It would make their job that much easier.

I could see what he meant. The loyal people of Lesotho sat in expectant ranks in front of me in the Holiday Inn's huge conference hall, where the meeting was being held. Early that morning, I had looked out of my hotel bedroom window to see streams of people riding down the mountains into town on their ponies, wearing their characteristic conical hats. I had seen them tying up their mounts outside, before striding into the hotel, with their hats still firmly on their heads.

I had an instinctive feeling that my speech, delivered in English, might fall on deaf ears. Simultaneous interpretation would improve matters no end.

I could see the row of interpreters sitting expectantly in their glass-fronted booths, like battery hens waiting for breakfast.

I handed the man my speech.

'Photocopy it and bring it back as quickly as you can,' I said. 'His Majesty the King is about to arrive and I don't want to have my head chopped off!'

'Yes, bwana. Of course, bwana. I will bring it back immediately.'

The King, alas, arrived promptly. He wore his royal robes, draped about his left shoulder but leaving his right shoulder bare. In his right hand, he carried the ceremonial elephant-tail fly swatter that denoted his kingly rank. He spoke first in Sotho (the national language of Lesotho). Then he switched to English. He was quite comfortable with English. He had been deposed several times in the course of his long reign and had on each occasion profited from his enforced absences from Lesotho by acquiring first a BA, then an MSc, and finally a DPhil at Magdalen College, Oxford.

'I now call upon the Honourable Mr Stanley Johnson to give the keynote address,' the King proclaimed.

I rose from my seat and strode over to the lectern. I had hoped, to the very last minute that someone would rush over from the interpreters' booths with the copy of my speech. But I should have known better. God knows, I have spent enough time in Africa over the years.

'Your Majesty,' I began, 'thank you very much for those kind remarks. Do you think you could possibly ask whoever it is that has got it whether they could very kindly come up to the lectern and give me back the text of my speech?'

Happily, the King's stern appeal had the desired effect.

I had hired a car in Johannesburg for the long drive down to Maseru the previous day. So Jenny and I drove to the palace that evening for the reception. It was half-term and Jo, then sixteen, had been able to join us for the trip to southern Africa. Night had fallen by the time we reached our destination. Maseru, at the time, was experiencing frequent black-outs. As we entered the palace all the lights went out. We found ourselves in a pitch-dark room.

'Hello, Mr Johnson. I'm so glad you found your speech in the end.'

'So am I, your Majesty.'

All I could see in the darkness in front of me were some magnificent gleaming white teeth.

Next day, while Jenny went shopping and Jo – with some success – gave the Holiday Inn Casino a whirl, I was taken by helicopter into the mountains to see the massive hydroelectric scheme being financed by the World Bank. The project involved, *inter alia*, the diversion of water from the Orange River, which currently runs from Lesotho straight into the Indian Ocean, so that it could be used in South Africa instead. Massive tunnels were being drilled through the mountain and pumps installed to lift the water hundreds, if not thousands, of feet to the top of the range, whence it would descend – by the force of gravity – to feed the thirsty fields and industries of the Orange Free State.

As we soared over the mountain peaks, an engineer pointed out the key features. The giant tunnels were already being dug. The turbines were ready to be installed. This was work in progress.

Leif Kristofferson, a huge blond Norwegian, came with me in the helicopter. I had known Kristofferson in Washington in the '6os, in my World Bank days. We had been Young Professionals together. Now he was the man in charge of the World Bank's southern Africa projects.

'Pity you didn't bring a spare copy of your speech yesterday,' Leif shouted above the noise of the engine. 'I was worried for a moment there. Still, the audience loved it when the King called on the interpreters to hand your text back. They thought it was a splendid joke.'

In November 1988, the first meeting of the Intergovernmental Panel on Climate Change (IPCC) was held in Geneva, in the splendidly baroque setting of the United Nations Palais des Nations.

The Panel was sponsored jointly by the United Nations Environment Programme (UNEP) and the World Meteorological Organization (WMO) and jointly chaired by the then heads of those two organisations, respectively Dr Mostafa Tolba and Nigeria's Godwin Obasi.

It is not fanciful to say that this was (and remains) potentially one of the most important intergovernmental meetings ever held.

As I saw it, Dr Tolba was very much the driving spirit. A scientist and politician, he had led Egypt's delegation to the first ever United Nations Conference on the Human Environment, held in Stockholm in June 1972. I had seen him in action then, since I had attended the Stockholm Conference as a delegate for the International Planned Parenthood Federation, while side-lining as a reporter for the *New Statesman*.

'Surely we don't need three articles, Stanley, to cover a two-week conference,' Tony Howard, the *New Statesman*'s editor at the time and a friend from my Washington days, had protested before I left for Stockholm.

'You need a special edition, Tony,' I had countered.

I shall never forget that balmy fortnight in June 1972. The highlight came when, one bright evening, we marched through the streets of the Old Town behind a giant inflatable whale.

'BAN WHALING!' we shouted, 'BAN WHALING NOW!'

It took more than ten years for the whaling moratorium to come into force and another thirty years for Japan to announce, as it did in April 2014, that following a judgment by the International Court of Justice it was going to give up its so-called 'scientific' whaling.

The Stockholm Conference of June 1972 had been masterminded by the Canadian Maurice Strong, and when Strong became the first executive director of UNEP, the new body the Stockholm Conference had recommended, Strong selected Tolba as his deputy. When Strong returned to Canada in 1975, Tolba succeeded him as UNEP's second executive director and stayed in that position for an amazing seventeen years.

Tolba had an extraordinary early success, driving through sometimes reluctant governments an international agreement to protect the ozone layer by reducing the emissions of dangerous chlorofluorocarbons. That agreement had by and large been respected by the participating countries and the threat to the ozone layer had been contained, though not eliminated.

The EU had played its part in the negotiations leading to the Vienna Treaty on Ozone and its so-called Montreal Protocol, with its director general for environment, Laurens Jan Brinkhorst, playing a key role. Brinkhorst's forceful (and ultimately successful) attempts to guide EU member states towards a strong pro-ozone 'common position' had led to more than one delegate having to make late-night calls to their capitals.

I attended the IPCC meeting that day in Geneva as one of the delegates from the European Commission. I couldn't help wondering, as I sat there with my headphones on and the Commission 'nameplate' in front of me, whether the brilliant, tough and sometimes bad-tempered Dr Tolba would be able to repeat his ozone victory given this new and even more complex challenge of climate change or 'global warming'.

Tolba told the meeting that day, 'Distinguished delegates, we hope that the panel will in the course of the meeting agree to establish three working groups. The first will look at the science of climate change: what is actually happening? The second will try to assess the impact in different parts of the world. The third, and perhaps the most challenging, will be to look at the possible responses.'

More than twenty-five years after that first meeting, the IPCC is still in business and the three-working-group structure that Dr Tolba outlined that day, and which was duly approved, is still in business too. The only problem is that, though great progress has been made in establishing the scientific facts of the problem and in assessing its impact, almost no progress has been made in establishing an effective response. Many people now believe that the meeting of the contracting parties to the United Nations Framework Convention on Climate Change (UNFCCC), which is to be held in Paris in 2015, represents the world's last best chance to deal with the 'global warming' issue. If we don't succeed in Paris in working out an effective international agreement, so the argument runs, we will see temperature increases far beyond the two-degree Celsius rise in average temperature levels that now seems to be inevitable.

Why didn't Dr Tolba take governments by the scruff of the neck and shake them vigorously, as he had over the ozone issue? The main reason is that governments decided not to let him. Far too many interests were involved. Realistically, many if not most people prefer to believe that if they just look the other way, climate change will disappear.

And even in the global warming stakes, not all the runners will be losers, not in the short term at least.

Not long after that inaugural meeting of the IPCC in Geneva, I attended the first meeting of Working Group 2, the group that had been set up to 'assess the impacts' of climate change.

WG 2 was chaired by an eminent Russian scientist, Dr Yuri Israel, a huge bearlike figure. Not surprisingly we met in Moscow, at the vast red-brick Rossiya hotel, which has been since demolished. Like many Moscow hotels of that era, the only way you could change the temperature in the super-heated bedrooms was to leave the window open.

The Russian delegation, of course, was a large one. They were on their home territory. They were also very determined not to be outplayed. Nine-tenths of Russia's land surface, so we learned, was frozen. A rise in global temperature might be much appreciated in the far-flung reaches of Siberia. Vast areas of newly productive land might emerge. New sea routes, for example, from Murmansk to Vladivostok, might emerge, thus avoiding the need for Europe-to-Asia shipping to be routed via the Cape of Good Hope or the Suez Canal.

So the tone of that first working group meeting was not at all alarmist. As I say, there could be winners as well as losers. The Soviet Union as it then was, or Russia, as it now is, could well be one of the winners. Some bright sparks in the Kremlin spotted this early on and I doubt if they have changed their mind since.

I was mulling all this over on the flight back to Brussels when an idea occurred to me. What about writing a novel about the geopolitics of global warming?

When I got home, and remembering my own Antarctic trip a few years earlier, I wrote my literary agent a letter. Imagine,

I said, that Scott of the Antarctic discovered some mineral during the course of his ill-fated last expedition, a mineral that contains the 'magic antidote' to global warming. Something, for example, that might be sprinkled on the plankton in the Southern Ocean to increase their carbon absorptive capacity. Let's assume that a chunk of that mineral is found in Scott's tent among the other geological samples the polar partly brought back. Might there not be a new race to the Pole, with Russia determined to grab hold of the supply of this magic new mineral (let's call it 'Falconite', after Scott's middle name) to ensure that no one else uses it to slow down global warming, which Russia believes is greatly beneficial – at least as far as their own national interest is concerned?

I even suggested a title. 'We could call the book *Scott's Rocks*.'

Quite soon, I received a letter back from Gillon Aitken. He had much enjoyed, he wrote, our long and fruitful relationship but he didn't in all honesty feel that he was likely to find a publisher for *Scott's Rocks*.

If I really wanted to write the book, he gently suggested I might have to look for someone else to represent me.

I realised, when I read the letter, that this was hardly a ringing endorsement of my literary prospects. But I could see Gillon's point entirely. By then, I had had eight novels published: six by Heinemann, two by Century Hutchinson. Only one, *The Commissioner*, had made any serious money and that was because we had sold the film rights.

I had written at least a dozen non-fiction books too, most of whose titles are too long to include here. Some of these had been well received, but none had been a great money-spinner.

But I didn't think Gillon's letter had been motivated by pecuniary calculations. Not wholly, anyway. He just didn't seem to believe in the story I proposed to tell.

That nettled. About halfway through my second stint in Brussels, as I have already mentioned, I had bought one of the first Amstrads.

It was this Amstrad that I had deliberately used to type out the text of the directives on animal experimentation, zoos, habitat and species protection etc. so as to foil colleagues who might have been thinking about proposing amendments. I surmised correctly that amendments which involved retyping large chunks of text would be dumped in favour of minor face-saving textual tweaks, if at all.

It was this same Amstrad, with its gently glowing green screen and primitive dot-matrix printer, that I now used to type out my 'global warming' novel.

I set the machine up on the dining-room table in our lovely Brussels house. I had a wonderful view of the azaleas in the garden, now in full bloom.

'Come and see the flaming azaleas!' I would shout to Jenny.

Jenny was more tolerant then of my jokes than she is today. Nowadays I try to avoid making jokes before breakfast anyway.

From where I sat, typing away, I could see the children, Julia and Max, playing on the lawn with Pixie, our little Jack Russell, or clambering precariously up on the great solid wood climbing frame that some Belgian DIY experts had kindly erected.

As it happened, I did sell *Scott's Rocks*, now renamed *Icecap*, to a publisher, but this was entirely by accident.

I was in Geneva for another UN environmental meeting, staying, as usual, in the Intercontinental Hotel, which was (and is) within easy walking distance of the Palais des Nations. One night, in the bar, I met a youngish fellow with an Australian accent.

He told me his name was Charles Haynes. He worked in London in publishing and was in Geneva scouting for material.

'We want to publish an important book on global warming,' he said.

My ears pricked. 'An important book on global warming.' Hadn't I just written one? My literary agent was no longer representing me, so I was perfectly entitled to strike a deal on my own. Being 'between agents' is a bit like being 'between marriages'. 'I think I've got just the book for you,' I said.

We shook hands on it several drinks later.

The following week I got a call from Nick May, managing director of Cameron May, inviting me to have lunch next time I was in London. It so happened that I had a trip planned in the near future, so we met at Bellamy's in Vauxhall, near where Cameron May had their offices.

Nick May, it turned out, was a cousin of James Cameron, a leading environmental lawyer and the main investor in Cameron May (hence the firm's title).

'Don't get me wrong,' Nick assured me when it was time for pudding. 'Charles has had to go back to Australia but James and I have talked about this. As far as we're concerned, a deal's a deal. Charles told us you shook on it and that's good enough for us. You've written a book on global warming and Cameron May have agreed to publish it. That's where we stand, don't we?'

I couldn't really see what Nick May was driving at.

'What's the problem, then?' I asked.

'No problem, really. It's just that Charles obviously thought he was buying some kind of legal tome about climate change legislation or whatever. That's what Cameron May does, you know. We publish environmental law books, at a pretty hefty price, I should add. Whatever the market will wear, as a matter of fact.'

'You mean you don't publish novels at all?' I gasped. 'No fiction whatsoever?'

'Not so far.'

I have to hand it to Cameron May. They listed *Icecap* in their autumn catalogue alongside weighty volumes such as *New Directions in Climate Change Legislation* and *Whither the IPCC?* They threw a launch party in one of the vaulted basement rooms of the Royal Society of Arts in John Adam Street. Some of my friends, like Peter Melchett and Charles Douro, came when they probably had better things to do. Greater love hath no man than to go to a friend's book launch when he truly, madly, deeply doesn't want to buy the book.

Cameron May even nobbled a few newspapers. Was *Icecap*, the (anonymous) *Economist* reviewer asked, the beginning of a new trend where fact combines with fiction?

Well, whoever (anonymously) suggested that some such new trend might be in the offing proved totally wrong, based at least on the evidence of *Icecap*'s sales. Nick May reassured me that *Icecap* had 'washed its face' but frankly I didn't believe him.

I sometimes remind James Cameron, when I meet him at various environmental gatherings (the last occasion was in Rio de Janeiro in June 2012 at the latest Earth Summit – more later about that) that I have had the honour of being published by the firm that bears his name. James has never reproached me for failing to make clear, in that late-night Geneva bar, that my book on global warming was purely a work of the imagination. Sometimes silence is more eloquent than words.

I don't actually feel particularly guilty vis-à-vis Cameron May. The time will soon come when they will be able to claim they were 'ahead of the curve' in publishing *Icecap*. As I see it, the main thesis of *Icecap* is beginning to look more and more plausible. As international agreements to 'mitigate' climate change by reducing emissions seem more and more elusive, attention is increasingly being devoted to geo-engineering solutions. We are beginning to look back nostalgically on the good old days when atmospheric pollution acted as a damper on global warming. We yearn for another volcanic eruption like, say, Krakatoa in 1883, which, though locally devastating (bad luck on Indonesia), achieved a massive and quite long-lived reduction in global mean temperatures.

Or else we can look for some other 'magic bullet', like giant reflective mirrors in space.

Twenty years after I wrote *Icecap*, scientists are once again focusing on the possibility of somehow scooping out carbon from the atmosphere. Maybe that pile of rocks which Scott and his men lugged back from the Beardmore Glacier and which, as far as I know, are still in the dusty basement of the Cambridge museum where they were consigned on their return to this country in 1912, will indeed soon be re-examined to see if, after all, they contain some miracle substance that might enable the world, once and for all, to bring global warming under control.

Chapter Seventeen

Saving the World's Forests

When I was eighteen, and in my gap year, I went to Brazil on an iron-ore carrier. Towards the end of my three-month stay in South America, I hitch-hiked on a lorry from Campo Grande to Brasilia.

It was a long haul. Campo Grande is in Mato Grosso do Sul, one of Brazil's more southerly states. Brasilia is in the heart of the Amazon. There was no metalled highway. Just a dirt road bulldozed through the jungle. In 1959, the new capital city was still being built. Giant yellow earth-moving machines shifted and levelled. The forest still loomed on every side, great diptherocarps hundreds of feet tall.

When I left England, I had taken the last £40 from my Post Office savings account but, even in the '50s, £40 did not last for ever. By the time I arrived in Brasilia I was seriously short of funds.

I got a job on a building site. Labourers had come to the Amazon from all over Brazil, looking for work. If ever there was a shanty town, this was it. And there was a palpable air of excitement about the whole place. 'Opening up the Amazon' was the new dream, the new political slogan.

I didn't occur to me then that I was witnessing, indeed participating in, the accelerating process of Amazonian deforestation that has, over the past fifty years, transformed the South American continent.

Admittedly, I was not then an 'environmentalist' in the way I am today. As a matter of fact, I don't think that, in the '50s, the word had even been invented. Guide books talked of '*Paris et ses environs*' but that was about it. I had been a classicist at school and I was about to go up to Oxford to study Greek, Latin and Ancient History for a further four years.

I read *The Iliad* – in the original and without a crib – on the ore-carrier on my way out to Brazil and I would, appropriately, read *The Odyssey* on the way home. My mother, bless her, kept all my letters home. When she died, my sister, Birdie, handed me a pile of them in a plastic bag. Rereading them now, or some of them at least, I cannot detect many traces of a budding conservationist.

In retrospect, however, that first journey to the Amazon, more than fifty years ago, proved to be a totally formative experience.

I had been in Brasilia only a few days when a police patrol stopped by the construction site on which I was working to check the papers of migrant labourers.

I had Homer and the last 100 pages of Disraeli's *Sybil: A Tale of Two Nations* with me (the early chapters had 'multitasked' as loo paper on a transcontinental journey that had taken me to Peru and back) but no valid work permit.

In the makeshift police post, the officer was firm.

'You can't work here without a permit. We'll have to fly you down to Rio on a military plane.'

I knew a bit of Portuguese by then, enough at least to say, '*Muinto obrigado, senor.*' Thank you very much!

If I had to put a precise date and time to it, I would say it was that first free flight over the Amazon in a Brazilian military transport (the authorities didn't charge me a single cruzeiro) that basically sealed the direction of my life.

I was the only passenger in the plane that day. I had the cargo hold to myself. I could walk from side to side, looking out of the windows in all directions. And what did I see? Just greenery. Greenery from one horizon to the other. For hour after hour, or so it seemed, there was nothing below me except the trees of the forest and the great oxbow rivers. I knew that tribal people lived 'down there', of course. In the *National Geographic* magazine, they printed photographs of naked 'Indians' pointing their blow-pipes at the sky, as though their venomous darts might bring down a passing plane. I knew that there were jaguars and pythons and the great web of forest life. But from the air it was just one great green unimaginably vast wilderness.

I came back to Brazil twice in the decade after I left Oxford. The first time was when I was writing my first non-fiction work, a long book about the population explosion, published by Little, Brown in the United States and Heinemann in Britain. To research that book I had travelled to more than a dozen countries in Asia, Africa and South America. The common factor was that all of these countries had launched population and family planning programmes.

The full title of the book was *Life without Birth: A Journey Through the Third World in Search of the Population Explosion*. Though I had been to Rio de Janeiro to interview the redoubtable Walter Rodriguez, President of BEMFAM, Brazil's national family planning association (an unenviable job given the power of the Catholic Church in Brazil and the recently published papal encyclical *Humanae Vitae*), I hadn't on that occasion revisited Brazil's Amazon regions.

The following year, however, researching my book on new agricultural developments (*The Green Revolution: The United Nations at Work*), I made up for this omission. I had the chance to fly down the whole length of the Amazon, from source to mouth. I began at Leticia, a frontier town in the most literal sense since it lies in

the Amazon forest exactly where the borders of three countries –
Colombia, Peru and Brazil – meet. I broke my journey in Manaus,
in the very heart of Brazil's Amazon region, then eventually flew on
to the coast, to Recife and Salvador da Bahia.

On that *Green Revolution* journey I experienced, once again, the
overwhelming sensation of the sheer immensity of the Amazon
basin. I began to understand more fully the need to keep it intact,
not just in the sense of safeguarding 'representative' biomes or
ecosystems or whatever, but throughout the whole of its range.

I have to admit that I didn't know much in those days about
the crucial role the world's three great tropical forest regions – the
Amazon, the Congo basin and the forests of south-east Asia –
play in the global climate system. In August 1972 the *New Scientist*
published a long article I had sent them, outlining some of the pressures the Brazilian Amazon was under. I didn't mention the climate
issue, concentrating instead on the ever-expanding impact of
cattle ranchers, logging companies and soya and sugar plantations.
I concluded my piece by saying, 'It seems to me that in the Amazon
the only tool "developers" seem to need is a box of matches.'

There were many opportunities, both as an MEP and as a
European civil servant, to work for forests. In Parliament, Hemmo
Muntingh and I, among others, tried to dissuade the Commission,
and the European Community as a whole, from supporting
schemes to dam the Amazonian rivers or vast projects to mine
iron ore in sensitive areas, such as Carajás in the Brazilian state of
Pará. Back in Brussels, and responsible for drafting the EU's Fourth
Environmental Action Programme, I made sure that a section was
devoted to 'tropical forest conservation'.

I pay tribute here to Tony Juniper and Simon Counsel, at the
time tropical forest campaigners for Friends of the Earth, who
visited me in my office in Brussels at a crucial moment.

'Just tell me what you want me to put,' I said. They didn't even have to buy me lunch.

In due course, we even sent a full-blown 'Communication to the Council on the European Community's Role in the Conservation of Tropical Forests' and the Council obliged by producing a useful resolution on the same topic.

But what for me turned out to be the game-changer was the new urgency that the deliberations of the Intergovernmental Panel on Climate Change had injected into the debate.

Quite apart from the extraordinarily important role the world's forests played in the conservation of species and as source of food and medicine (e.g. the cancer-curing potential of the forest plant known as the rosy periwinkle), quite apart from the vital 'environmental services' they provided on a local or regional basis (e.g. prevention of floods and erosion; water supply; provision of shelter, food and firewood), the world's forests were increasingly being recognised as a vital element in the global climate system. Up to 20 per cent of all CO_2 emissions were estimated as being due to the destruction or degradation of tropical forests. By eliminating those emissions, the world would be taking a giant step in dealing with the global warming issue, quite apart from all the other benefits saving the forests would bring.

As I sat there in my office in Brussels, only a year or two short of my fiftieth birthday, waiting for my secretary to come back from the cafeteria with my afternoon cup of tea, I couldn't help wondering whether the world shouldn't be aiming at some comprehensive international agreement for the conservation of forests.

Basically, as far as I could see it, what was needed was an international forest treaty, preferably worked out under the auspices of the UN, under which the tropical forest countries would make legally binding commitments to protect their forest areas and the rich industrialised countries would make legally binding commitments to help the developing countries develop in other ways that didn't involve the massive destruction of their forests.

It wasn't a stupid idea. And it wasn't an original idea. Many people were thinking along the same lines.

The problem was, towards the end of the '80s, the international calendar was looking rather crowded. The International Union for the Conservation of Nature (IUCN), for example, had produced a first draft of a Convention on Biological Diversity. IUCN's Wolfgang Burhenne and his wife, Françoise Burhenne, were the moving spirits behind that draft. A first informal discussion was scheduled to take place in the margin of the IUCN Conference, which was to be held in San José, Costa Rica, in February 1988.

The weekend before the conference began I visited Tortuguero, on Costa Rica's Caribbean coast. Costa Rica was in the vanguard of 'environmentally conscious countries'. I stayed at an eco-lodge near the beach. I say 'near' not 'on' the beach because Tortuguero is one of the key breeding grounds for the endangered green turtle.

I am not a scientist. I wish I was. I don't even have a single O level in a scientific subject. What I learned about turtles that weekend taught me how little I know about even the basics.

One day, at dinner in our eco-lodge, Ivan Hattingh, a WWF veteran, also visiting Tortuguero before going on to the meeting, explained the real reason for the decline in turtles on Tortuguero's beaches.

'It's deforestation,' he said.

I tried to work it out, but I couldn't so I said, 'Tell me why?'

'Alimentary, my dear Watson,' Hattingh replied. 'The turtles come up out of the sea, year after year since time immemorial, to lay their eggs on this beach. But the eggs, increasingly, are being scavenged by the jacaranda cats. In the old days, before the forests along this part of the coast were cut back, there were plenty of jaguars and they preyed on the jacarandas. But now, with the disappearance of the forests, the jaguars have gone, the jacarandas thrive and the turtles face a crisis.'

I drove on up to San José feeling chastened. So much to learn. So little time to learn it!

The informal meeting to discuss the Burhenne draft convention on biological diversity was useful. It was clear that the United Nations Earth Summit, scheduled to be held in Rio de Janeiro in June 1992, twenty years after the famous Stockholm Conference, would have the adoption of a world treaty on the conservation of biodiversity high on its agenda.

But it was also clear to me that there was no chance that a new UN biodiversity treaty would address forest conservation head on. The draft I had seen covered issues such as 'access to benefits', 'biosafety considerations' and the 'preparation of biodiversity action plans'. These were important and often contentious questions in themselves. The proponents of the biodiversity treaty would not be keen to see its scope enlarged to deal head on with the conservation of forests. If that happened, there was a good prospect that the whole thing would go down the drain.

As it turned out, another more promising opportunity presented itself. After that first plenary meeting in Geneva, the three IPCC working groups had been beavering away. Much attention was, of course, focused on Working Group 3: the 'response' option, viz. the actions to be recommended nationally and internationally to stop or at least reduce the impact of global warming. In this context, recognising the importance of forests as far as CO_2 emissions were concerned, the UN scheduled a meeting of a 'special sub-group of the working group' to discuss some of the key issues.

The meeting was to take place in São Paulo, Brazil, in January 1990.

I rang my daughter, Rachel. 'Do you fancy a trip to Brazil?' I asked. 'I've got to go to a meeting in Sao Paulo. But we could go to Manaus and Rio first. Then, while I'm at the meeting, you could go on down to Iguaçu, if you like.'

I'd been to the amazing Iguaçu waterfalls, on the Brazil-Paraguay-Uruguay border in June 1984, in the margins of a trip to the International Whaling Commission's Annual Conference, which was being held that year in Buenos Aires. (You could still see the posters in the Argentine capital: '*Los Malvinas son Argentinas*'!)

I told her about the falls. 'You can walk right in behind the great wall of water. Hundreds, thousands, of swifts nest there.'

Rachel, who had left Oxford and just started work on the *Financial Times*, was only too delighted to take a break.

'Count me in, Dada.' Rachel still calls me 'Dada', which is fine by me. Her children call me 'Grandaddy'. That's fine too.

Rachel and I arrived in Manaus in time to take a boat upstream on the Rio Negro (which joins the Amazon at Manaus) to stay in the famous 'Canopy Lodge' or 'Tree House'. You have to climb up rope ladders to reach your room. When you wake up in the morning, you actually look down on the treetops below. If you don't keep your windows closed, the monkeys will make off with your belongings.

At sunset, cocktails are served 250 feet above the ground.

I made a joke about canopy canapés. My first joke of the day, actually. Flying can take it out of you sometimes. Or else I was getting old.

'Is your life always like this, Dada?' Rachel asked.

'Pretty much,' I replied.

We went that night with a guide in a dug-out canoe, paddling along the creeks, or *igarapés*, as they call them in Portuguese. When the guide shone a torch, we could see the alligators lining the banks, their eyes glinting red in the beam.

We didn't see just one alligator. We saw hundreds. At one point, our guide actually leapt onto the bank, grabbed an alligator, bound its snapping jaws shut with a rope, and hoisted it back into the dugout for us to inspect at close quarters.

Nowadays, I suspect there are eco-guidelines advising against this kind of behaviour but we enjoyed it at the time.

Ivo Dawnay, the *FT*'s correspondent in Brazil, took us out to lunch the day we arrived in Rio. Though Rachel hadn't yet met her *FT* colleague, I knew Ivo from my days in Brussels when he had worked in the *FT*'s European bureau.

I had rung him from London (those were the pre-email days) and he had sportingly agreed to interrupt his busy schedule. It was a long interruption. We went to a magnificently tiled restaurant that Ivo told us had been 'much loved by the Nazis'. While Ivo went back to the office, Rachel and I – somewhat the worse for wear took the cable car to the top of Sugarloaf Mountain. Some months later, Ivo returned to Britain to work for the *FT* in London. He re-met Rachel. They married, had three children and lived happily ever after.

If that Brazil trip was, obviously, a momentous one for Rachel, it also represented a turning point in my own career.

The 'special meeting on forests of the subgroup of IPCC's Working Group 3' not only took place in Sao Paulo. It was also chaired by a high-level official from Itamaraty, the Brazilian Foreign Office. To me, this was a very significant development. I saw it as indicating that the Brazilians, in the run-up to the Rio Earth Summit, were ready to discuss and perhaps to agree to the adoption of some kind of international legally binding instrument for the protection of forests.

The report of our 'special sub-group', unanimously agreed, called for a well-worked-out Forest Protocol to be attached to the

Climate Change Convention, if and when such a convention was adopted by the international community.

Rachel's 500-word report of our meeting didn't make the coveted 'Page One, Above the Fold' slot in the next day's *Financial Times*, but it was well placed in the paper and apparently well received by the hierarchy. Strictly speaking, the Sao Paulo date line was accurate for, though Rachel had been at Iguaçu during the meeting itself, she had returned to Sao Paulo before filing the story.

Rachel is not the only one of my children to have produced a useful report at a crucial moment. Boris, who to our delight was posted to Brussels as the *Daily Telegraph* Europe correspondent towards the end of the '80s, wrote some immensely helpful pieces about elephants, zoos, leg-hold traps, whales and so on. Frankly, I have no idea where the notion that 'Boris is a Eurosceptic' comes from.

Boris and Allegra, Boris's first wife, set up home in Woluwe. Jenny and I lived in Rhode St-Genèse, on the other side of the Bois de la Cambre. We resurfaced our tennis court. At half-term and holidays, there were gatherings of the clan and the sound of first (and often second) serves crashing into the net.

I realised, as I approached the end of my second term in Brussels, that 'the children' had all become grown-ups or were well on the way to achieving that status. As a matter of fact, they were overtaking me by leaps and bounds.

It was about time, I thought, for another quixotic career move.

The White House Global Change Conference, held in April 1990, gave me the opportunity I was looking for. By then I had left the Environment Directorate-General (then known as DG XI), having been promoted to the post of 'director of energy policy' in the Energy Directorate-General (then known as DG XVII). In French, my title was *Directeur de la Politique Energetique*!

The White House Energy Conference was, as its name implies, actually held in the White House. You went through all the security checks to get in, you got a tour of the 'private' rooms. Best of all, you had your photo taken with the President himself. And not just a group photo – a proper one-to-one shot. George H. W. Bush is much taller than I am. The photo, which I received some weeks later in Brussels, bears the inscription 'For Stanley Johnson, with best wishes, George Bush'. It shows me gazing up into the President's face with a 'devoted admirer' expression.

As I sat there at the White House Conference, listening to US President George H. W. Bush expounding on the US approach to climate change, I realised that one of the reasons the White House had called the conference was to signal their opposition to any international agreement that sought to limit their God-given right to emit as much carbon into the atmosphere as they jolly well pleased. Whichever way you dressed it up, that was the bottom line. That was the reason lobbyists all over Washington were pouring thousands of dollars, millions of dollars, into the coffers of senators and congressmen. *Daily Telegraph*, eat your heart out!

Whatever the reality was and is, most of the world's governments also care about perceptions. President George H. W. Bush, the forty-first President of the United States, was not some hillbilly upstart. He was the scion of an upper-class East Coast family. Appearances were important. The USA, under Bush 41 at least, didn't want to be the dog in the manger, the spectre at the feast. Not if it could be avoided. It seemed to me that they were looking, truly looking, for something to put on the table, something that, for the time being at least, might keep others off their back, particularly those pesky Europeans. Whatever that something was, it had to be plausible. And achievable.

Back in Brussels, not long after the White House Energy Conference, I played squash one lunchtime with Tom Niles, the US ambassador to the EU, in a squash club off the Chaussée de Waterloo. Tom was a much better squash player than I was and he thrashed me soundly.

After the game, we had a light, non-alcoholic lunch. I put forward my plans tentatively.

'Let me make it clear, Ambassador,' I said, 'that I'm not speaking for the Commission, not for the Energy or Environment DGs, certainly not for the EU as a whole. I just think the time is right, and that an initiative of this sort might get the USA off the hook. After all, the next G7 summit is in Houston, the USA is chairing the meeting. President Bush will presumably announce the official conclusions. This could give him a face-saver.'

I went on to say that, with Brazil the host country for the forthcoming UN Earth Summit, with the precedent of Brazil's potential support for a Forest Protocol, as evidenced by the Sao Paulo meeting (he had seen the excellent *FT* report, hadn't he?), the idea of the G7 calling for an international forest convention was not totally off the table.

'And if Brazil and some of the other key players line up behind the G7 idea, we could be on a roll.'

Niles was not convinced. He pointed out that the EU was hellbent on getting some tough language about the need to reduce energy consumption in the Houston communiqué.

I countered that by saying some of the EU countries, Germany especially, were pushing hard for a forest treaty.

'You could do a trade-off,' I argued. 'Let the USA give the EU some language about the forest convention; in exchange, the EU could drop its insistence on the energy and climate stuff, or at least tone it down.'

I added one last caveat. 'I don't want my fingerprints on this one, Ambassador. I'm just acting as a freelance here. You understand that, don't you?'

'Count on me, Stanley.'

Tom Niles picked up his squash bag and headed back to the office. He exuded confidence. What the hell, I thought. It was worth a try.

I don't in any way want to claim that this idea of linking the forest issue with the energy issue was my idea alone. Certainly not. Other people must have had more or less the same thought at the same time. The conclusions of the G7 summits (still G7, not G8 in those pre-glasnost days) are not just plucked out of the air. 'Sherpas' work on them in advance.

That said, I do claim to have played a small part in the outcome. The text of the communiqué issued after the G7 summit held in Houston on 11 July 1990 had a substantial section on the environment.

With the time difference between Brussels and Houston, I didn't actually get the wording till late afternoon.

We didn't have a fax at home; we didn't, obviously, have email because emails hadn't been invented then. I phoned a friend in the EU's Washington office and got him to read out the official text as it came in.

Frankly, I couldn't believe my ears. The text as I wrote it down, sitting at my desk in our Brussels sitting room, with the magnificent azaleas still in bloom in the garden outside, read as follows:

We are ready to begin negotiations, in the appropriate fora, as expeditiously as possible on a global forest convention or agreement, which is needed to curb deforestation, protect biodiversity, stimulate positive forestry actions, and address threats to the world's forests. The convention or agreement should be completed as soon as possible, but no later than 1992. The work of the IPCC and others should be taken into account.

'This is the jackpot!' I exclaimed. 'This is the absolutely effing jackpot!'

A couple of days later, Laurens Jan Brinkhorst, the European Commission's director general (Environment) and my former boss, rang me. He didn't sound his usual cheerful self.

'I've just got back from the Houston G7 meeting,' Brinkhorst said. 'I was arguing hard on behalf of the European Community to try to get the USA to sign up to some stronger language about reducing CO_2 emissions. And they said, "If we help out on the forest issue, will you back off a bit on energy?" So I said firmly that this was not the Community's official position. Then one of their team pushed over a piece of paper about forests which clearly came from you, all about having an international forest treaty. I've got to say that I was embarrassed to say the least.'

'Uh-oh!' I thought.

I was about to do some serious grovelling when Brinkhorst went on, 'I'm not going to take this any further, Stanley. But I just wanted you to know.'

Phew! I heaved a sigh of relief. Had I handed Tom Niles a piece of paper that day we played squash? Well, maybe I had. Did that piece of paper obviously emanate from me? Well, maybe it did.

Was there a moral to the story? Just the usual one. Never put things in writing. I should have known that, of course, after all these years, but sometimes you get sloppy.

Chapter Eighteen

Return to Oxford

I would like to record that the reason I left a plum job in Brussels, as the Commission's newly appointed director of energy policy (*Directeur de la Politique Energetique!*), was simply that I wanted to work full time on developing the 'world forest convention', but it wasn't as simple as that. The real reason was altogether less heroic. It was the issue of schooling.

The children of my marriage to Jenny, both Julia and Max, were growing up. If I stayed on in Brussels, what schools would they go to?

The earlier Johnsons, viz. Boris, Rachel, Leo and Jo, had all gone as boarders to Ashdown House, a well-regarded prep school in Sussex, and would in due course move on to public school and university. They all seemed to get on very well. Charlotte and I showed up at speech days and sports days and, on the whole, shared the kids during the holidays. If this was 'hands-off parenting', it seemed to work.

Jenny was not keen on the boarding school option. If the children were going to be at a non-boarding school in England, she wanted to be in England too.

Julia already had a place as a day girl at Bute House, St Paul's Junior School, but that would have meant going back to London. Could we afford London? If we put our house in Brussels on the market, what might we hope to get for it?

I rang Madame de Groot, a local estate agent.

'The house could be wonderful when it is habitable,' she said.

I thought that was a bit rude but I let it pass. You have to make allowances. In my view, Joseph and his Polish team had done a tremendous job of 'refreshing our ancient villa'.

I showed Madame de Groot the new lightning conductor, the *paratonnere*, installed at considerable expense, which ran from our house's Gothic tower to the ground outside the kitchen. I didn't show her the dead rats in the cellar. As a matter of fact, I didn't show her the cellar at all.

'Normally, of course,' Madame de Groot said, 'anyone who buys this property will knock the house down and build a new villa.'

She looked round the garden appreciatively. 'Forty ares, almost half a hectare! That's something! This would be a palace. Someone from the Congo would pay a lot of money for this.'

We sold the house that summer, for more than we paid the Ullens de Schootens but quite a lot less than Madame de Groot suggested it might fetch, warts and all.

I wasn't sure we would have enough money to buy a house in London but we could probably afford Oxford. In those days, houses in Oxford were cheaper than houses in London, though apparently not today.

'Julia could go to the Dragon in Oxford,' I said. 'Max too, in due course. Martin Jay went to the Dragon. All the Jays did.'

A year or two earlier we had been sailing with both Peter and Martin Jay, their wives and numerous children, off the coast of Turkey. Peter Jay, former UK ambassador to Washington, had his own boat. Martin, his brother and my Oxford contemporary, was 'between boats' and had hired one that year. A third boat belonged to a friend appropriately called Nelson. When I was campaigning in the Isle of Wight for my Euro seat back in 1979, I had a slogan: 'One man, one boat!' It came in useful now.

We had formed a little flotilla as we cruised around the Aegean.

It was a great holiday, though on a windless day it could be hot. The problem was Martin didn't believe in putting the awning up. He wanted to be ready to sail as soon as there was the least puff of wind.

There was one bad moment, near Dalyan, south of Fethiye, when Tabby Jay (the younger of Martin and Sandra's two daughters) had been bitten by a hornet and had gone into anaphylactic shock. But Sandra Jay, her mother, happened to be a doctor and knew exactly what had to be done. Tabby had to have an injection of something or other to counteract the hornet's sting. And she had to have it fast. Really fast.

There was, amazingly, a first-aid post half a mile away. Leo, as fit then as he is now, performed some sterling rescue work, literally carrying Tabby down the hornet-ridden cliff, and over the intervening rocks to the emergency unit.

In the circumstances, I felt I could call on Martin Jay for a reciprocal favour. I telephoned him from Brussels.

Martin could not have been more helpful. 'Ah, the Dragon. Wonderful school. Happiest time of my life. Talk to Inky or Guv. Do use my name. They'll be delighted to have Julia.'

'Inky' and 'Guv' were the joint headmasters of the Dragon.

In due course, I spoke to 'Guv' by telephone from Brussels.

'Hello, do you have a place for my daughter, Julia, this coming September? She's going to be eight next January.'

'Guv' knew how to deal with pushy parents, even when they are calling long-distance. 'Our waiting list is years long. Children have to be put down at birth.'

Put down at birth! That sounded a bit drastic but I let it pass.

'She could be a day girl,' I said.

'She would have to be. I'm afraid there aren't any girl boarders.'

'Martin Jay never told me that.'

'Oh, are you a friend of Martin's?'

'We went sailing together in the Aegean last summer. Peter Jay too. Lots of little Jays. They've all been to the Dragon, I believe.'

Suddenly Guv was all sweetness and light. 'I'll see what I can do. I'm sure it will be all right.'

So Julia went to the Dragon. Max went to a little school called Greycotes, off the Bardwell Road.

With the money from the sale of our Brussels property, we bought a house in Polstead Road, which runs left off the Woodstock Road after St Margaret's Road, assuming you are heading out of Oxford. It took Julia about five seconds to spot that Polstead was an anagram of 'tadpoles'.

Pixie, our Jack Russell, came with us from Brussels to Oxford. One day my father came to stay bringing his own Jack Russell, Pepper. Pixie was on heat at the time. I came down to the kitchen in the morning to find the dogs coupling. Pixie in due course had four puppies. One died and we gave two away. But we kept Harry. No. 13 Polstead Road was very handy for Port Meadow. You could let the dogs off the lead there without losing them. I had form where losing dogs was concerned.

While the children went to school, Jenny went back to university, signing on for a BA in French and Philosophy at Harris Manchester, once a Hall, but now a fully fledged College of Oxford University. She already had a BSc from the Open University, having taken the OU courses during our time in Brussels.

The Principal of Harris Manchester, Dr Ralph Waller, could not have been more encouraging. He and his wife, Carol, went out of their way to make students like Jenny feel at home.

Another bonus of the move to Oxford was that, though Boris and Rachel had already left, Leo was still 'up'. He had a splendid set of rooms at New College. Having gained a first in Classical Honour Mods, he was now in his last year reading PPP – Politics, Psychology and Philosophy.

As soon as Leo went 'down', Jo arrived (Balliol). So Oxford, in the early '90s, for me at least, began to seem very much a family affair.

Not that I was in Oxford much. I worked for the FAO's Forestry Department in Rome from Monday to Friday. Strictly, I worked from Monday lunchtime to early Friday afternoon, since I caught the first plane out to Rome on Monday morning and a return flight from Rome to London around mid-afternoon on Friday. It wasn't as expensive as it sounds. The trick was to start the journey in Rome on the Friday, so that you spent the weekend in England, with the return flight to Italy being on the Monday. Back-to-backing, it was called.

I rented a flat in the Via Capo di Africa, a rundown street, not far from the Colosseum (and the main FAO building next to the Circus Maximus or Circo Massimo). The offices of the FAO's Forestry Department were in the Avenida Cristofero Colombo, about twenty minutes' walk from the FAO HQ.

Hollis Murray, an amiable Trinidadian who headed the Forestry Department, and Gerald Moore, the FAO's chief legal officer, were jointly my sponsors. Technically, I was on leave of absence from the European Commission, with the FAO footing the bill.

In those first months in Rome, in the second half of 1990, I helped the FAO draw up a draft international treaty on the conservation of the world's forests.

I would argue that this was, and remains, a serious and substantial effort to achieve a legally binding international regime for forest protection. (The title of the draft I produced used the phrase 'forest conservation and development' because, however keen I was on the conservation aspects, my colleagues in the FAO never let me forget that the FAO was a 'development' agency, part of the UN system.)

Even though the draft I produced was, in my view, a good one, in reality its political death-knell had been sounded almost as soon as I put pen to paper.

I had made a massive career switch on what was basically a false premise. It soon became apparent that the countries that actually had tropical forests were not at all ready to submit to an international forest regime on the say-so of the G7 countries, which – they were quick to point out – didn't actually have any tropical forests.

The FAO's Committee on Forestry (COFO), the principal intergovernmental forum on forests, was due to meet in Rome at the end of September 1990. Hollis Murray and Gerald Moore were convinced that if COFO gave my draft a fair wind, then the FAO could get its skates on, set up an intergovernmental negotiating committee (INC) and, if all went well, bring the text to Rio for adoption alongside the Climate Convention, the Biodiversity Convention and the voluminous 'sustainable development' guidelines then being worked on, known as Agenda 21.

These high hopes were soon dashed.

If the G7 in Houston had led the charge for a world forest convention, the counter-charge at the COFO meeting was led by Malaysian's ambassador to the FAO, Madame Ting Wen Lian.

Madame Ting clearly had no intention of being diplomatic. Her instructions came from the highest level, from the Malaysian Prime Minister himself. She wasn't called the Dragon Lady for nothing. She looked around the room that afternoon at the COFO meeting in Rome and she breathed fire and flame.

Officially, of course, the FAO's plans were not dead. At the end of November, I went to Geneva for the Second Climate World Climate Conference. Saouma sent a message, repeating his desire to see an international agreement on forests, but I had no sense that the process of launching negotiations for a World Forest Convention was running smoothly. This particular ship wasn't even on the slipway.

Not that the second World Climate Conference was dull. Far from it. From my point of view, one of the highlights of that meeting was Mrs Thatcher's own speech. She was accompanied on that occasion by Crispin Tickell, now Sir Crispin. Attentive readers may recall that the Tickells had very kindly given me the use of their London flat during my brief 'between marriages' phase. Sir Crispin had now returned to London, as head of the UK's Overseas Development Agency. He was widely credited as being Mrs Thatcher's 'green guru' as a result, apparently, of some decisive interventions he had made at a crucial climate change seminar held at Chequers.

At all events, Mrs Thatcher, in Geneva that day, was very much on message, urging rapid and effective action on climate change and global warming. 'Just as philosophies, religions and ideals know no boundaries, so the protection of our planet itself involves rich and poor, north and south, east and west. All of us have to play our part if we are to succeed. And succeed we must for the sake of this and future generations.'

She ended her speech, rather touchingly, by quoting some lines of 'Man' by George Herbert:

Man is all symmetry.
Full of proportions, one limb to another,
And all to all the world besides;

Each part may call the farthest, brother;
For head with foot hath private amity
And both with moon and tides.

Mrs Thatcher went on to Paris from Geneva. It was there, in the courtyard of the embassy, that she famously came out to confront the crowd of journalists, with her brave but futile act of defiance: 'We fight on. We fight to win.'

I didn't have a television in my flat on the Via Capo di Africa but I had a transistor radio that more or less worked if I went into the loo, stood on the seat and pointed it to the heavens through the open skylight.

Next day it was all over. A tearful Mrs Thatcher left Downing Street for the last time. John Major took over as Prime Minister, with Michael Heseltine becoming Deputy Prime Minister, a constitutional innovation that in the context of the current coalition government has proved particularly useful.

One weekend, I didn't fly back to England. Jenny came out with the children and we stayed with the Fairweathers. Patrick Fairweather was now 'our man in Rome'. The residence of the British ambassador was the magnificent Villa Wolkonsky, set in a vast well-shaded garden, with the remains of an ancient Roman viaduct running through it. If ever there was a romantic setting, this was it.

There was a splendid swimming pool too. 'Just one thing,' Patrick said, 'Princess Margaret likes to use the pool when she's in Rome, so please be sure to be out of the water in good time.'

During that long weekend, we kept a wary eye out for signs of a royal presence. By some ill chance, we were still splashing around in the pool when Her Royal Highness arrived. We stood not on the order of our going, but went at once, leaving tell-tale ripples on the surface of the pool and wet prints on the marble surround.

By coincidence, a few weeks later Jenny and I were introduced to the Princess at a fundraising reception held in the splendid dining hall of St John's College, Oxford, in support of a charity of which Her Royal Highness was the patron.

'I'm so sorry we swam in your water, ma'am,' I blurted out.

She looked at me blankly, totally puzzled. There wasn't time for me to explain, since there were others behind me waiting to be introduced.

To be frank, the exchanges I have had with royalty had, up till that point, not been particularly illuminating. In 1970, I had met the Duke of Edinburgh at a meeting in Strasbourg at the start of European Conservation Year. Critics who at that time thought the nascent environmental movement was a lot of 'blah-blah' joked about European Conversation Year, but Prince Philip in his keynote speech gave them a firm talking to.

He also talked about the need for birth control. 'Put pills in the bread, if you like,' he told a startled audience.

Years later, Charles and Antonia Douro invited Jenny and me to a party at Apsley House. There was music and dancing and a splendid buffet. Both the Queen and the Duke of Edinburgh were there.

I found myself standing next to the Duke at the buffet. As he reached for a baguette, I suddenly remembered listening to his famous remarks about birth control.

'I so much enjoyed your point about pills in the bread, Sire.' I thought 'Sire' struck exactly the right note.

The Duke spent a moment examining his plate, as though there might be something wrong with it, and moved swiftly on.

Ironically, even though I was now living in Rome, at least during the week, I had little time to visit, let alone inhabit, the property that Jenny and I had bought in the Maremma, not far from Grosseto.

Inspired by the fact that our old friends, Brian and Disie Johnson, were in the process of acquiring a house near Scansano, in the Maremma, Jenny and I (while we were still living in Brussels) had made a flying visit to Tuscany. For years I had been talking about 'buying a house in the sun'. I was ready, I thought, to take the process one step further.

We viewed several Maremma properties that weekend, all farm-houses, some newly restored, others in various stages of dilapidation.

There was one property in particular that had appealed to me, an old typically Tuscan farmhouse near Grosseto, not far from the Ombrone River. The family lived on the second floor, accessed as usual from outside by a wide stone staircase. The ground floor consisted of huge vaults where the wine, tractors and other farm implements were stored, as well as livestock in the worst of winter.

The house didn't much appeal to Jenny, who pointed out that there was (a) a large electricity pylon in front, (b) no guarantee that the authorities would permit the construction of a swimming pool and that (c) the house would need a lot of money spent on it anyway before she was going to live there.

When I decided anyway to revisit the property, called Rattaioni, a few weeks later, to take another look, she made me promise not to buy the place.

'Don't worry,' I said, 'I just want to take another look.'

I flew to Pisa with Jo, who was then in his last year at Eton, hired a car at the airport there and drove to Grosseto. It was one of those blissful afternoons when the Tuscan landscape can be spectacularly beautiful. The Maremma, of course, is one of the wilder parts of

Tuscany, but for me, coming from Exmoor, that made it all the more appealing. This was a place where wild boar and wild deer abounded.

Rattaioni was about 15 miles from Grosseto, You approached it down a long winding dirt road. It reminded me of the bumpy track up to Nethercote, though the road was in marginally better shape.

The owners, a peasant family who had lived at Rattaioni for generations, had the *vino santo* waiting for us when we arrived.

'*Nostro proprio vino, signori,*' the old lady said as she refilled our glasses. She looked old anyway. The sun and years of hard work had taken their toll.

That night I rang Jenny from the hotel. 'We sat at the kitchen table and the old couple served us wine and home-cured ham. I'm afraid I signed a *compromesso*. It seemed such a good idea. They say we needn't worry about getting permission for the pool. Apparently you just get a digger in and dig a hole and say it's for agricultural purposes and it's quite all right.'

'What about the pylon? Are they going to move the pylon?'

'I'm afraid I forgot about the pylon.'

Once I explained that a *compromesso* was a legally binding document, and that I had actually put down a substantial deposit with the balance to be found on completion, Jenny expressed herself quite forcefully.

'We already have one decrepit farmhouse at the end of a long bumpy track. Why do we need another?'

'I'm afraid it's ours already. That's the system here. We actually owned it from the moment we signed.'

'*You* signed!' Jenny pointed out.

It took over a year to sort things out. While I was working for the FAO in Rome, we found a buyer for Rattaione, a man from Florence who loved the place and was ready to spend what it took. So we engaged an expensive lawyer from Monte Argentario to ensure that, in one seamless transaction, we somehow bought and sold our 'Tuscan dream' on the same day. Back-to-backing again, I suppose.

Looking back, I would say that Rattaioni would never have worked for us. There were the problems I have already mentioned, viz. the pylon and the pool. It was also too far from the sea. We really wanted the sea. Ideally a place where you could stroll down to some quiet cove through the olive groves. Your own olive groves, preferably.

Of course, I pretended at the time that the old farmhouse was right next to the sea.

Jo and I did a trial run, the moment we left the property, the ink not yet dry on the *compromesso*.

'The sea's only half an hour away,' I claimed, as we screeched into the concrete parking area by the beach at Castiglione della Pescaia. 'Not more than that, surely?'

I was wrong. Fuelled by beakers of the warm south, it had still taken us forty-five minutes to get from Rattaioni to the coast. And who wanted to go to the beach at Castiglione della P anyway? I had been there before. A typical Italian seaside resort. Sometimes you could actually see the sun oil floating on the water.

Did I learn my lesson, as far as searching out 'that little place in the sun' is concerned? Of course not. But that comes later.

Chapter Nineteen

Desperately Seeking Jo

The FAO did not throw in the towel at once, as far as a world treaty on forests was concerned, but its interest was fading fast. At the beginning of January 1991, I attended an 'expert' meeting in Bangkok that got nowhere. There was no political impetus and without that, 'experts' may as well save their breath.

In practice, Maurice Strong and the team now preparing for the Earth Summit, officially known as the United Nations Conference on Environment and Development (UNCED), had already taken up the reins. Officially, the idea of negotiating some kind of a legally binding 'instrument' (by then we were all shying away from the t-word, where 't' meant treaty) was still on the table. Realistically, Nitin Desai, a high-level Indian diplomat who served as Strong's deputy, and who now effectively took over the pre-Rio forest discussions, was aiming for a 'Statement of Forest Principles', some document that might at least set out some general guidelines and could be proclaimed officially as one of the important 'outcomes' (a new buzzword) of the Rio conference.

Of course, Malaysia and its allies insisted even in this context that any such 'Statement of Forest Principles' should be 'non-legally binding' and actually labelled as such.

I left Bangkok feeling somewhat disillusioned. I had given up a perfectly good job in Brussels to take up an assignment in

Rome that, basically, had fizzled out. What a way to start the New Year!

To cheer myself up, I decided that I would stop off in Delhi on the way back to Europe from Bangkok. Actually, not in Delhi itself. My third son, Jo, was in his gap year, having left school before Christmas, and was now teaching at Mayo College in Ajmer.

I didn't have the faintest idea where Ajmer was, but I imagined I could take a taxi easily enough from Delhi airport. Apparently, Mayo College was fairly well known. A kind of Indian Eton.

Outside Delhi international airport, I got into one of those yellow and black 'Ambassador' taxis that look a bit like the old Morris Minors. The vehicle had clearly seen better days. So had the driver, an elderly Sikh.

He loaded my luggage in the boot and held the door open for me. 'And will you be kindly telling me your destination, sahib?'

'Mayo College. Mayo College, Ajmer.'

'Ajmer is over 300 miles from Delhi, sahib,' the driver said, 'and the road is not always being superbly excellent. It will take us many hours to reach Ajmer and even then I am not knowing precisely where this Mayo College is.'

Of course, I should have looked at the map. I had somehow imagined that Mayo College was within easy striking distance of the airport.

We drove through the afternoon and evening and into the night. As always, on the roads in India, you take your life into your hands. More accurately, someone else takes your life into their hands. Basically Mr Singh drove with one hand on the wheel and the other on the horn.

From time to time he suggested that we should call it a day and find a place to stop for the night, but I was determined to press on.

The moon came up as we entered Rajasthan. We drove through the desert. There was no heating in the ancient vehicle and the outside air was cold. I was still wearing my Bangkok outfit.

About two in the morning, with the moon still shining brightly, we entered Ajmer.

Singh, though tired by then, seemed optimistic. 'Quite soon we will be finding the college.'

We drove around for another half-hour and eventually came to a sign saying 'Mayo College'. A guard was on duty.

I had no idea where Jo was housed, so I got out to enquire. 'Jo Johnson? English boy? A teacher-wallah. Can you tell me where to find him please?'

I don't think the man was very impressed. The taxi was hardly a Mercedes and both the driver and I were showing signs of exhaustion.

He waved his *lathi* and pointed. I didn't properly hear what he said. It sounded like 'pavilion'. What on earth could he mean? Pavilion?

I got back into the car. 'Let's find the pavilion.'

So we drove round some more. The grounds of Mayo College are impressive. The battle of the Khyber Pass or wherever was probably won on the playing fields of Mayo. Suddenly I saw a big white cricket score board. The totals were still on the board. MAYO COLLEGE 318, LAST MAN 47. VISITORS ALL OUT 275.

The penny dropped. I looked around the ground, and suddenly I saw it, the cricket pavilion! A huge white structure, almost as big as the pavilion at Lord's.

We drove over and parked in front. Could Jo possibly be housed here? Shome mistake, shurely?

I got out of the car and yelled, 'Jo, JO!'

There was no sign of life. I yelled again, 'Jo, JO!'

At last a door, right at the top of the pavilion, under the eaves, opened and my third son stepped out, blinking and bleary-eyed, into the moonlight. He was quite surprised to see me, having had no advance notice.

'Why are you sleeping in the pavilion?' I asked.

Jo explained that it was, he hoped, only a temporary billet while other accommodation was being prepared.

He lent me his *charpoy* that night and, nobly, slept on the floor. Next morning he was teaching classes early, so I came along to sit in.

It was a difficult session. Ajmer is a Muslim city and many of Jo's pupils were Muslim. They were in an angry, truculent mood. The reason soon became apparent. Overnight, while I was traversing a large slice of northern India, looking for Jo, President George H. W. Bush, my hero from the White House Climate Change Conference, had launched an all-out attack on Iraq. There was no television in the classroom, but several of the boys had radios and they did not like what they were hearing. This wasn't just an assault on Iraq. It was a blatant assault on Islam.

Jo assessed the situation. 'Let's get out of here. Why don't we head back to Delhi?'

We found Mr Singh fast asleep in the back of his taxi.

'*Jalde,*' I said. It's one of the few Hindu expressions I know, apart from the obvious ones like dahl and bindu ghosh and chicken tikka masala. It means 'get a move on'. '*Jalde jalde!*' I repeated.

Singh groaned and opened his eyes.

'Where to, sahib?'

'Back to Delhi. The Oberoi Hotel.'

David Housego, an old Oxford friend, was at the time the *FT* correspondent in New Delhi, a post that Jo himself would occupy a few years later. He invited us to come with him that evening to the Foreign Correspondents' Club where huge television screens were showing the American air strikes in real time, i.e. as they were actually happening. You could see the flashes and hear the crump of the bombs.

The place was packed, but the waiters in their smart turbans and tunics still managed to push their way among the tables, carrying trays of drinks.

'Another Cobra beer, sahib? A whisky? Black Label or Red Label Johnny Walker?'

It was a weird experience.

With Maurice Strong and Nitin Desai and the well-oiled UNCED machine now effectively in charge of the forest issue, as least as far as the preparations for the Earth Summit were concerned, my full-time assignment to the FAO came to an end, though I stayed on as a consultant attending meetings of the UNCED preparatory committee and its subsidiary groups, as and when required.

Nitin Desai performed brilliantly on the forest front. He set up a group to work on the Statement of Forest Principles and kindly invited me to submit some thoughts. I was pleased to note that when, finally, the Earth Summit adopted the Rio Forest Principles, alongside the Climate and Biodiversity Conventions, and the ever-more massive Agenda 21, most of the ideas, and even much of the language, reflected that early draft of an international forest treaty that I had prepared for COFO almost two years earlier.

Just how sensitive the forest issue was, even at Rio, can be seen from the full title of the Forest Principles, which was, officially: *The Non-Legally Binding Authoritative Statement of Principles for a Global Consensus on the Management, Conservation and Sustainable Development of All Types of Forests* (1992).

I don't have enough space here to go into the forest discussions at the Earth Summit itself, but I gave a full account in my book on the Earth Summit, published in 1993 by Kluwer Law International. In essence, the fight to have a treaty, or at least the beginning of a process leading to a treaty, went on till the very last moment in Rio and only some resolute chairmanship by Klaus Töpfer, the German

Environment Minister, ensured that a 'compromise' in the form of the Forest Principles eventually emerged.

I caught a glimpse of President Bush at one moment. He was sitting in the front row of the audience when President Castro strode to the podium. Was this, I wondered, the closest the two men would ever get to each other?

Castro held up his right hand, four fingers splayed, before he started to speak.

The US President was apparently heard to mutter, 'Oh my God, he's going to speak for four hours.'

Castro must have heard or sensed the joke, because he shook his head laughing. He planned to speak for four minutes, not four hours.

He did precisely that.

In spite of the disappointment as far as my principal interest, viz. getting a forest treaty, was concerned, I still regard the 1992 Rio Earth Summit as a useful meeting.

Though international efforts to deal with climate change have got precisely nowhere over the twenty-six years since the IPCC was set up, the adoption of the climate treaty in Rio in 1992 has at least ensured that discussions continue and, who knows, maybe the Paris meeting of the climate treaty partners, scheduled for December 2015, will at last achieve a breakthrough.

The Convention on Biological Diversity, it must be said, has proved a disappointment, not least because of the failure of the treaty, as agreed in Rio, to include mandatory provisions for the protection of habitat and species. The EU by then had adopted its own far-reaching legislation, the habitat and species directive. Though some countries, in the course of the negotiating process, had attempted to insert similar provisions in the UN's biodiversity treaty, this had proved impossible. As a result the CBD remains a toothless instrument, as far as the protection of nature and the world's wild places is concerned.

The jury, amazingly, is still out on the forest issue. For more than a quarter of a century, discussions have continued in one forum or another, about a possible international forest instrument. We have seen a UN Forest Forum, an Intergovernmental Panel on Forests and a UN Forest Initiative, to name just three. But these have been talking shops. What we haven't seen is real progress in combatting deforestation. In the end, of course, the process will be self-limiting. Deforestation will end when there are no more forests left to destroy. If discussions continue along present lines, that is one certain result. On the other hand, a major forest fire in, say, the Amazon, consuming millions of square kilometres, might, just possibly, act as a spur to effective last-minute action.

Oddly enough, Rio's most lasting legacy may well prove to be Agenda 21. I consider it to be a brilliantly presented, brilliantly argued document. It covered virtually the whole range of environmental issues, including population, and even now can be mined for useful insights. The trouble is Agenda 21 is over 700 pages long. It is not bedtime reading.

One evening, when the Earth Summit was going on, my good friend Derek Osborn, then director general at the UK's Department for the Environment, invited me for dinner at the Copacabana Palace.

'Michael Howard will be there,' he said. 'I thought you might liven things up.'

I don't think Derek meant to imply that Michael Howard, then a Cabinet minister and Secretary of State for the Environment, was a dull dinner companion, since that was and is far from the case. We certainly had a jolly evening. Little did I know that, only a few years later, Michael Howard would be the leader of the Conservatives seeking to end more than a decade of Labour rule and that I would be one of the Conservative parliamentary candidates 'fighting' to help him do precisely that.

We went out onto the seafront to take the air after dinner. When I first came to Brazil, in 1959, the ocean came right up to the hotels. Sometimes the waves broke right across the Avenida Atlantica and swamped the hotel lobbies. Now the beach has been dramatically widened. The ocean is many yards away and, most often, the sound of the waves is just a distant roar.

But still you have to take care. When you go swimming off Copacabana, the waves can knock you over and spin you around and thump you down on the sand so your head aches, even if you don't drown.

Chapter Twenty

Death of a Patriarch

L aurens Jan and Jantien Brinkhorst were staying with us in
Oxford at the beginning of May 1992 when my father rang
up one morning. My father didn't often use the telephone. That
was not his way. He believed if you had something to say to a
man, you would probably be able to find him in the pub. If you
didn't know which pub he was likely to be in, you might have to
do the rounds till you found him. In our part of Exmoor, there
were several obvious possibilities – the Royal Oak, Winsford; the
Royal Oak, Withypool; the Crown or White Horse, Exford; or
the Sportsman's Inn, Sandyway, to name but a few. It was always
better to talk face to face, my father believed, if you had something to discuss.

So I was a bit surprised when I heard his voice.

'Hello, Stan. Bit of trouble here, I'm afraid. My kidneys have
packed up. I'm going into hospital. I shan't have dialysis though.
No point in that. Not at my age.'

My father was eighty-two that year. I couldn't see that ruling out
dialysis was necessarily the right option.

'I'll come down straightaway.'

'No, don't do that. No need for that.'

'Of course I will.'

I didn't realise when I put the phone down that this was the last conversation I would ever have with my father. In fact, it was the last time I would hear his voice.

I should have cancelled the lunch party we had laid on that day, but I didn't. I'd asked Martin Parry, the head of Oxford's newly established Environmental Change Unit, to come over with his wife to meet the Brinkhorsts. There were some other guests as well. They were all about to arrive.

We were just sitting down when the phone rang again. It was the hospital in Taunton. Nothing desperately urgent. They just thought I would want to know that my father was not in the best of shape.

I waited for the first course to be over, made my excuses, and then drove like hell to Taunton.

My sister Birdie, who had done so much for both my mother and father over the years, was there.

'Pa died ten minutes ago.' She put her arm round my shoulder. 'They think it was a heart attack, or some kind of seizure. You can go in, if you like.'

I went in and laid my hand on my father's still-warm forehead.

Boris, as the oldest grandchild, gave the address at my father's funeral in Winsford Church. This is what he said.

Winsford Church, 15 May 1992, by Alexander (Boris) Johnson

Johnny, Pa, Grandaddy or Granbeer as he was known to his Australian grandchildren, liked to see the horizon. As one thinks about his life of adventure, farming as a teenager in Canada, playing rugby in Egypt before the war, flying bombers with distinction in Coastal Command and then, even in his seventies, stuffing a mattress in the back of a station wagon and driving around the Australian outback, talking to whoever he met, living on meat pies and beer, one thinks about his resourcefulness.

For the last forty years, that energy was concentrated here. In the valley at Nethercote, with his wife Buster, he created a kind of semi-paradise, not just for the dogs, peacocks and horses, the legendary figures of the Johnson bestiary, with whom we can imagine he is now in some sense reunited, but also for his family, whom he loved, and by whom he was loved back deeply.

You needed strength and perseverance to run Nethercote, by the way. We were all amazed as children at how, even with arthritis, he could crank the engine from cold. He understood the natural and mechanical world. When Grandaddy assured you that one of the cars, long immobile in the yard, moss on the wheels, would soon be roaring up the motorway with the addition of a single sprocket, it was plausible.

Though not from these parts, he had a deep respect for the Exmoor way of life. He didn't like to leave the valley much, unless it was for something important like the pub or a point to point. He wanted nothing so much as to have a working family farm and it was with a bemused pride that he watched his children make their own separate lives.

He dug deep roots here and they will remain. On a day like this, especially on a day like this, he would have been happy to be remembered in the place he loved so much.

After the service we all went back up to Nethercote. The whole family was there, including my sister, Hilary, who had flown in from Australia. We set up trestle tables in the yard, a scene that I described in a poem I sent to the *Exmoor Review*, entitled 'In Memoriam Wilfred "Johnny" Johnson (1909–1992)'.

The day dawned bright and clear
With a touch of frost.

Had he been there,
Most probably he would have ventured
A confident 'It'll be warm
By noon.' It was a good day to go.
The valley had seldom seemed
More beautiful. In so many ways
It was his valley, stamped
With his mark. After all,
He had lived there forty years.

After the funeral,
They came back with us for a drink
And stood around in the yard.
In our farming days, it used
To be full of mud and muck
But now the grass has seeded itself
And it's more like a lawn.

Most of the village was present,
As well as the family, of course.
One of the local huntsmen
Who had ridden through often enough
In the past doffed his cap
As he took a glass of beer from the tray,
'If I'd had my horn with me,' he said
'I'd have blown 'Gone away'.

In practice, though my father lived in our valley at Nethercote for forty years, as I mentioned in the poem, he was actually a full-time Exmoor farmer for less than two decades.

The long-term effect of his wartime injuries, combined with

sometimes crippling arthritis, meant that he had to give up active farming in 1969, at the age of sixty. I remember the farm sale we held in one of the fields at the top of the farm one windy October day. I took the train down from London with the then five-year-old Boris, hired a car at Taunton, and got to the farm in time for the opening bids.

Some of the stock escaped from the pens and there was much hollering as the locals, some of whom had ridden over to the sale that morning, galloped off to round them up again.

My father once told Jenny that the day of the farm sale was the 'saddest day' of his life.

He was not a 'gentleman farmer'. And we were definitely not 'county'. In all my time we were farming, I can't remember my parents either going out to a dinner party or giving a dinner party themselves. It was not that they were standoffish. Far from it. 'Entertaining at home' simply didn't fit in with an Exmoor farmer's life. There was neither the time nor the money for it.

The evening meal was 'high tea'. If it was summer, you went on with outside work; in winter months, you stoked up a huge fire in the 'middle kitchen'. My mother, on the whole, didn't go to the pub with my father. Her hearing wasn't good even when she arrived on Exmoor, aged forty-four, and it deteriorated over the years (not helped, as I have mentioned earlier, by the habit the terriers had of chewing her hearing aids). During the holidays, of course, we stayed in with her, but during term-time she was often on her own in the evening. We profited, of course, from that, because that was when she wrote us her long weekly letters to our respective schools, universities or, in later life, homes of our own.

Nowadays, Exmoor has seen some serious 'gentrification'. People are constantly whizzing around, going out to lunch or dinner, and then having the people who have invited them back for a return match. Fortunately our own drive is still so bad, in spite of the efforts I have made to improve it over the years ('money down the drain'), that even now we tend to think twice before venturing out. And I am sure others think twice or even thrice before 'venturing in'.

There are still, for example, people who don't like driving over Nethercote Bridge, which crosses the Exe just before you reach the farm. Sometimes they arrive in our yard saying their 'nerves are in shreds'. In response, I observe that any time the river tops the bridge, bringing down tree trunks and other debris in its path, new railings are swept way.

My parents, living at Nethercote Cottage in 'retirement', had a lot of peacocks. They started out with two, but the flock, if that is the right collective noun for far too many peacocks, soon expanded. There were more than a dozen, anyway. Maybe twenty.

The peacocks made a tremendous noise. They also made a tremendous mess. There were peacock droppings everywhere, moist and smelly objects, like large slugs.

We were having lunch one summer day in the garden at West Nethercote. Ever since I had sawn down the overhanging branch by accident on my fortieth birthday, the garden was now a bright sunny place to eat. We made the most of it. I would sit at one end of the long table, Jenny would sit at the other, with family and friends lined up at either side. An idyllic scene, you might say.

Not totally idyllic on that particular occasion. The peacocks had been over that morning. They had woken us early with their ear-piercing shrieks and yells. Eventually I had got out of bed and shooed them out of the garden.

We had fishcakes, for lunch that day. Moist, soft fishcakes, with a spray of parsley. The culinary detail is important.

With a fishcake neatly pronged on my fork, I was making some important point that involved a certain amount of arm-waving. The fishcake became detached from the utensil and fell to the ground. Without wishing to interrupt myself in mid-flow I leant down with one hand, grabbed the soft round sticky object lurking near my foot, and popped it in my mouth without looking, firmly believing it to be the fishcake I had dropped.

I was in bed with a high fever for days. One of my Turkish cousin's stepchildren, Halim Tanzug, arrived to stay but I was too ill to receive him. I could merely groan a gloomy 'Merhaba!' through the bedroom door.

Nowadays, if you told a doctor a story like this one, you'd probably find yourself on a 'watch list' of some kind. It would get onto his or her notes anyway and into the system and sooner or later the press would know all about it, whatever the Data Protection Act says. I can see the headlines. EXMOOR MAN SERIOUSLY ILL FROM EATING PEACOCK POO.

We got rid of the peacocks soon after that. A man came from Norfolk to get them. We herded all the peacocks into the barn and the 'peacock man' caught them one by one, popped them into a sack, and then decanted them into a small trailer. I was amazed how many birds he was able to get into such a small space.

'They'll have plenty of room in Norfolk,' the peacock man said.

Sometimes I miss the peacocks. They were truly beautiful birds, particularly when they spread their tails. Once I herded them back to the cottage from halfway down the drive. They were quite biddable and they didn't mind about the lack of railings on the bridge. Not as far as I knew, anyway.

At night, they roosted in the trees. One moment they would be on the ground, the next – as dusk fell – you'd hear a great explosive noise as the peacocks made their literally vertical take-off into the trees.

The foxes would get them from time to time. My father kept his Purdey by his bed. He once shot a peacock-loving fox out of the bedroom window.

And he sometimes fed the digestive biscuits that he kept for the peacocks to Max, who as a toddler had a habit of wandering over to the cottage in the early morning, often when it was still dark, to ask his grandfather to start the diesel engine so that he, Max, could watch television.

Jenny asked my father whether Max's visits were a bother. My father denied this vigorously. 'No bother. Good to see the little chap.'

Chapter Twenty-One

Consultancy Assignment

As an ancient Chinese proverb put it, 'When one door shut, other door open.'

My FAO job had no sooner come to an end, than my Coopers and Lybrand job began. I didn't have to commute to Rome from Oxford, just to London.

Coopers and Lybrand nowadays is part of Pricewaterhouse-Coopers (PwC), one of a handful of big international firms specialising in taxation, audit and management consultancy. (My second son, Leo, is a Partner in PwC's 'Sustainability Practice'.)

I knew nothing, of course, about taxation and audit. I barely got Maths O level. I also knew I knew nothing about management consultancy but Coopers obviously believed otherwise.

I had two jobs at Coopers. On the one hand, I was Coopers' new senior environmental adviser, reporting to David Miller, a former managing director of the firm's management consulting practice. On the other hand, I was recruited by Francis Plowden, the partner responsible for government relations, as a European affairs adviser.

There was not enough room for all that on one business card, so Coopers made me two separate business cards to add to my growing collection.

Francis Plowden could not have been more charming. He came from a family of distinguished public servants. Both his parents had held major civil service appointments and both had been awarded life peerages.

I don't think I did anything particularly useful for Francis Plowden during my time at Coopers, except to provide some 'insider' insights into life in Brussels and how best to penetrate the European Commission's seemingly impermeable thickets.

On the other hand, I do think I pulled my weight as far as the environmental side of the business was concerned.

In management consultancy, as I quickly learned, there are some important tricks of the trade. The key thing is to use bullet points when bidding for a job. Whole paragraphs are totally useless. In fact, they are counterproductive. As a matter of fact, even whole sentences are frowned upon. It is better to have several, but not too many, bullet points. Short. Sharp. Positive!

David Miller, a large, immensely cheerful Merton man, was already a very experienced management consultant. He understood the system perfectly. He not only wrote in bullet points, he thought in bullet points.

Coopers soon won a major contract, viz. to evaluate the performance of the United Nations Environment Programme (UNEP), the UN agency that had been set up after that first world environment conference in Stockholm in 1972. The first phase of the project was due to take eighteen months and would cost upwards of US$1 million.

The Coopers team for this assignment consisted of David Miller himself, as team leader and responsible 'partner'. There was the environmental adviser, viz. me. There was Geoff Lane, a senior associate, and some younger consultants too, both male and female. By day we paced the corridors of the UNEP building at Gigiri, on the outskirts of Nairobi, interviewing people and making notes. By night we gathered at the Norfolk Hotel and 'brainstormed' over some expensive claret. David Miller knew his way round a wine list and the Norfolk had a good one.

Winning a job is one thing. But you still have to write the report. The key thing here is to find out what your client's real agenda is.

Luckily, I had a 'mole' inside the organisation.

All countries that are members of UNEP have their permanent representatives to the organisation. These 'perm reps', as they are called, sometimes double up as ambassadors to Kenya. Looking through the diplomatic list, I noted that my old friend Willem Hoogendoorn (the man who had been so helpful to me in Brussels over the animal experimentation directive) was now the Netherlands' permanent representative to UNEP in Nairobi.

I had a quiet dinner with him one night soon after we arrived in Nairobi. Hoogendoorn explained, 'Basically, the perm reps decided to authorise this management consultancy project – a lot of money by the way, I can tell you, and UNEP is not a rich organisation – as a means of dealing with the "succession" issue.'

I had the feeling that we were hitting pay-dirt and I was right.

Hoogendoorn continued. 'Dr Mostafa Tolba succeeded Maurice Strong as the executive director of UNEP in 1976. And where are we now? The beginning of the '90s. And who is still in charge? Dr Mostafa Tolba. Of course, Tolba has done a great job, a tremendous job, but there comes a time...'

Hoogendoorn's voice trailed off.

'You mean the perm reps want someone else to do the dirty work?' I asked. 'Isn't that a pretty roundabout way of going about it?'

'It's the only way,' Hoogendoorn said. 'No single country, no group of countries, is going to get out in front on this one, and say it's time for him to go. Basically they're scared of Tolba. He's a powerful man.'

I knew that, of course. Over the years, I had seen quite a bit of Dr Tolba. I had seen how brilliantly he had managed the ozone issue, bullying the producer nations to cut back on CFCs, not just by getting the ozone treaty in place but, just as important, ensuring that the funds were there to back it up.

I had seen how he had, ruthlessly and single-mindedly taken over the draft biodiversity treaty from IUCN, and made it his, and UNEP's, own. The fact that the CBD had the weaknesses I have described earlier couldn't be laid at Tolba's door. No man could have tried harder than he did to get some teeth into that treaty.

But clearly Tolba had made enemies along the way. Too many enemies. They just didn't want their fingerprints on the dagger.

Once we knew what the 'real agenda' was, the rest of our assignment was easy.

Of course, we made the usual management consultant-type proposals about organisational structure. Do you have the projects (marine pollution, chemicals, biodiversity etc.) on the X axis of the organisational matrix, and the areas (Asia, Africa, Latin America etc.) on the Y axis, or do you do it the other way round?

At one stage, as we sat over dinner in the hotel, I think we even brainstormed about a 'three-dimensional matrix', though I don't think any of us really knew what we were talking about. We put in lots of comments about 'core values' and 'key staff'. We suggested a different 'governing structure' for UNEP with more countries being on the Governing Council. We thought up new ways for UNEP to raise money.

But, frankly, a lot of this was padding. The money shot was always going to be how we dealt with what Hoogendoorn had described as 'the succession issue'.

Normally, I would be back in Oxford before 7 p.m. I liked to get home in time to say goodnight to Julia and Max.

But that particular evening, when we were trying to finalise the Coopers Report on the Future of UNEP (Phase I) after our return from a field trip to Nairobi, it was after midnight before I picked up my bike at Oxford station and pedalled back to Polstead Road.

Before I put pen to paper that evening in Coopers' Charing Cross HQ, I agonised about how to produce a text that (a) did what the client wanted (the number one priority), (b) was nevertheless intellectually coherent and substantively accurate, and (c) was fair to Dr Tolba who, by my yardstick, was a great man and who had done a great job.

Next day the report was Fed-Exed to Nairobi. A few days later, David Miller and I flew out to Kenya to a specially convened session of the UNEP perm reps.

We were invited onto the dais in the huge plenary meeting room in the Gigiri building. I wouldn't say the place was full, but there was far more than a quorum of delegates.

Miller summarised the summary, projecting loads of bullet points onto the screen. I added some words about 'governance' and 'funding' and sat back to await the turn of events.

A lively discussion ensued about some of the minor points, the 'paper-clip' or 'nuts and bolts' issues , but no one talked about the 'succession' or referred to my 'Tolba' paragraphs. Silence said more than words. Silence, as far as I could see, meant assent.

In May 2013, when I was working on my book about UNEP's first forty years, mentioned in Chapter Thirty-Six, I had a long meeting with Dr Tolba in Nairobi. Our interview was televised and the recording is to be found in UNEP's archives, along with the tapes of the other interviews I conducted with former UNEP executive directors.

I have looked again at the transcript of our interview. Dr Tolba didn't comment, one way or another, on the Coopers report. I don't find that surprising. Tolba, by the time of that interview, was well over eighty. With the video camera running, we sat under a shady tree on the lawn at his hotel. Tolba's new young wife and their two young children were only a few feet away. Though Tolba's recall of dates and events decades earlier was still razor-sharp, for him life had clearly moved on.

The Coopers report was not at the forefront of his mind.

Well, it *was* at the forefront of my mind as I sat there that day, talking to one of the 'environmental heroes' of our time. We had wielded the stiletto, not the axe, but the effect had been the same.

Soon after the Rio Earth Summit was over, Dr Mostafa Tolba retired after seventeen years at the helm of UNEP. If any man deserved a graceful exit, he did.

Chapter Twenty-Two

The Rocking Horse House

Halfway through 1994, we moved from Oxford to London. The house we bought in Regent's Park Road, Primrose Hill, NW1, was known in the neighbourhood as the Rocking Horse House. This was because, as far back as anyone could remember, there had been a rocking horse in the window. Any new owner either brought his/her own rocking horse or persuaded the previous owner to part with theirs.

The vendors were two charming doctors, both called Dr C. Williams. Though this must have led to confusion as far as sorting out the morning post was concerned, there was a good reason for it. Dr Christopher Williams was an oncologist, dealing with cancer of the internal organs. Dr Christina Williams looked after wounds to the head, and the damage to the brain caused thereby.

The Williamses, though most helpful in all other respects, were not keen to sell us their own rocking horse.

'Our children have grown up with it,' they explained. 'We really don't want to part with it.'

I could understand their point of view. Theirs was a splendid beast. No. 60 Regent's Park Road was so strategically placed that you could hardly fail to notice the house (painted bright pink) and the magnificent horse in the huge bay window directly overlooking Primrose Hill.

For the first few weeks, after the move to London, we did without a horse in the window but every few days someone would ring the bell.

'Excuse me, can you tell us what has happened to the rocking horse?'

We even received letters addressed to: 'The Rocking Horse, Primrose Hill'.

I opened one of the letters. 'Dear Rocking Horse, what has happened? Where are you? We miss you! Love and kisses, Brenda!'

Jenny was adamant. 'If people want a rocking horse in the window, they can jolly well pay for it.'

I recognised this, of course, as an intellectually valid approach. Tropical forest countries frequently argue that 'if the world wants to preserve the rainforest, the world must pay for it'.

The trouble is the tropical forest countries haven't had much luck so far with this line of argument. This is a point I shall revert to in Chapter Thirty-Five in the context of Ecuador's 'Yasuni' initiative.

Of course, we gave in to neighbourhood pressure in the end. Who were we, mere newcomers, to break a tradition stretching back into the mists of time?

Jenny, having conceded the point, wasn't going to be satisfied with some two-a-penny rocking horse. The firm to go for, she was advised, was Stevenson Bros near Ashford in Kent.

I telephoned them to make the necessary arrangements.

'Please bring a copy of *The Times*,' I was advised, 'when you come for your appointment.'

We drove down to Kent *en famille*, the party consisting of myself, Jenny, Julia, Max, Pixie and Harry. Harry barked in the back of the car all the way to our destination. I had to yell at him in the end.

Stevenson Bros, proud purveyors of rocking horses to the royal household, don't go in for mass production. On the contrary, you choose your own design from a number of options.

The decision made, you shake hands, and sign on the dotted line. Going, going, gone at £3,257.68, including VAT!

At this happy point, an antique gentleman, who may well be one of the original Stevenson brothers, produces an almost equally antique Polaroid camera.

'I'll take the group photo now,' he says. 'Hold up the newspaper in front of you. Smile please! Yes, let's have the dogs too!'

Each Stevenson Bros rocking horse receives its own individual number, which is recorded by the firm and will in due course be inscribed on a bronze plate to be attached to the finished product.

Long before that, the photo showing the 'commissioning family' and the newspaper bearing witness to the 'commissioning date' will be placed inside the basic square wooden box, about which the rocking horse will be constructed. That box is then permanently sealed, like the tomb of Tutankhamun, to be opened only in some dim and distant future.

'Do you want a name, as well as a number on the plaque?' Mr Stevenson asked. 'Many people do.'

We had already fixed on a name. 'Tarquin,' I said.

'What about an inscription?' the rocking-horse man asked.

We had thought about that too.

I replied, 'Please can you write: *Quadrupedante putrem sonitu quatit ungula campum*. Five dactyls and a spondee.'

It would have been great if the old boy had snapped back with 'Virgil's *Aeneid*, if I am not mistaken.'

Alas, he didn't but he noted it down quite correctly and when we finally took delivery of Tarquin, neatly caparisoned with a bright red leather saddle and matching bridle, we admired the gleaming bronze plaque on the solid oak stand saying TARQUIN, with the Virgilian hexameter in italics underneath.

When I was about ten years old, at prep school in Devon, R. L. Schuster, the headmaster, who was also my Latin teacher, used to cite this particular line as being a particularly felicitous example of onomatopoeia.

'Can't you hear the horse galloping?' he would ask us? And then he would translate in case we hadn't done our homework.

'*A hoof shakes the crumbling field with a galloping sound.*'

Of course we could hear the horse galloping. I can hear that horse now.

R. L. Schuster taught us, even at that tender prep school age, many of the rhetorical tricks that today seem to have fallen into desuetude.

We learned, for example, about ellipsis, zeugmas and anacoluthons.

'Anna who?' I once asked, putting my hand up in the approved fashion.

'Come and see me after prayers, Johnson,' was Schuster's reply.

There were two huge tomes on R. L. Schuster's desk. One was titled *The Glory That Was Greece*. The other was called *The Grandeur That Was Rome*. The headmaster's cane was suspended between them.

Schuster didn't hesitate to use it. Those were the days!

When, in 2007, we sold the Rocking Horse House on Primrose Hill to move through ignorance or inadvertence (the jury is still out) to another house smack in the path of the HS2, we took Tarquin down to Nethercote. We felt he would be happier in the country.

For the time being, Tarquin rocks on the landing, next to the billiard table where the rats used to play after lights out.

Jenny, in her own 'last year' at Manchester College, made regular trips from London to Oxford for lectures and tutorials. When she graduated, her mother, Lois, as well as Julia, Max and I, attended the ceremony in the Sheldonian. Jenny had turned out in full regalia, mortar board included, and looked very fetching.

Later, we bought a video tape of the event. It cost £8 and came in a natty box labelled 'Degree Ceremony 1995' with a cover picture of delighted young men and women wearing gowns, some of them tossing their mortar boards in the air.

We went down to Somerset for the weekend soon after. My sister Birdie came over for coffee and a 'replay' of the great day. I put the tape on the floor while I was figuring out how to turn on the video.

Max, then eight and duly primed by me, came and stood on the box.

'Please don't stand on ceremony, Max!' I admonished him.

I don't want to give away the tricks of the trade, but some jokes have to be 'set up' in advance if they are to work at all. This was one of them.

The best jokes, of course, can't be set up.

I was at the Victoria Falls in Zimbabwe once when a bunch of lions walked out of the trees through the spray ('the smoke that thunders'). 'Pride comes before a fall' was the obvious one-liner.

I am convinced that the real reason I was selected as a Euro candidate back in 1979 for the plum Wight & Hants East seat was because of the joke I told at the final selection meeting.

We were down to the last three. The other two candidates, Bill Cash (yes, *the* Bill Cash) and Sir John Peel (no, not *the* John Peel) had both arrived with their very presentable wives. I was 'between marriages' and had to walk into the hall unaccompanied.

'And will Mrs Johnson', the chairman asked, 'be coming to live in the constituency if you are elected?'

'Mrs Johnson may very well be coming to live in the constituency,' I replied, 'but, I fear, not with me!'

A moment's pause, a sharp intake of breath, and then a full-throated burst of laughter.

Phew! I said to myself. Not for the first time, and certainly, not for the last.

I don't know whether it was Jenny's example in gaining her degree as a 'mature student' at Oxford which spurred her on, but my sister Birdie a few years later was accepted by Sussex University to do an MA in Oral History. Though this was an unusual step in the sense that Birdie took a postgraduate degree without ever taking an undergraduate degree, it made sense. While living on Exmoor, Birdie wrote and published a brilliant book about old Exmoor characters, lavishly illustrated and accompanied by a CD of the many 'oral interviews' that she arranged and taped. I now add MA after her name when I write.

By the time we moved to London, I was a director of ERM. The full name was Environmental Resources Management and the CEO was Robin Bidwell. I had known Robin for years. Soon after I first joined the European Commission, back in the '70s, we commissioned ERM (then ERL) to make a comprehensive study of the Law and Practice of Environmental Legislation in the (then) nine members of the European Community.

ERM had gone from strength to strength. I joined John Horberry's international team, concentrating on international agencies that might be looking for some consulting advice.

One evening John Horberry and I had dinner in Washington with Martin Riddle, then working for the International Finance Corporation, an affiliate of the World Bank. Leo, who happened to be in Washington at the time, was able to join us. Not long after that, he moved to Washington to take up a job with IFC.

I was probably more use to Leo, at least in linking him up with Martin Riddle and IFC, than I ever was to ERM. He also met his future wife, Taies, in Washington (she was working at the

World Bank), then started his own firm before, as noted above, joining PwC.

I have to admit that consultancy, even environmental consultancy, was not really my bag.

Robin Bidwell decided that the whole company should become certified under ISO 14000. ISO stood for the International Standards Organization and ISO 14000 referred to an accreditation procedure designed to ensure that certain office practices and procedures were properly carried out.

You had for example to log faxes, and, because faxes faded, having logged them, you had to photocopy them onto non-fade paper and file them, even if they were total rubbish.

I asked Robin whether ISO 14000 rules would also apply to company directors.

Robin is a very wise man. His hair even then had a distinguished silvery tone to it. He tended to think before he spoke. And he usually voiced his opinions in a slow and deliberate way.

He was slow and deliberate then. 'I'm afraid the whole company has to be examined before accreditation is granted. That includes the directors, of course.'

To help us understand what was required, we were all issued with a book called *The Crosby Quality Control Manual*. It came nicely shrink-wrapped.

Robin sent a message to all ERM staff inviting them to study the manual carefully. 'Read, learn and inwardly digest' was the gist of it.

On the appointed day the examiners came round. I had sharpened my pencils and tidied up. As far as I knew all recent faxes had been photocopied and filed.

One grey-haired lady – she reminded me of matron at school – came over to my desk. Her eye fell on the still shrink-wrapped manual. I had, as usual, placed my mug of coffee on the most convenient surface.

'I see you are finding the Crosby manual useful?' she commented.

ERM passed muster anyway, though I'm not sure I did.

I realised, as time went on, that I lacked the objectivity to be a good management consultant. Yes, you can use a report someone else has commissioned to promote some message you yourself are keen on, and I didn't hesitate to do so if the opportunity presented itself, but that was not the primary purpose of the exercise.

I also lacked the commitment. However much you dress it up, the business of business is business.

I have sold some books, i.e. books that I have myself authored or co-authored (more than twenty at last count). I have, on one occasion as already mentioned, sold the film rights to a novel. As a management consultant, I helped land one important contract (UNEP) and maybe contributed to other successful bids. My time was 'billed' to clients when I worked on various assignments. But, frankly, my billing record left a lot to be desired. If the norm was that a consultant should bring in his salary multiplied by x where x is more than 10, I fell woefully short.

I have kept the farm going over the last several decades in the sense that Nethercote still 'washes its face' financially. Of course, I do not actively farm it, in the way my father did. I do not dock, dip or sheer the sheep; I do not help cows calve or round them up on my pony with a lot of hollering as I used to do when I was home from school or university. I have graziers who look after *their* stock on *our* land.

Whichever way you look at it, I am not an outstandingly successful businessman. The CBI is not going to give me a medal.

In such circumstances, when the International Fund for Animal Welfare invited me to be their 'director of European affairs', with a flat in Brussels and a season ticket on the Eurostar, I didn't hesitate to accept.

And, anyway, I liked the idea of being back in 'campaigning mode'.

I had known IFAW for years. They had been one of the crucial NGOs, if not *the* crucial NGO, behind the 'save the seals' campaign. Though the name might imply that the organisation was mostly concerned with animal welfare rather than conservation issues, the reality was that IFAW covered both.

IFAW was a hard-hitting campaigning body. It knew where to find the pressure points. It had a record of delivering the goods. It wasn't just seals that IFAW sought to protect. IFAW's anti-whaling campaign helped keep up the pressure on Japan, year after year, to give up its so-called 'scientific whaling'. That campaign, by the way, seems finally to have paid off. Japan, formally at least (as noted earlier), seems to have accepted the ruling of the International Court of Justice against their version of 'scientific whaling'. It remains to be seen whether Japanese whaling vessels will once again head south to the Antarctic under some new (but equally spurious) formulation of 'scientific whaling'.

An example of IFAW activism on the animal welfare front was their campaign against the way dogs in South Korea were being 'tenderised' for human consumption by being beaten to death.

The EU, as IFAW rightly saw it, was a crucial player in so many areas. In setting up a European Affairs Office, their plan was to put more pressure on the EU institutions, particularly the Commission and the Parliament, to 'up their game' as far as both conservation and animal welfare issues were concerned.

For example, was the EU's elephant-ivory ban going to hold up against pressures from those countries in southern Africa, e.g. South Africa, Zimbabwe and Namibia, who were pushing for a 'downlisting' in CITES? IFAW would do its utmost to make sure the EU ivory ban stayed in place.

Was the EU going to push for a ban on imported timber, where that timber has been produced under clearly unsustainable conditions, even if the World Trade Organization ruled against such a ban? IFAW would encourage the EU to defy any WTO challenges.

One of the things that persuaded me to accept IFAW's offer was that Hemmo Muntingh had already joined IFAW as a special adviser.

When Hemmo and I met up again in IFAW's new European office in the Rue Taciturne, not far from EU headquarters, it truly was an emotional reunion.

Lesley O'Donnell, IFAW's office manager, who basically would hold the show together for the next six years, joined us as Hemmo and I went round the corner to Kitty O'Shea's to celebrate.

'You can say one thing,' Hemmo commented, as the barman drew us tankers of Mort Subite, possibly the strongest brew known to man, 'the Belgians certainly know how to make beer.'

Chapter Twenty-Three

Turtles in Seattle

IFAW was by no means alone as a campaigning organisation. Though it was sometimes, as in the seal campaign, very much in the lead, there were other issues where it was happy to join in a coordinated NGO effort.

At the CITES meeting, which was held in Harare, the capital of Zimbabwe, in June 1997, the NGOs grouped together to fight off a possible 'delisting' of elephants. South Africa, Zimbabwe, Namibia and Botswana had all asked to be allowed to sell their stockpiled ivory on the market. President Mugabe himself, at the official opening ceremony, had banged the table and insisted 'that the voice of southern Africa be heard'.

The NGOs present in Harare feared that if the southern African proposals were adopted, a huge breach would be blown in the ivory ban as agreed in Lausanne in 1989. Illegal ivory would 'piggy-back' on legal ivory. Customs and enforcement officers would not be able to tell the difference. In Harare, Will Travers, head of the Born Free Foundation, brilliantly coordinated NGOs protests, but when the final vote was taken, the ivory traders won.

I shall never forget the sound of the Zimbabwe National Anthem being chanted that day in the conference hall by President Mugabe's henchmen as the tally was announced.

This was not CITES's finest hour by any means. Almost twenty years later, as noted earlier, the illegal killing of elephants has reached crisis proportions.

At the CITES meeting held in Santiago, Chile, in November 2002, IFAW and other NGOs tried hard to ensure that whales remained on Appendix 1, meaning international trade in whale meat and whale products is banned. There was a real fear that if CITES relaxed its ban, the International Whaling Commission's moratorium on whaling, first mooted at the UN's Environment Conference in Stockholm in June 1972 but only finally approved by the IWC in 1982, would collapse. With whales at least, the dam held. But it was tough sledding. It always is.

After the Santiago meeting I flew down to Punta Arenas in Tierra del Fuego. Apart from Argentina's Ushuaia, Punta Arenas is the world's most southerly town. This is the port Adrian Berry and I had set off from in the *John Biscoe* during our trip to Antarctica in 1984. Nothing much had changed in the intervening decade and a half. I hired a car and drove north to spend the weekend in the Torres del Paine, Patagonia's amazing National Park, where the mountains seem to jut straight up from the icy plain and where the condors swoop and soar in the wind.

On the way back, still about 180 miles north of Punta Arenas, I stopped at the famous Cueva del Milodón, a cave that contains a full-scale replica of the 'milodon', a giant prehistoric bear with the head of a camel, which once roamed these parts.

Most recent 'wildlife extinctions' have been caused by the impact, direct or indirect, of human populations. The demise of the milodon almost certainly falls in that category. How many more extinctions would we be responsible for, I wondered? Were we even keeping count?

I found it tremendously refreshing to be batting on the NGO team. There was absolutely no need to take a 'balanced view'. Deep down I have always distrusted people who talk of the need for a balanced approach, of 'striking a compromise between environment and development'. If you do that, it seems to me, you are already shifting your stance towards the middle ground. There are quite enough people trying to occupy the middle ground as it is.

As a politician, as a civil servant, it is sometimes advisable to appear to be 'objective'. A campaigning NGO is under no such restrictions. You may and must press your point as hard as you can.

In December 1999, for example, Patrick Ramage, IFAW's communications director, and I dressed up in turtle suits to join the protesters in the streets of Seattle when, famously, the NGO movement actually succeeded in derailing the World Trade Organization's proposals for a 'new trade round' for almost twenty years.

My old friend Brian Johnson's daughter, Jacoba, who was living in Seattle at the time and working for a local environmental organisation, challenged me as soon as I arrived.

'Why don't you get out on the streets?' she exclaimed. 'If this new trade round goes through, the existing trade bans may be struck down and no new ones will be allowed. You won't have the ivory ban. You won't be able to protect the dolphins from the tuna-fishers. You won't be able to discriminate legally against timber that is imported from unsustainably managed forests and other timber. What WTO's proposing will be a total disaster for the environment. And it may be too late to stop it.'

'Are *you* going to be out there in the streets tomorrow, Jacoba?' I asked.

'Of course I am! Thousands of others will be out there too!'

Jacoba had two spare turtle suits and Ramage and I put them on.

Next day, we joined the crowd parading in the streets and chanting, 'WTO! No! No! NO!'

They turned the water cannon on the protesters, but it didn't make any difference. The Seattle 'riots' gained worldwide attention and the resolve of the official delegates began to crack.

By the end of the week, the much-heralded launch of the 'new round' had been put on hold and the WTO conference itself came to a premature end.

As noted earlier, there are, of course, no permanent victories in this game. You can hope only to stave off defeat. In Bali this year, the 'new' WTO rules were finally concluded and they will be, by all accounts, just as bad for the environment as the rules that we managed to put on ice, at least for the time, in Seattle.

Some existing measures, like the EU seal-import ban or restrictions agreed under CITES, may survive challenge but what about new proposals? What if new trade measures to protect wildlife are brought in unilaterally (by a country or even a group of countries, such as the EU) and then challenged under the WTO? Will these survive? I doubt it. Years ago, the Danes tried to ban beer in plastic bottles and the Danes had to fight like hell to resist the legal challenges that were thrown at them. Austria tried to ban the import of illegal timber but had to back off because of WTO rules. And I can't help remembering the devastating treatment meted out to the EU's directive on the import of furs from animals caught in leg-hold traps, a directive that (as noted in an earlier chapter) had actually been approved by the EU Council and Parliament.

As I see it, there is – now more than ever – a case for NGO groups, and for 'civil society' as a whole to take to the streets, to the press and media, to Twitter and Facebook or whatever. If we don't make a stand, who will?

That's why organisations like IFAW, and Greenpeace, and WWF and FOE (Friends of the Earth), deserve support.

Does IFAW, and campaigning organisations like it, sometimes go too far? That depends on your point of view.

I learned the hard way that groups such as IFAW make enemies as well as friends.

The IUCN conference held in Montreal in October 1996 was one of the most painful professional experiences of my life.

IFAW's application to become a member of IUCN had already been turned down by the IUCN Council, on the grounds that IFAW's primary objective was not conservation but animal welfare. But under IUCN rules an organisation applying for membership, if rejected by the Council, had a right to appeal to the supreme body – the triennial IUCN Conference – against the Council's decision.

It fell to me to make the case in Montreal.

I knew it was going to be a hard fight, when Canada's Prime Minister Jean Chrétien in his opening remarks on the first day of the IUCN meeting, held in Montreal's giant modern conference centre, appealed to the gathering to reject IFAW's bid.

It got worse. The centre had huge gleaming metal escalators that carried delegates from street level up to the main floor. Those elevators were decorated with banners and posters: KEEP IFAW OUT OF IUCN.

My old friend Ian MacPhail was with me that day. On official occasions Ian usually sported the MacPhail tartan kilt. He did so then. He was bare-kneed and magnificently irate, ripping down the offending posters whenever he had a chance.

'Why on earth did IFAW choose to make a fight of it here in Canada?' he spluttered. 'They hate our guts here.'

'Maybe we'll win the floor fight,' I tried to sound hopeful but in my heart I already felt it was a lost cause.

It wasn't just the posters we had to contend with. IFAW's opponents circulated some of IFAW's campaigning literature. There
was one A4-size sheet, for example, that showed a prune-like object
which purported to be a photo of 'Bobbitt's penis'. John Bobbitt's
wife, famously, had cut off her husband's penis in a fit of rage and
he had been rushed to hospital to have it sewn back on. Mrs Bobbitt
had become something of a hero in the women's lib movement

'This is what they do to seals,' the IFAW handbill stated. 'They
cut off their penises and sell them to China.'

Factually, of course, the IFAW poster was completely correct.
With the EU seal ban, Canada had looked for other markets for
its 'seal products' and China was importing seal penises in growing
numbers.

But this was hard-hitting, 'in your face' stuff. IUCN prided itself
on being a 'scientific' body.

Another IFAW handbill showed a picture of (now former) EU
Commissioner's Carlo Ripa di Meana's glamorous wife, Marina,
completely naked, except for a vigorous sprouting of pubic hair. The
poster proclaimed the message: 'The only fur I'm proud to wear.'

Marina's 'fur' doubled as a scratch-card. Like a new PIN number
the bank sends you when you have forgotten your old one, if you
scraped the 'fur' away, you were able to read the message: 'Donate
NOW to IFAW's anti-fur campaign.'

As I said, IFAW was a hard-hitting campaigning organisation.

The great shoot-out, the gunfight at OK Corral, was scheduled
for the last Thursday of the conference. IFAW had some friends in
the hall. Maneka Gandhi, for example, India's former Environment
Minister, and the widow of the Indian politician Sanjay Gandhi,
who had founded her own animal welfare organisation in India,
was superb.

She came with me to bilateral meetings with hostile delegates where I tried to explain that IFAW's record on the conservation side was good, and that Bobbitt's penis and Marina's bush were not the whole story.

'Stick to your guns, Stanley,' Maneka urged.

Alas, Maneka Gandhi's help, energetic and persuasive though she was, was not enough to turn the tide.

I could sense which way things were going, so I sought instructions from IFAW headquarters in Cape Cod. There too the message seemed to be 'stick to your guns'. Reluctant to be blamed for the impending fiasco, I sent the full text of my speech to the Cape for prior approval.

The leafleteers were out in force again that morning as Ian MacPhail and I rode the elevators up into the conference centre, like old gun-fighters riding into town. Up on the dais, the chairman banged his gavel and read out the rules.

'Each side will have ten minutes to make the case, one side in favour of IFAW's membership of IUCN, the other side against,' the chairman intoned. 'There will be no discussion. Once the two speeches have been delivered, the meeting will proceed to a vote.'

I knew I had lost before I even started to speak. The leafleteers had come in from outside to take their seats in the body of the hall. As I stood up, a large number of delegates raised yellow placards in the air: KEEP IFAW OUT!

If you read the official report of the IUCN Montreal plenary, you might conclude that I had made a perfectly convincing speech, stressing IFAW's record as a conservation organisation.

'IFAW has campaigned, Mr Chairman, distinguished delegates, ladies and gentlemen, for whales, for dolphins, for elephants. We have fought like tigers for tigers, and, yes, we have fought for seals.'

Perhaps I shouldn't have mentioned seals, even though opinion polls showed that a substantial majority of Canadians were against the seal hunt.

Finn Lynge, a Member of the European Parliament and a leading Inuit politician from Greenland, seized on IFAW's seal campaign and the damage (he alleged) it had done to the Inuit communities of Greenland who had seen the market for seal products collapse after the EU seal ban.

There was a large Inuit contingent in the hall that morning, specially bussed in from Ultima Thule, and they burst into 'spontaneous' applause.

'Poor Inuits, my foot,' Ian MacPhail, sitting next to me, hissed. 'Look at Lynge's great gold wrist-watch. And I bet he drives around in a skidoo!'

MacPhail had been in a cantankerous mood all week.

Finn Lynge kept his deadliest shot to the end. He gazed round the room. IUCN prided itself on being, above all, a professional body. There were many distinguished scientists present that morning, men and women who knew their way around the highways and byways of Linnaean taxonomy without the need of a satnav to help them. Some of them, the exalted few, had even actually had species or sub-species or sub-sub-species named after them.

Though it was quite warm in the hall, Finn Lynge strode up to the podium that morning wearing a sealskin coat. His very presence reminded his audience of journeys they themselves might have made, many moons ago now, to far-flung parts – the Arctic, the Amazon, the High Pamirs – searching out nature's secrets.

Lynge's message was clear enough but he spelled it out anyway

'How can an organisation that circulates pictures of Bobbitt's penis and a lady's private parts be admitted to this venerable and renowned scientific organisation?' Lynge thundered.

There were giant screens behind the podium. If you were up on the stand speaking and you turned your head to look behind you, you could see yourself, massively multiplied, doing precisely that.

I hoped against hope that Finn Lynge wasn't going to project those damned IFAW posters onto the screen. The idea of Bobbitt's penis or Marina's bush invading the chamber at that moment as a gigantic *deus ex machina* was too much to contemplate.

I don't know whether Finn Lynge just didn't think of it, or whether a sense of compassion held him back. Whichever it was, I felt grateful.

When the vote was called at the end of the shoot-out, forty-three IUCN members actually voted in favour of letting IFAW join. Admittedly, 189 voted against. But the result was a great improvement on that earlier vote in the IUCN Council (as opposed to the Assembly, where the tally had been 33–1 against!)

I sent a message to Cape Cod, outlining the arithmetic. 'Some progress made with IFAW's application in terms of votes received. Montreal not the most favourable venue under the circumstances. We may need to review our strategy here. If IFAW is not for IUCN, maybe IUCN is not for IFAW.'

To be honest, I felt bruised and battered by the week's events.

The good news was that Leo and his soon-to-be-bride Taies flew up to Montreal from Washington. My spirits soared. Leo and Taies were clearly meant to happen. One night we went to a Chinese restaurant that doubled as a karaoke bar. Leo sang 'Hey Jude' with more than a touch of professionalism. Then it was my turn. I had never tried my hand at karaoke before. I didn't realise that when you slowed down, the backing tape slowed down too.

It took me thirteen and a half minutes to get through 'American Pie'. Leo timed it.

Not long after the Montreal fiasco, Maneka Gandhi took me to visit the Indian Prime Minister, Mr Atal Bihari Vajpayee. It was a

Saturday morning and we called on him at his house on Racecourse Road, Delhi. We planned to convince the Prime Minister to support the development of an International Convention on Animal Welfare. The Indian government, we urged him, could convoke a diplomatic conference to agree on a draft. We would cover wild animals, farm animals, the transport of animals, animals in zoos and circuses, even pet or companion animals.

Maneka Gandhi had a tremendous record in the field of animal welfare. As a government minister, she had banned the dancing bears that toured the towns and countryside. She had built sanctuaries for the poor abused animals as they started a new life. She had set up her own animal welfare NGO.

'India should take the lead, Prime Minister,' she urged.

The Prime Minister seemed keen. Or maybe it was difficult for him to say 'no' to such a powerful and persuasive lady, the widow of Sanjay Gandhi.

Anyway, he shook his head from side to side, which in India can be quite a positive sign.

'Of course, we must do it,' he said.

We had our photo taken with him in his sitting room and he walked us to the door.

That initiative too, I fear, came to grief. The Indian Trade Minister sent Maneka a firm note, which she forwarded to me. Because of 'trade and commercial considerations', the Indian government would not be in a position to host a plenipotentiary meeting to adopt an international animal welfare convention.

Not long after, Maneka Gandhi came to London, so I invited her to our house on Primrose Hill for tea in the course of which I asked her about this apparent volte-face on the part of the Indian government.

'I think the minister believed that India's leather exports might run into trouble,' she said, 'if India supported a convention.

There are states in southern India, like Kerala, where the cow is not a sacred animal, and where they have a big leather industry. The conditions the animals are slaughtered under are sometimes horrendous. The minister may have feared other competing countries with their own leather industries would seize on the animal welfare issue as an excuse to block Indian leather exports.'

As far as I can see, the International Convention on Animal Welfare is an idea whose time has both come and, unfortunately, gone.

Chapter Twenty-Four

9/11

In 2001, at the end of the summer, my fourth son, Max (then aged sixteen) and I flew to Brazil to visit an Earthwatch turtle project on the Ilha do Bananal in the State of Tocantins. I had travelled through Tocantins on my way to Brasilia in the course of my gap year in 1959. There was just a dirt road through the jungle then. I could hardly believe how much had changed. The conversion of forest to farmland was obviously proceeding at breakneck speed.

But the Ilha do Bananal, a vast area that, as its name implies, was actually an island surrounded by the Amazon and its tributaries, was still primal jungle.

Max and I camped with the Earthwatch volunteers at the side of the river. We rose early to count the turtle eggs buried deep in the sand. The point of the project was to establish a correlation between the depth at which the eggs were buried and the sex of the hatchlings. Does a turtle have more chance of emerging as a female hatchling the deeper the egg is laid, or is it the other way round? Temperature seems to be the key here, the incubation temperature varying according to the depth at which the eggs are laid.

Basically, you had to walk along the sandbanks in the early morning looking for the tell-tracks which indicated that a turtle had emerged from the water to lay her eggs. You then had to follow the tracks, which wasn't always straightforward since the turtles seldom went straight from A to B. When you found the nest, you marked it with a bamboo pole. The researchers, the serious scientists, would then come along and do their stuff, with measuring rods and thermometers and so on.

This was all very wondrous. But as the sun rose higher in the sky the heat on the river's sandbanks became almost unbearable.

Being an Earthwatch trustee, I knew the official guidelines. You have to make a 'risk assessment'. I had a word with the lead scientist, known in Earthwatch terms as the Principal Investigator.

'Piranhas are not all they're cracked up to be,' I advised. 'I'm sure it's okay for the team to splash around in the river to cool off, as long as they don't go in too deep.'

Some risk assessments are straightforward.

Max and I went on from the Ilha do Bananal to the Pantanal, one of the world's last great wetlands, to stay for a few days at the Fazenda Rio Negro, where there was another Earthwatch project. As the Cessna lands on the airstrip by the ranch, you can see a cluster – fifty or sixty birds – of hyacinth macaws, some flying around, some in the branches of the trees.

Hyacinth macaws! Some of the most beautiful birds on earth. And some of the rarest.

By day, we paddled down the river in a canoe. Caimans by the thousand, giant river otters, capybaras and peccaries – I couldn't believe I had passed through this wonderland in the course of my gap-year travels back in 1959 without even realising it was there.

Of course, there are caipirinhas as well as capybaras and Max and I had a few, sitting on the verandah of the fazenda at dusk, listening to the macaws macawing.

Max had to return to the UK in time for the school year, but I flew on. First to Colombia, where IFAW amazingly was still funding some projects in spite of the political turmoil, then on to Boston.

Brian Davies, IFAW's founder and first CEO, had moved the organisation to Cape Cod when the Canadian government, angry about IFAW's campaign to end the seal hunt, let it be known that its presence in Canada was no longer welcome.

I don't know whether leaving Canada diminished IFAW's effectiveness in terms of protecting seals but, as a place to 'relocate', it was certainly a good choice.

In the early fall, Cape Cod is particularly agreeable. The water is still warm enough to swim in, the leaves on the trees have begun to turn, and the summer crowds have departed.

When Fred O'Regan, Brian Davies's successor as IFAW's CEO, decided it would be a good idea to hold a staff retreat to discuss 'Who are we? Where are we going?', early September was the obvious pick.

I was not the only one to have made a long journey to Cape Cod that year. As a growing international organisation, IFAW now had antennae in many parts of the world. Grace Gabriel had come in from IFAW's Beijing Office, Vivek Menon from Delhi, Sally Wilson from Sydney, Hemmo Muntingh and Lesley O'Donnell from Brussels, Cindy Milburn from the UK office. Professor David Lavigne, a distinguished marine mammal expert from the University of Guelph, came down from Canada.

The home team included, of course, Fred O'Regan, Azzedine Downes, his deputy, my 'turtle friend' Patrick Ramage and Chris Tuite, who had recently joined IFAW from The Nature Conservancy, another US-based NGO.

Round about 9 a.m. on the morning of 11 September, we all gathered in good spirits in the conference room at IFAW's HQ, cups of coffee in front of us and notepads to hand. Fred O' Regan had just embarked on a longish 'overview' of IFAW's present and future prospects when Vivek Menon came into the room.

'Sorry to interrupt, Fred,' he said. 'I heard on the way in that a plane just flew into one of the Twin Towers in New York.'

There was no television in the office so many of us adjourned to Chris Tuite's newly purchased home in nearby Barnstable. Chris sent out for pizzas.

By lunchtime it was clear that Fred O' Regan was not going to have a chance to finish his 'overview'. We didn't even reconvene.

I had been on the road a long time, having – as explained above – visited South America, en route to Cape Cod. I wanted to get home.

All US airports were shut down. Logan Airport, Boston, where it seemed the hijacked planes had taken off from, would not reopen for days.

I rang Air Canada to learn that there was still a seat on a 9 a.m. plane the next morning from Toronto to London.

Toronto is around 500 miles from Cape Cod. David Lavigne and I hired a car and drove through the night, listening to the radio.

At one point, they played a tape of Todd Beamer, aboard United Airlines flight 93, talking to his wife on the phone. We heard him say, 'OK, let's roll.'

United Airlines flight 93, of course, crashed in Pennsylvania. Its target was thought to have been the White House itself.

About four in the morning, we stopped for a break at Niagara Falls. By seven we had reached Toronto. I then caught the 9 a.m. British Airways flight back to London.

Chapter Twenty-Five

Have I Got News For You

For a variety of reasons, I decided at the beginning of 2002 that, if the opportunity presented itself, I would like to go back into politics.

Of course, to say 'go back into politics' is a bit of an exaggeration. I hadn't officially been a politician since I left the European Parliament in 1984, which was quite some time ago. But when I looked at things in the round, as I did post-9/11, I couldn't help feeling that there was some unfinished business. My oldest son Boris, I noted, had – in May 2001 – been elected MP for Henley, one of the safest seats in the country.

I thought the punchline of his acceptance speech, 'Go home and prepare for breakfast', delivered around five in the morning after a long sleepless night in Henley Town Hall, was right up there in the A-list of one-liners. Might there be room for another Johnson in Parliament? Though sons had followed fathers into Parliament, their careers on the green benches sometimes overlapping (as in the case of David and Andrew Mitchell), there didn't seem to be any precedent for a father actually following his son (or daughter) into the hallowed halls of Westminster.

I had to go up to Milton Keynes for what was known as the Conservative Party's Parliamentary Assessment Board (PAB). I had never been to Milton Keynes before, nor to a PAB. I found it an interesting experience on both counts.

The assessors at my own PAB were, as I recall, David Maclean MP, a Conservative Chief Whip (now Lord Blencathra), and Oliver Heald MP, a senior front-bencher.

David Maclean was and is a brave man. Suffering then, as now, from multiple sclerosis, he used a large shepherd's crook to help him get around. At Milton Keynes, he would come into the room, crook in hand, to make sure we all had the right papers before us.

Many of the questions being put to potential MPs in those days at least were what is known as multiple-choice questions, e.g. 'How much do you like your mother-in-law?' and you had to give an answer on a scale of 0 to 5 where 0 was 'not at all' and 5 was 'very much'.

There was no time to think because you had to answer 100 questions in about sixty seconds. Good practice for being an MP. I decided that on the whole the best thing was to go for the middle range of values except of course for the mother-in-law question where I ticked the 'very much' box.

Then there was the 'inbox' simulation exercise.

'An MP,' Maclean explained, waving his crook, 'will have a very full intray. He or she' – there were several female wannabe politicians on the group as well as men – 'will have to deal with their intray quickly and efficiently. Let's hear how each one of you would hope to deal with your intray when you come in to your office in the morning.'

When it came to my turn, I explained that, when I was a Euro MP, dealing with one's intray was fairly straightforward. I waited until a large pile of letters had accumulated, I then put them all in a large plastic bag, tied the bag to the back of my bike and cycled around London.

'Why would you do that?' one of my fellow candidates asked.

'Well, basically,' I told her, 'most of the letters I received should have been addressed to the local MP, or the local council, or else were junk mail.'

'But why put them in a bag on the back of your bike?' she persisted.

'I found that the bag sometimes fell off in the course of the day's cycling – if I was swerving to avoid a bus, for example,' I replied.

A few days later, Jonathan Isaby, then working on the 'Peterborough' column of the *Daily Telegraph*, and today the CEO of the Taxpayer's Alliance, telephoned me: 'I hear you've joined the candidate's list. Congratulations.'

'Thanks for telling me, Jonathan. I hadn't heard. As always, the *Telegraph* is first with the news. Actually, I haven't joined the list. I have re-joined it. Richard Sharples MP first put me on the list in 1972 as I remember. They sent him off to be Governor of Bermuda, where, alas, he was assassinated, along with his aide de camp and his Great Dane.'

'We may not be able to get all that in the column,' Jonathan said. 'We're quite pushed for space today.'

The real boost to my political 'relaunch' came not from the 'Peterborough' column but from appearing on *Have I Got News For You* in May 2004.

I sat next to Anne Robinson at dinner one night and, later, she kindly mentioned my name to Denise O'Donoghue, then – with Jimmy Mulville – the boss of Hat Trick Productions, the company that makes the programme.

A few weeks later Denise welcomed me to the studio. She couldn't have been more charming.

'William will be chairing the show tonight,' she said.

'William who?'

'William Hague, of course.'

The future Foreign Secretary was a natural presenter. That wry smile! That beguiling Yorkshire accent! That readiness to help a poor floundering novice!

After introducing the in-house team, the brilliant Paul Merton and Ian Hislop, who have delighted viewers of *HIGNFY* for decades with their rapier wit and lightning repartee, Hague turned to the guests.

'With Ian Hislop tonight we have the lovely CLAUDIA WINKLEMAN!'

Claudia brushed back a straying lock, gave a little self-deprecatory wave at the studio audience and looked utterly enchanting.

The Hat Trick researchers obviously hadn't been able to dig up anything of interest in my CV, because Hague went on, reading from the autocue, 'And, on my right, with Paul Merton, we have STANLEY JOHNSON, BORIS'S DAD!'

Not long ago, a wonderful charity, known as the Rainbow Trust – it helps harassed and overwhelmed parents look after their disabled children – kindly invited me to compère their annual fundraising Carol Concert, held in St Paul's, Knightsbridge.

The charity's chairman concluded her brief introduction that evening by saying: 'Stanley is, of course, best known as Boris's dad!'

'I wonder,' I began, after climbing up into the pulpit to embark on my MC role, 'whether God is occasionally irritated at being introduced as "Jesus's dad"!'

This was, of course, just a warm-up quip. In reality, I am never 'irritated' at being introduced as 'Boris's dad'. Far from it. I am pleased as punch. If, in the TV studio that day, quick as a flash, I pressed my buzzer, I intervened simply for the sake of accuracy and in the interests of transparency.

'Well, actually, chairman,' I said, 'I am not just Boris's father, I am also Rachel's father and Leo's and Jo's and Max's and … Er. Er.'

My mind went blank. Hague looked at me. 'Well, how many more are there?'

Of course, the studio audience loved that. The ice was broken. A good time was had by all.

The show's 'odd one out' segment showed photographs of four houses. Three of them were white, including the White House, home of the US Presidents. One of them was pink. I immediately recognised it as our own house on Primrose Hill. I could clearly see Tarquin the rocking horse in the bow-fronted window.

'That's my house!' I exclaimed. 'That's the odd one out. It's pink. All the others are white!'

'Stanley, you're brilliant!' William Hague said.

This was high praise indeed. I heaved a sigh of relief. Got that one right, at least.

The show went on the air the next day. Back home in our (pink) Rocking Horse House on Primrose Hill, we gathered round the screen.

I watched Hague introduce Merton and Hislop (APPLAUSE) and Claudia Winkleman (MASSIVE APPLAUSE). Claudia, I felt sure, would go far. And I was right. It has just been announced as I pen these words that Claudia Winkleman is going to host *Strictly Come Dancing*. You can hardly go further than that!

Then we all watched that floundering exchange I had with William Hague as I tried to remember the names of my children. Julia let out a sudden scream and rushed from the room. Both Pixie and Harry ran after her.

'How could you, Dada?' she sobbed. 'How could you forget my name like that?'

Of course, it was unforgivable. My strong advice is: if you are going to appear on television and you think that, in the heat of battle, you may forget some key fact (e.g. the names of your children), ink the info on your knuckles or on the palm of your hand before you go into the studio.

A few days later some burglars, no doubt grateful for the information supplied on air free, gratis and for nothing, climbed into our house through an open window at the back and helped themselves to the silverware.

Chapter Twenty-Six

Bitten by the Tumbu Fly

While waiting for the call from some (preferably safe or at least 'winnable') constituency's Conservative Party association anxious to interview me as their prospective parliamentary candidate *(60+-year-old male, former MEP, good sense of humour, seeks poorly remunerated but highly fulfilling employment)*, I was asked to help the United Nations Environment Programme (UNEP) with its newly established Great Apes Survival Partnership, otherwise known as GRASP.

In June 2002 I had attended the UN's environment and development conference held in Johannesburg, at which GRASP had been officially launched. Klaus Töpfer, then UNEP's executive director, explained that GRASP aimed to unite governments and non-governmental bodies together in one concerted effort to save the great apes.

He didn't mince his words. This might be the world's last best chance to save the gorillas, the chimpanzees, the orang-utans and the bonobos, the four 'great ape' species.

Robert Hepworth, a former senior official at the UK's Department of the Environment (DOE), was now in charge of UNEP's Division for Environmental Conventions. GRASP was one of his responsibilities.

Hepworth's job was to put some flesh on Töpfer's idea, and to create a lasting structure that really did ensure the 'buy-in' of both governments and NGOs.

Hepworth told me when I met him in Nairobi, 'We need a proper strategy for GRASP and a workable constitution which enables the GRASP partnership to work.'

It occurred to me, as I settled down to work on this new and challenging assignment, that the number of great apes I had actually seen in the wild, as opposed to in zoos, was actually zero. So I made a quick side-trip from Nairobi to Kampala, where Richard Ssuna, who worked for a local wildlife NGO, met me.

Kibale, a Ugandan National Park with a still healthy chimpanzee population, is in the south west of Uganda, near the border with the Democratic Republic of the Congo. We arrived late afternoon, hot and sticky from the long drive.

The facilities were far from primitive. We had tented accommodation of a high standard.

'Please give me any laundry,' the steward said. 'You will have it back tomorrow. Would you like a sun-downer?'

Next morning a guide took us into the forest. We had trekked some distance before we had the good fortune to see half a dozen chimpanzees scuttling, more or less at ground level, through the forest ahead of us. They looked as though they knew where they were going and what they wanted to accomplish. It was almost as though they were on the warpath.

'Chimps can be pretty aggressive,' Richard said. 'You have alpha males. Alpha females too.'

Alpha females! I've met a few of those in my time.

Our laundry was ready for us when we got back to camp. It was good to put on clean socks and pants etc.

With a day to spare before I had to fly back to London, Richard said he would like to show me the chimpanzee sanctuary on Ngamba Island, which lies in the middle of Lake Victoria. He negotiated with a local fisherman in Entebbe, and we set out in a steep-sided 'artisanal' fishing boat. Lake Victoria can be quite rough when the wind gets up, and a flat, shallow craft could be easily swamped.

We spent a couple of hours on the island. Of course, the chimpanzees are not really in the wild in the sense that the food they gather from the trees has to be supplemented by food brought in from outside. These are animals that have been caught up in frequent human–animal conflicts.

That visit to Ngamba was a memorable experience. On the way back across the lake, we were still some miles from shore, when Richard observed that we were crossing the Equator.

'At this very moment?' I asked.

'Pretty much.'

It seemed an ideal moment to celebrate. I stripped off, and dived in. Here was a golden opportunity and I didn't want to miss it. How many people actually get to swim across the Equator?

The problem was getting back into the boat. The steep sides defeated me. If they had a rope they could perhaps have towed me back to shore, but I don't think I would have survived. The water was far colder and choppier than I had expected. And we were a long way from home.

I could see Richard Ssuna and the local fisherman, whose boat we had hired, grinning down at me as I tried to get back in. I agree that I must have looked a funny sight, lunging up to try and catch onto the high side of the boat, so as to haul myself in.

Actually, it wasn't funny at all. Quite soon, they started to look alarmed. They tried to help me up but that didn't work. They couldn't get hold of my outstretched hand. I couldn't get hold of theirs. I was too heavy for them anyway.

I am sure there is a moral to this story. Something like 'never jump out of a boat, unless you know you can get back in if you have to'.

I could feel my heart rate rising. Was it the effort of trying to get back in or was it – let's face it – the first hint of panic?

In the end, they found an old tyre and lowered in over the side of the boat, so I was able to use that as a kind of stepping stone to get back on board.

Back in England, I went to the GP in the Primrose Hill Surgery.

'My upper back leg seems to be very swollen,' I said.

Dr Barlow, who was keen on cricket, was intrigued.

'Upper Back Leg? Is that somewhere near Long On or Deep Leg? Let's take a look.'

Dr Barlow wisely referred me to the Tropical Diseases Centre, off Tottenham Court Road, where an Asian doctor examined the swollen limb.

'Umhh…' he mused. 'Did you hang your clothes up to dry somewhere when you were in Africa?'

I suddenly remembered that the steward at the Kibale tented camp had taken my laundry. I had seen it hanging on the line as we set out on our morning trek.

'Precisely!' Dr Amarasinghe seemed delighted to have his suspicions confirmed. 'They hang the clothes up to dry, and the tumbu fly comes along and lays its eggs in the clothes. If they ironed the underpants as they should, there should be no problem. The hot iron would kill the eggs.'

We had had a comfortable stay in Kibale. I didn't want to cast unwarranted aspersions.

'I'm not sure everyone irons underpants nowadays. And these were Travel Lite drip-dry pants from that shop in Covent Garden.'

Dr Amarasinghe stuck to his guns.

'The tumbu fly laid its eggs on your underpants. Next time you put your pants on, the larva buried deep into your flesh. That's why you have the swelling. But the larva still has to breathe. So it has a long thin tube like a periscope, which it sticks out through the surface of the skin. In normal circumstances, when the larva is fully formed as an insect it will claw its way up to the surface, break the skin and fly away.'

'Wow!' Enthusiastic conservationist that I was, I had never imagined that my destiny was to provide a refuge for the endangered tumbu fly. 'We can, however, interrupt nature's cycle,' the doctor continued. 'I am going to spread some Vaseline on the swelling. That should block up the larva's breathing hole and, literally, suffocate it. If you come back tomorrow, we will deal with it then, removing the corpse. No problem. Of course, the larva may come out at night, while it fights for air.'

When I explained to Jenny that evening that there was a possibility, just a possibility, that the tumbu fly larva might make a break for it while we were in bed, she wisely suggested I should sleep in the next room.

The following morning, as I was waiting to see the astute and most knowledgeable Dr Amarasinghe, the receptionist waylaid me: 'There's a BBC *Horizon* film crew in the building this morning. They're making a programme about rare tropical diseases as experienced in Britain. They want to know if they can film you having the tumbu fly larva extracted. Apparently, incidences of tumbu fly bites are very rare in Britain.'

'What are they actually hoping to film?'

'Oh, it will all be quite anonymous,' the young lady informed me cheerfully. 'They won't show you, just your buttocks.'

'Buttock, actually,' I corrected her. 'I was bitten on only one side.'

The BBC film duly arrived and Dr Amarasinghe duly extracted the surprisingly large tumbu larva. He held it at arm's length with a pair of tweezers and showed it to me. It looked large and fleshy, well nourished, I would say. I guess it must have been half an inch long, and almost as wide. The doctor had plucked it out from a position very near the surface. It had obviously been making a last desperate effort to fight for life and air.

The *Horizon* film was shown in due course. They dwelt at some length on the ravages caused by the tumbu fly. By way of illustration, they showed a film of a young Tanzanian woman, who had come to London for a holiday and who had developed a strange swelling on her head.

Dr Amarasinghe, who had his eye in by now, had spotted that one too and had dealt with it with his patented 'large blob of Vaseline' treatment.

In my view, the *Horizon* team made the right decision. That young Tanzanian woman was far prettier than the rear view of my upper left leg.

UNESCO was a co-founder of GRASP together with UNEP. We had a big meeting in Paris at the end of November 2003, to sketch out the main themes of the GRASP strategy and the main planks of the Constitution.

Jo, by then married to Amelia Gentleman, was working in Paris as part of the *FT*'s Paris bureau. He wrote a long and helpful piece in the paper about the United Nations' efforts to save great apes on the morning the Paris meeting was due to begin.

Nick Nuttall, who worked for UNEP in Nairobi as 'director of communications', rang me on my mobile as I walked from my hotel to UNESCO's headquarters where the meeting was being held.

He sounded peeved. 'Please give me a head's up in the future when you're planning to plant another big article about UNEP in the press!'

No good deed goes unpunished.

Chapter Twenty-Seven

Finding a Seat

Anne Robinson, who had so kindly promoted my TV career, such as it was, now took a hand on the political front as well.

She rang up one day. 'I'm putting together a team for the Cotswold quiz night. Nicky Haslam's coming to stay for the weekend. Can you and Jenny come too?'

I am not much good at quizzes, but Jenny is. And Nicky Haslam was brilliant. Much dudgeon was caused in the locality when the Robinson team won not only the quiz but, thanks to Nicky Haslam's inventiveness and attention to detail, the 'best-dressed table' prize as well.

Anne gave a big lunch on Sunday for her victorious team and various neighbours, including David and Samantha Cameron. David Cameron, elected MP for Witney in 2001, was at the time closely involved with the Conservatives' planning for the next election, being the Conservative leader Michael Howard's 'chief of policy coordination'.

Rachel Whetstone, another of Michael Howard's key allies (she had worked with him when he was Home Secretary), was at that lunch too.

I found myself sitting next to her at table. I told her that, though I was on the candidate's list, I had not yet caught the selectors' eye.

'Have you been interviewed yet?'

'I was interviewed in South Thanet, Jonathan Aitken's old seat. The first question the chairman asked me was what I knew about Thanet.'

'And what did you say?'

'I said, "I'm afraid you've got me stumped there, chairman."'

Rachel Whetstone, to do her justice, thought that was quite funny.

'Why don't you put in for Teignbridge, down in deepest Devon?' she suggested. 'You have West Country links. Don't you? The current candidate has just withdrawn and they're looking for a successor. Go and talk to the agent. Apparently she's quite a character.'

The summer was about to begin. We planned to spend a lot of time on the farm.

'I'll follow that up,' I said.

I drove over from Exmoor to Newton Abbot to meet the Conservative's Party's agent for the Teignbridge constituency. Audrey Warren was a veteran campaigner. Well over seventy, she regarded me as a mere stripling.

'Follow me. I'll take the car because I'll go straight on to Bovey after lunch.'

She jumped in her Mini and shot off along the narrow high-hedged country lanes, with me doing my best to keep up with her, to a country pub on the edge of Dartmoor.

Over a well-lubricated lunch, Audrey explained that Teignbridge, a parliamentary constituency that included a slice of Dartmoor as well as towns such as Newton Abbot, Teignmouth, Dawlish and Bovey Tracey, had been a Tory seat once but the Lib Dems had won it.

'Ugh!' she shuddered. 'Lib Dems! How I hate them! Put in for the seat. You'll make an excellent candidate. I'm sure you've got a good chance.'

I worked hard to win that nomination. We had the usual three-step selection process that August (2004). A large number of candidates were quizzed at the first session by small selection panel. A smaller number was interviewed at a second session by a larger group of party activists, say thirty or forty. The final short-list (just three) had to appear before all the members of the local association, or at least those of them ready to give up their time to participate in this manner in the democratic process. For this last phase, Audrey had (wisely) booked the Langstone Cliff hotel in Dawlish, whose conference room was capable of seating well over 200 people.

I swanned through the first round. Audrey, though officially neutral, was pleased with me. 'Keep it up,' she urged, 'and you'll definitely be shortlisted.'

I almost blew it on the second round. My first joke had gone down well.

One little old lady had asked me, 'I do hope, Mr Johnson, if you are selected and elected, that you won't forget us in your busy life. We very much hope you will speak in Dawlish often.'

'Of course I will,' I reassured her, 'though I usually prefer to speak in English!'

A second joke didn't fare so well.

A man sitting in the front row raised his hand. 'Mr Johnson, you say you have strong local connections, but I'd like to ask how long it will actually take you to get back to your farm on Exmoor this evening.'

'That depends on how fast I drive,' I replied, 'and how long I stop in the pub on the way home.'

I could see Audrey rolling her eyes as I spoke. Later she came up to me and hissed, 'Didn't you know he was a retired policeman.'

When the third and final round came, I kept my eye on the ball, blocked the tricky questions and hit the softer ones to the boundary.

Balloting at such events often takes a while. Unless you win on the first round, there can be several counts. Jenny and I had just ordered dinner in the hotel dining room when word came that we were needed. They hadn't needed a second-round ballot or subsequent rounds. I had won more than 50 per cent of the votes first time round so that was that.

Winning the nomination is one thing; winning the election is something else. I rented a flat in Dawlish because, whatever I had said at the meeting, it really was too far to drive over from Exmoor every day. My flat had a splendid view of the famous red sandstone cliffs. On a rough day, I could see the waves and the spray breaking over the railway tracks below. (In early 2014, as I was writing this book, a storm knocked out the line altogether and it took several weeks for it to be repaired.)

As far as the campaigning end of things was concerned, I did what candidates are meant to do. I got stuck in. For example, in the early autumn of 2004, with only a few months to go before the election, George Strickland, Winsford's long-time resident carpenter (his father was the vicar when I was still at school) joined me in walking along the Two Moors Way from Winsford on Exmoor to Widecombe-in-the-Moor on Dartmoor to raise money for new bell ropes in the local churches. 'Money for new rope' was our slogan. We succeeded brilliantly, raising over £4,000.

At one point on that walk, somewhere near Rackenford, I had plucked a passing blackberry without noticing there was a wasp attached. The wasp stung me and my throat swelled up. George, who is a tall man with long legs, had been striding on ahead, but I called him back to help with a strangled cry.

'I can either open your windpipe with my pen-knife,' he advised, 'or I can rip your tongue out!'

I opened fêtes galore (including some fêtes worse than death!) and ran in the famous Newton Abbot pancake race. I actually won one of the races. Afterwards a woman came up to me.

'Are you a practised tosser?' she enquired.

I visited schools and old people's homes, farmers and factories. When the balloon finally went up and the election was actually announced I was raring to go.

I thought the Conservatives had a good message. A clear message. I liked Michael Howard's bullet points. More police. School discipline. Lower taxes. Cleaner hospitals. Controlled immigration. Easy to memorise.

Even so you could sometimes get it wrong and find yourself talking about 'taller police' and 'cleaner taxis'.

Channel 4 had asked me to write a blog for them during the campaign every day, and this I duly did. It was a lighthearted take on the day's events. Here, for example, is the entry for 19 April 2005, as posted on the Channel 4 News website.

Tuesday 19 April

In a housing estate high above Teignmouth, I rang the bell of a house called The Haven and had a good talk with the lady who answered the door. I found out that her name was Mrs Martha Finch. I don't like actually asking people straight out whether I can 'count on' their vote. It seems a bit intrusive. In this transitory life, who can 'count on' anything? But she was friendly enough. After we had talked for a few minutes, I marked her down as a P (for 'probable Conservative').

When I had left The Haven, I walked round the corner and rang the next doorbell. The person who answered the door seemed vaguely familiar. I think she must have recognised me too, or perhaps it was just the rather large blue rosette I have been wearing.

Thank God I remembered her name. 'Mrs Finch? It is Mrs Finch, isn't it?' Having first called at the front door, I had somehow managed to call at the back door of the same house. I was covered in confusion.

'Don't worry,' she said, 'you can ring my bell any time. And, yes, I will be voting Conservative.'

Several of the Conservative Party's bigwigs very kindly came down to speak for me – Andrew Lansley and Oliver Letwin, for example. Boris also came down, followed by a *Newsnight* team, who filmed a charity squash match he and I played in the local squash club.

Next day I wrote in my Channel 4 blog on 22 April:

The father-and-son squash match has been well-reported in the press. The *Today* programme even alluded to it as the 'key sporting event so far in the election campaign'. I will therefore content myself with saying that it was, as I anticipated, a fiercely fought contest. I lost the first two games, won the third and lost the fourth 8–10, at which point we called it a day.

The upside was that Boris was able to catch the 5.40 train. I would like to record here my gratitude to him. Conservatives are, as we all know, the party of the family, and Boris certainly came up trumps.

David Cameron kindly came down, too, an event that Simon Hoggart memorably described in *The Guardian*:

'David Cameron is coming here today, to push my campaign – over the edge!' said Stanley Johnson. 'Sorry, over the finishing line!'

Stanley, father of Boris, and perhaps the first man to follow his son into the Commons, was in the Devon village of Chudleigh Knighton, at a pub. 'We have campaigned in every village – at least every village that has a pub!'

David Cameron is the Tories' shadow cabinet member in charge of policy coordination, whatever that is. He's tipped as a future party leader. If the Tories lose badly, and they decide again to skip a generation, he could be there this year. Though I don't see him in a baseball cap, or boasting about 17-pint benders.

He descended on Teignbridge like one of those American tornados that wreck trailer parks. He had been all over south Wales in the morning, flew to Plymouth and was driven to the pub for lunch. Inside it was chaotic. Some nineteen people were clustered round him and Stanley – aides, agents, hacks, photographers, drivers and hangers-on. Mad conversations ensued.

'And I spent an hour on the local radio talking entirely about nappies.'

'Who was the stilton ploughman's then?'

'So you see, reducing council tax is a massive issue here. And slaughtering infected badgers.'

'Two ham ploughmans and one ham sandwich, or is it the other way round?'

'I did rather well in a pancake race, and one lady asked me, "Are you a practised tosser?"'

Cameron looks and behaves like a junior minister, and already talks the talk. 'I found that Cardiff was blue, and Barry was blueing up … the momentum is in our direction. We're talking about what we're going to do in government, while the other two parties are talking tactics. "Don't let the Tories in by the back door." After eight years, that's pathetic!'

We raced on, leaving behind enough ploughpersons' grub to feed a small African village. We descended on the market town of Bovey Tracey where Cameron roared up the high street introducing voters to the candidate, who didn't like to say that he'd worked the shops before and, yes, most of them knew him already.

We passed a pub with a placard outside saying 'Eat the rich' – not natural Tory territory perhaps. It turned out to be the name of a rock group. A canvasser leapt out. 'We've got a swayer here!' he declared. Old Terry was exactly that, literally and figuratively. 'Dunno how I'll vote,' he said, unsteadily. 'You could buy me a pint.'

'No he can't, it's illegal,' said Cameron. 'Old Terry, always pissed as a handcart,' the Tory agent confided.

'Margaret in the fruit shop is hovering!' we learned, and, faster than a speeding bullet, Cameron was there to tether that vote. Once outside, he charged back down the street. An ex-policewoman came up: 'I would rather cut my arm off than vote for those lying scumbags who are in power now.'

Not Labour, clearly, and the party was a poor third last time. Stanley Johnson is just 3,000 votes – 5 per cent – behind the sitting Lib Dem, Richard Younger-Ross.

'We've got to go, David!' said the driver. We dashed past a stylist's salon. 'I fight shy of hair dryers,' he said. 'And banks. Never disturb people when they're with their money!'

Finally, the driver dragged him away. 'Stanley, that was huge!' said Cameron, as he left, a term which perplexed the candidate slightly. He watched the next leader (or next but one) go with gratitude but some relief. 'We can slow down now. I don't know, people from London…'

Esther Rantzen was also in Newton Abbot during the election on ChildLine business but she wisely decided to stay clear of politics.

After two bottles of Montepulciano d'Abruzzo in a local restaurant, I thought I had persuaded her to support my campaign. Eventually she wrote a message for me on a paper napkin. 'I am a floating voter and I have not yet decided which way to vote, but I always enjoy Stanley's company.'

It was, ironically, an article by another *Guardian* journalist that was responsible for the major blip in my campaign.

My campaign team was taking a well-earned break in the Ship Inn, Cockwood, on the Exe Estuary, when my mobile telephone rang.

'This is Simon Goodley of *The Guardian* Diary,' a voice said.

I wasn't sure I had heard it correctly. 'Do you mean the *Manchester Guardian?*'

A pause. 'We haven't been called the *Manchester Guardian* for years.'

'You were last time I read the paper, back in the '60s.'

Goodley very quickly levelled the score by pointing out that a couple of typos in my campaign literature had recently come to his attention.

'I'd like to talk about your election address.'

'No secret,' I replied. 'It's on the ballot paper. Flat 2, Shell Cove, Seaview, Dawlish. I can give you the postcode too, if you like. I'm definitely a local man.'

'No, I mean the printed address you circulated to the electors. You've left out the D in Teignbridge.'

I decided that this was a telephone call whose intimate details others did not need to hear, so I went outside where the sun shone and the wildfowl pottered about on the mudflats. You wouldn't have thought that there was an election on.

'Are you sure there is a D in Teignbridge?' I parried. 'This is pretty rich coming from *The Grauniad*!'

Goodley had kept his best shot till last. 'You also say, in paragraph 4, that the Conservatives believe in "more talk and less action".'

Now I'm not trying to argue that my failure to win back Teignbridge for the Conservatives was entirely due to the unhelpful column that *The Guardian* ran the next day. I suspect other factors played a part.

One day, for example, I wrote in my blog that, if I was asked on the doorstep or at public meetings what I would do if I was elected, I tended to reply, 'Not too much, I hope.' MPs, I went on, should resist the temptation to reach for the statute book at the slightest opportunity. They should pass fewer laws, while repealing many existing ones.

A week before the election, my Liberal Democrat opponent took out full-page advertisements in the local press in which he not so subtly distorted my meaning. 'Tory candidate says he won't do much if elected,' ran the headline.

Here are another couple of passages from my Channel 4 News blog:

Monday 25 April

My last full week of campaigning begins with an interview with the BBC Radio 4 *Today* programme in the car park at Newton Abbot railway station. Ed Sturton, the presenter, has spent the last two weeks in Rome covering the funeral of Pope John Paul and the election of Pope Benedict. He gives a passable impression of being pleased to be in Teignbridge on a wet morning.

With me, standing in the rain beside the *Today* radio van with its futuristic satellite aerial, is Trevor Coleman, the UKIP candidate, a tall serious gentleman who, like me, was born in Cornwall.

Ed kicks off by playing a clip from an interview with Richard Younger-Ross. I can't hear what RYR is saying since neither Trevor or I have headphones on. It is not a long clip because, after a minute or so, Ed thrusts the microphone towards me and says, 'Well, Richard Younger-Ross calls you a "minor celebrity". A carpetbagger, eh? What do you say to that?'

… I wish I had thought at the time of saying that it is better to be a minor celebrity than a major nonentity but I didn't. Ed Sturton steers the conversation on to Europe, which he calls the non-issue so far of the campaign.

Wednesday 27 April

'Vote Conservative on May 7th,' I boomed as I drove the battle bus down the coast road from Dawlish to Starcross. I have got the hang of the loudspeaker now. The secret is (a) to switch it on before you start speaking and (b) to switch it off when you have finished.

'It will be too late by May 7th,' one of our canvass team corrected me, as I stowed the mike. 'You should have said May 5th!'

'Ooops,' I said, switching the machine back on. 'I meant May 5th. VOTE CONSERVATIVE ON MAY 5th!'

I know why I said May 7th: May 7th is – or was – my mother's birthday. Had she still been alive, she would have been ninety-eight.

The whole family (except Boris who was once again standing in Henley and therefore had to be present at his own 'count') came down to Teignbridge for the count, held at the Newton Abbot racecourse though not, obviously, on the course itself.

I am not sure that long evening at the Newton Abbot racecourse, with Jenny and five (out of a possible six) children present, was the best way to end a political career. I realised quite early that things weren't going as well as they needed to go, if I was to stand a chance of winning. A roving TV camera recorded me as saying that I was 'cautiously pessimistic'. I had reason to be. It was clear that the stacked piles of votes assigned to me were smaller by some margin than those cast in favour of Richard Younger-Ross, the sitting MP and my Lib Dem opponent.

The last entry in my Channel 4 News Blog read as follows:

Friday 6 May

I have just returned from handing back the battle bus, and saying good bye to many friends who gathered this morning in the Teignbridge Conservatives Association's headquarters.

We lost to the Liberal Democrats last night by a margin of over 6,000 votes. Even if all the UKIP votes (almost 4,000) had come our way, we would not have been 'first past the post'.

That said, there was a discernible swing to the Lib Dems in the West Country, augmented by the collapse of the Labour vote, so I did not feel totally humiliated. 21,593 people voted for me which was better than a slap in the face with a wet fish.

The below photo shows me making a brief speech at the count, thanking all those who had supported me including any who may have mistaken me for Boris! (Boris himself posted an increased majority in Henley on a more than 7 per cent swing.)

There was a valedictory tone to this morning's occasion at Teignbridge HQ. I quoted Emperor Hirohito's remarks on 14 August 1945, as he accepted the Potsdam Declaration:

'Despite the best that has been done by everyone – the gallant fighting of our military and naval forces, the diligence and assiduity of our servants of the state and the devoted service of our 100,000,000 people – the war situation has developed not necessarily to Japan's advantage, while the general trends of the world have all turned against her interest.'

I have much enjoyed writing this blog and am grateful for having had the opportunity to do so.

Chapter Twenty-Eight

Katz and Dogs

One of the advantages of not being elected to Parliament is that you don't have to be an MP.

I was walking on Primrose Hill one morning a few days after the election. It was not a very good day, as far as I was concerned at least. I was looking for Harry, son of Pixie, our Jack Russell terrier. Somehow, I had let him out of the house when I went to fetch the newspaper and he hadn't returned.

I had reached the top of the hill and, from this vantage point, was surveying the scene looking for a small white dog, when my mobile telephone rang.

It was, as it happened, another man from *The Guardian*, Ian Katz, who ran *The Guardian*'s G2 section and is now in charge of BBC's *Newsnight* programme.

'Did you say CATS?' I said. 'What a coincidence! I've been thinking about DOGS all morning. I've lost Harry. It was definitely my fault – I saw him flash by when I opened the door to pick up the paper. I should have gone after him at once.'

Ian Katz wisely decided to ignore my nervous banter.

'I've been reading your Channel 4 News blog,' he said. 'I wonder if you would like to write a weekly column for *The Guardian*. Would you like to drop by our offices to have a chat?' Forgetting about Harry, I said I would get on my bike and be there – *The*

Guardian's offices were then in Gray's Inn Road – in about twenty minutes.

My first *Guardian* column appeared a few days later under the heading: '*The Guardian* ruined my political career.' In the first few paragraphs, I told the story of that fateful telephone call from the *Guardian* reporter in the course of the election campaign informing me that I had left out the D in Teignbridge. I also mentioned my friendly, but politically unproductive dinner with Esther Rantzen in Newton Abbot. Then I continued:

> Well, we've all passed a lot of water under the bridge since 5 May. The Conservatives are yet again in the throes of a leadership contest, one which is of more than academic interest. David Davis, the shadow home secretary, has set out his stall, and I must say that I find his vision of a low-tax, legislation-lite future with a strong emphasis on civil liberties attractive. The fact that he has had his nose broken a couple of times also appeals to me. As Kipling might have put it, a man who can break his nose when others are all about him picking theirs could go far.

Since this was my very first column and I didn't want, perhaps inadvertently, to give the impression that I was deep-down, to paraphrase Tony Blair, a 'pretty serious kind of guy', so I decided that I would end it on a lighter note:

> The other day, as we were driving down Parkway in the direction of Camden Town, my wife, Jenny, said, 'I think we should split up.'
>
>   I knew it had been a bad day (our Jack Russell terrier had gone AWOL), but I didn't know it had been that bad. I carefully put the car into neutral at the traffic lights. There was an ominous silence. 'Yes, I definitely think we should split up,' Jenny continued. 'Why

don't you go to the print shop to get a 'missing dog' poster made, while I go to Marks and Spencer?' Phew!

Harry, I am glad to say, was found. The 'missing dog' posters that we had printed did the trick. Jenny and I were at our house in Greece when the telephone rang.

'They've found Harry,' Julia was overcome with emotion. 'A lady saw the poster Max and I put up outside the school. She says someone sold Harry to her and she didn't realise he was stolen.'

Julia went to the woman's flat in Camden and retrieved Harry. She rang us again. Harry was in fine shape, apparently, though a bit thin.

I heaved a sigh of relief. Honestly, I hadn't had much faith in the posters.

I ought to explain about Greece.

The sea – or rather, the lack of it – had been the crucial element in our decision to sell that old farmhouse in Tuscany, which we had barely owned. The unspoken subtext of my by now decades-old refrain about buying 'a little place in the sun' was that the residence in question should be near the sea. Actually, not just near the sea. It had to be within walking, even spitting, distance. It simply wasn't good enough, we decided, if you had to pile in the car and drive there. You had to be able to get to the sea under your own steam, viz. Shanks's pony (and back again). And the sea had to be crystal clean and, preferably, warm.

So how did we end up in Pelion?

One summer, a few years earlier, we had rented a villa near Milina, a small seaside town two-thirds of the way down the Pelion peninsula in Greece. We fell in love with the place. Pelion is full of chestnut forests and alpine meadows and perfect beaches on the Aegean, as well as being on the Pagasitic Gulf side of the peninsula.

You can ski in winter and sail and swim for at least six months of the year. There are a score of mountain villages that reminded me, when I saw them, of the first time I travelled in Greece – in my gap year at the end of the '50s. Think *Captain Corelli's Mandolin* with old men sitting under the plane trees in the village square drinking ouzo and cups of thick, black coffee.

Soon after we returned from that holiday, our old friends, Patrick and Maria Fairweather, who already owned a house there, told us that there was some land for sale very near where they had their holiday home, just above Horto, one of Pelion's old fishing villages. In Greece, you need a minimum of 4 stremmas of land to build a house – that's about an acre. There were actually 2 acres of land for sale, within a few hundred yards of where our friends lived, which made it an especially attractive prospect.

'Dona will build a house for you on your half of the land,' Patrick told us, 'and a house for herself on the other half.'

Before committing ourselves, I telephoned Dona. A trained architect, she is half-Greek, half-Italian.

'What we need to be sure of,' I said, 'is that you can actually see the sea over the olive groves. We don't want to buy the land and build the house and find out at the end of it all that we can't see the sea.'

'I give you my word,' Dona said. 'You will have one of the finest views you could ever imagine.'

Dona was as good as her word. In fact, she was better than it. The four-bedroom house, named Villa Irene after my mother (though she was always called Buster, she was christened Irène) is built in the traditional Pelion style, on two floors with a roof of grey stone tiles. The view from the wide terrace is spectacular. You can walk down to a perfectly secluded little beach through the olive groves in seven minutes.

Miraculously, Dona managed to hook us up with the mains water supply, no mean feat in Greece. She built a pool that, being terracotta in colour, blends in with the surroundings. In the height of the summer, if you get hot walking back up from the sea, you can plunge into the pool to cool off.

One great sadness is that Maria Fairweather, alas, is no longer with us in person, having died of cancer in 2009. But she is with us in spirit. We love her and miss her.

When Ian Katz had offered me a job as a weekly *Guardian* columnist, an offer that I was pleased and proud to accept, he explained that this was not likely to be a permanent assignment. *The Guardian* was in the process of changing its format to the 'Berliner' model, which as far as the format of the paper was concerned, meant about halfway between the broadsheet and the tabloid. There would probably be a reshuffle of the columnists.

After sixteen of what I like to think were well-turned 750-word contributions to the nation's breakfast table (some filed from Greece, others from more distant parts), my career as a *Guardian* columnist came to an end.

Happily another, equally brief career, as a TV presenter, unexpectedly arrived on the scene.

In the summer of 2005, Channel 4 announced that it would soon be launching a new TV channel called More4. Among the shows being proposed for the new channel was a nightly news and comment magazine-type programme to be known as *The Last Word*.

They must have got my name from somewhere because I received a call from the production company inviting me to a 'screen test'. They said they were trying to build up a list of people who might be able to come on the show, as guests, from time to time.

'We've seen your bio. You could talk about Europe or the environment, I suppose. That kind of thing.'

'Who's the presenter?' I asked.

'Well, it's not official yet but we're looking at a team of present-ers: David Mitchell, Hardeep Singh Kohli and Mark Dolan,' the other end said.

I'm not particularly familiar with the media world but I realised that More4 had fingered some well-known personalities. David Mitchell's Channel 4 sitcom *Peep Show* had rave reviews, Hardeep was a brilliant radio comedian and Mark Dolan was hosting a popular TV show with the gripping title *Balls of Steel*!

'What a line-up!' I exclaimed. 'Three comedians already. Do you need a fourth?'

The weekend before the screen test, Jenny and I had stayed in a weird little hotel, more like a B&B, on the Sussex Downs, having been invited to a party near Lewes.

'I went out into the hotel garden,' I explained as the camera rolled during my screen-test, 'and by mistake I peed on the cat. It started rubbing its back on my legs when I was in mid-flow as it were. When I walked back into the sitting room through the French windows, the cat – it was a large marmalade pussy – followed me. The landlady happened to come into the room at that moment. "Why's the cat all wet?" she asked.'

A few days later I was down in Somerset, driving across Winsford Hill to Dulverton when my mobile phone rang. This took me by surprise. There is no mobile phone reception in the Nethercote Valley, and reception elsewhere on Exmoor is decidedly poor.

One of the big cheeses from More4 was on the line. 'We loved the story you told about peeing on the cat. We don't want you to be on just as a guest from time to time. We think we can do much better than that. We'd like you to be one of the regular presenters.'

'You mean with David, Hardeep and Mark?'

'*Stanley*, David, Hardeep and Mark!'

There is only one possible line to take in a situation like that.

As I rattled over the cattle grid at Mounsey Hill Gate on the way to Dulverton, I said, 'You'll have to talk to my agent.'

It's a great line. *'You'll have to talk to my agent.'* I wish I had a chance to use it more often.

More4, television's newest and latest channel, opened for business in October 2005. The four presenters of *The Last Word* worked on a rota, each of us doing one week (five shows) a month. We thought of ourselves as the Four Musketeers.

I had to go to a specialist to have an earpiece modelled to fit my right ear. Not that my right ear is an unusual shape. It is, as far as I know, perfectly normal.

The technician explained, 'We're going to fit you with an earpiece modelled on your own ear, but with a hole in it and a short plastic tube to fit your own hearing canal. You'll be able to listen to the producer, while at the same time talking to your guests.'

Ah, my guests!

Basically the studio lined up the guests but, as the presenter, you can put up some names.

One evening, at my suggestion, my guests were Anne Robinson, yes, *the* Anne Robinson, who – as I have already explained – had once put me up for *Have I Got News For You* when William Hague was chairing it. Then there was Susie Orbach, a well-known psychotherapist. Finally, there was my daughter, Rachel, already an established journalist and author.

It turned out to be a lively half-hour.

The topic of conversation, as I remember, was childcare. I was sure Susie Orbach, who was trained as a psychotherapist, would have strong views. Anne Robinson would too. Anne has strong views about many things. So I let them both crack away.

But, as the presenter, I wanted to bring Rachel in. I was sure she had strong views too. She certainly did when she was a baby.

'What do you think, Rachel?' I asked. 'You've got two ... er ... er, yes, two children, haven't you?'

'Actually, Dada, I've got three children and you jolly well ought to know!'

Ouch!

Anne Robinson intervened to lighten the air of tension that had begun to hang over the studio.

'That's the first time I've heard one of the guests call the presenter "Dada".'

Later in the show Anne accused me of being 'patronising'.

'That's a very long word for you to use, Anne!' I said.

There were moments, during my time as one of the presenters of *The Last Word* when I found myself resenting the comments and instructions I received through the bespoke earpiece.

One evening the topic of prostitution came up. There had been a story in the press that day to the effect that 'more men were paying for sex'.

On that particular occasion in the specially designed *The Last Word* studio, I had three male guests.

'Ask each of your guests in turn whether they have ever paid for sex,' the voice in my ear instructed.

I wanted to say 'No, I bloody well won't. I wouldn't dream of doing such a thing!' but of course, the red light was glowing, we were on air and every word I spoke could be taken down and used in evidence against me.

So I ripped my special earpiece from my ear, glowered in the direction of the producer, safely ensconced behind the glass, folded my arms, and took no further part in the proceedings.

My guests were only too delighted, chatting happily among

themselves until it was time for the late-night news round-up and lights-off in the dorm.

As I left the studio, Peter Swain, the show's executive director, threw his arm about my shoulders. 'Wonderful! Your best show so far! Just great the way you let them talk. That's the secret of being a good presenter. The light touch!'

I was very proud of picking up a 'presenter's baton', as it were, on my first serious venture into TV. And I was very proud to have such illustrious co-presenters. Someone sent me a photo of a double-decker bus in Birmingham. There we were, plastered all over it.

I rang up Hardeep. 'We were completely plastered!' I told him.

Basically, I think Hardeep Singh Kohli believed I could be quite funny, or at least funny-ish, if I worked on it. I don't think the others shared his confidence.

With all the publicity, I couldn't help feeling that maybe my new career was headed somewhere.

How wrong I was! After six months, we were all asked to leave and More4 brought in Professor David Starkey instead.

How Starkey managed to do, single-handed, a job that had previously occupied four of us, I don't know. The word on the street was that he had signed a contract worth a lot of money with Channel 4, and Channel 4 was determined to get its pound of flesh.

I have checked with Wikipedia. The anonymous authors are rather coy about the Starkey takeover. The Wikipedia More4 entry says: 'The channel featured a nightly discussion programme *Starkey's Last Word* hosted by David Starkey during the autumn line-up. This show was originally called *The Last Word* and hosted alternately by Stanley Johnson, Mark Dolan, Hardeep Singh Kohli and David Mitchell and occasional special guest hosts such as Morgan Spurlock.'

I'm glad the Wikipedia compilers gave Morgan Spurlock a special mention. The man was just superb. He came on the show one night to promote his new film *Super Size Me* and to tell the story behind it.

'I ate nothing but McDonald's for thirty consecutive days,' he told us. 'Over the course of my McDiet, I consumed thirty pounds of sugar from their food. That's a pound a day. On top of that, I also took in twelve pounds of fat. Now, I know what you're saying. You're saying nobody's supposed to eat this food three times a day. No wonder all this stuff happened to you. But the scary part is: there are people who eat this food regularly. Some people even eat it every day.'

I have admittedly had occasional work in television since that tantalisingly brief More4 assignment.

I appeared on *Newsnight Review* once, for example – that's the BBC programme where guests take the train up to Glasgow and engage in serious 'live' discussion, about a film, a play and a book, all of which they are meant to have seen in the previous week.

I saw the film and the play, and worked out something to say about them both, in case Kirsty Wark, the regular presenter, asked me a question, as I imagined she might, since I was going all the way up to Scotland. As for the book, this was a serious tome by David Willetts, MP, called *The Pinch*.

I knew Willetts. He was MP for Havant. He was also colloquially known as 'Two Brains' on account of his vast intellect. I realised there could be no shirking the task in hand. I bought a copy of *The Pinch* at the station bookstore, knowing that I would have a full four hours to absorb its message on the train on my way to Glasgow.

Unfortunately, more or less as the train entered the tunnel that runs beneath Primrose Hill on its way north out of London, I fell asleep.

I was woken at Crewe by a phone call from Scotland.

'This is *Newsnight Review* calling from Glasgow. We're just about to brief Kirsty on tonight's show. It would be very helpful if you could give us an indication of the line you're planning to take.'

I came up with some reasonable stuff as far as the film and the play were concerned.

'Great!' the voice at the other end said. 'What about the Willetts book? Is the older generation really stealing the heritage of youth?'

'I'm sorry,' I shouted. 'I can't hear you. The line's breaking up. Whoops, we're just going through a tunnel!'

Actually, we had a very good discussion that evening, although Glasgow seemed quite a long way to go for it. I suppose it depends where you're starting from. Apparently Kirsty Wark lives in Scotland, so from her point of view it's probably quite convenient.

The Willetts book, in particular, provided food for thought. Willetts, I thought, argued convincingly that the 'oldies' had never had it so good. With a far higher propensity to vote than the younger generation, the oldies ruthlessly ensured that, whoever was in power, spending on pensions and health would go up and up, while they themselves accumulated wealth in far-too-big-for-them houses that they were shamelessly unwilling to vacate.

I had never thought if it like that before. If it's true, I'm surprised the younger generation doesn't make more fuss. Maybe they realise that they too will be old some day.

I did actually make one full-scale hour-long documentary.

My old friend, Sally Doganis, a BAFTA-winning TV producer herself, persuaded *her* old friend, Dorothy Byrne, in charge of news and current affairs at Channel 4, to send me off to Europe to report on the EU and in particular on the way the best-intentioned EU legislation can have unintended consequences.

I travelled to western Greece to film the tobacco growers of Agrinio, who receive subsidies from one department of the

European Commission while another department tries to ban smoking. I visited Spain where my old colleagues from the European Commission's environment department were busy trying to save the endangered Iberian lynx, while other departments were funding hydroelectric schemes that flood the vital habitat on which the lynx depended. Still in Spain, we filmed so-called 'fish farms' off the coast of Murcia, where the young tuna are actually wild-caught, the whole activity contributing to the catastrophic decline in tuna stocks in the Mediterranean.

Back in the UK, we looked into the issue of church organs.

Organ pipes are made of lead, but the EU had declared that lead, a toxic substance, could no longer be used in the manufacture and repair of organ pipes.

C4 filmed me talking to the Vicar of St James, Piccadilly. The organ's wonderful Grinling Gibbons surround was in fine shape, but the instrument itself desperately needed repairing.

'What we really need is a whole new organ or to rebuild this one totally,' the vicar explained.

'You need a very rich organ donor,' I said.

Next day, still on the organ story, we flew to Brussels and the team filmed me interviewing the Swedish Environment Commissioner, Margot Wallström, in her office of the thirteenth floor of the Berlaymont, the European Commission's headquarters.

This was the building where I myself had had my office (on a lower floor, *naturellement*) when I first joined the staff of the Commission at the beginning of April 1973. It was quite a strange feeling. I'd spent so many years in Brussels, looking out from the ivory tower. Now I was looking in.

'What will the good citizens of Nuremburg think,' I asked the Commissioner, 'if, thanks to an EU directive, they are no longer able to hear Buxtehude played on the great organ in the Frauenkirche?'

I didn't pluck that particular example out of thin air. Years ago, in the run-up to Christmas, I was driving back to Brussels from a meeting in Munich. I stopped in Nuremberg on the way home and that evening went to a service in the Frauenkirche. Sometimes, when I am tempted to think all religion is rubbish, I remember the way a Buxtehude organ prelude sounds, played on a wintry evening in a fourteenth-century church in southern Germany.

I asked the Commissioner, straight out and with the cameras rolling, why the Commission didn't give a special exemption from the provisions of the EU's toxic waste directives when lead was needed for the manufacture, replacement or repair of organs.

'We'll do it. We'll definitely do it,' Margot Wallström said.

The Commissioner's chef de cabinet looked worried. His main task in life was to make sure his boss didn't go off piste.

Before we left, I presented the Commissioner with a copy of my novel: *The Commissioner*.

'The Commissioner in my book is actually English,' I explained. 'He is called James Morton and he's played by John Hurt in the film of the book. He has an affair with the Portuguese Commissioner, called Elena, and almost gets blown up by a bomb. Wittamer, the chocolate shop in the Sablon, is completely destroyed in the explosion. Of course, when I wrote the book, there weren't any female commissioners. I had to imagine one.'

Margot Wallström was blonde, petite, very pretty and about forty years younger than me. Imagining her wasn't hard work.

'I shall look forward to reading your book,' she said. Then she added, 'The Belgians take chocolates very seriously, as we all know. Losing Wittamer would have been a big blow.'

Mrs Wallström lived up to her promise. She made sure that the 'organ-pipe' exemption was properly enshrined in the EU directive on the use and disposal of toxic substances.

When I heard the news, I rang Sally Doganis. 'The Commission has agreed the exemption I proposed. Lead can still be used for church organs and so on. Mrs Wallström must have worked hard to get that one through.'

'I guess she pulled out all the stops,' Sally said.

Chapter Twenty-Nine

Climbing Kilimanjaro

One of the high points (literally) in my life has been climbing Mount Kilimanjaro. As a matter of fact, in the past few years I have climbed Africa's highest mountain not once but twice.

Why, one might ask, would anyone want to climb Africa's highest mountain twice? Isn't once enough? Some people might say that once is more than enough.

As far as I am concerned, the short answer to the 'why twice?' question is the telephone call I received one morning from my cousin Colin Williams. Colin had just read my 'My Week' column in the *Sunday Times*. Strictly speaking, I had not actually penned the article myself. The piece was headed, 'As told to Audrey Ward'.

Audrey Ward is not some pen name, like William Hickey, Ephraim Hardcastle or Sebastian Shakespeare. She really exists. We had a very jolly talk on the telephone soon after I arrived, footsore and weary, back in London.

Here is the article as it appeared in the *Sunday Times* on 27 February 2011 (as it happened, Jenny's and my thirtieth wedding anniversary):

I've just returned from scaling Mount Kilimanjaro. You might wonder why I would do such a thing at the age of seventy and rightly so. Last year I became chairman of the Gorilla Organization, a body dedicated to saving the world's last remaining gorillas from extinction. I wanted to raise money for the organisation – these animals are dying out fast; we're down to 700 mountain gorillas in the Virunga Mountains in east Africa.

I've been lucky enough to see the gorillas in the eastern Congo in a wonderful park called Kahuzi-Biega, but gosh, that was quite hairy. I was there in the middle of a war involving the other kind of guerrillas, the human ones, and they were shooting off in all directions.

I was absolutely thrilled by how many people said, 'You're bonkers' when they heard my plans. They made remarks such as 'What about altitude sickness?' and 'Don't you know that the tennis player Martina Navratilova had to be airlifted off the mountain?'

I was never going to be affected by altitude sickness – I played a lot of rugby as a schoolboy and I have a fairly large chest.

I told them I would do some serious training, which I did. It involved climbing up Primrose Hill in north London a couple of times. The Kuoni travel company agreed to sponsor my climb and people have been very generous with their donations. At least one person wrote to say: 'I'll give you even more money if you stay up there.'

When I arrived in Tanzania two weeks ago I was assigned a superb guide, a cook, a waiter and four porters, one of whom was permanently assigned as a loo porter. He carried the loo and a tent, so I had my own personal tent as well as my own personal loo. If the Tanzanians still had a diplomatic honours list he could have been dubbed 'Loo Porter OBE' for services rendered.

Kilimanjaro is one of twelve national parks in Tanzania and getting to the summit is just the icing on the cake. The route we followed, the Rongai route, took us through the rainforest and the moorland and the scenery was spectacular.

Having set off on a Wednesday, I did some very long days of walking and on the Saturday night I made my final push to Gilman's

Point. Fortunately there was a full moon and the rocky route was well illuminated.

By 10 a.m. on Sunday I had reached the summit. It was a brilliantly sunny day. In the distance I could see the other great volcano, Mawenzi, sticking up out of the clouds.

I'm afraid I had no profound thoughts on reaching the top of the mountain. As I get older my mind is blank most of the time.

However, I do remember thinking: 'This is jolly good but what a pity I left my mobile phone in the front pocket of seat 27C on the plane to Nairobi. It will take me some time to get the news of this great exploit out to the world.'

It was a long haul down. I finally got back to the base on Wednesday. By then my feet were absolutely killing me and when I landed at Heathrow last Thursday morning I could barely limp off the plane.

Fortunately, when I arrived at the terminal there was an elderly Indian lady who had booked a buggy. She looked about ninety years old and I asked, 'Do you mind if I share your buggy?'

She agreed, so I got in and the lights flashed and the engine blipped and bleeped as we drove along. I'm so glad there was no one I knew there to witness my undignified arrival in a mobile wagon.

The *Sunday Times* printed a photo of me, carrying a large banner with the words: 'The Gorilla Organization – Saving Gorillas from Extinction.' It was the photo that caught my cousin's attention. Colin had been a very generous supporter of my fundraising effort on behalf of the Gorilla Organization.

Here is how the conversation went.

'Hello, Stan. I gather from the paper this morning you're safely back. Congratulations! How are the feet?'

'Much better, thanks, Colin. And thanks for all your support. Terrific!'

'Just one thing, Stan,' Colin continued. 'I've been looking at the photo they printed with the article. What's that peak behind you, covered in ice?'

I have to admit that I was slightly miffed but I didn't show it. I didn't want Colin asking for his donation back on the grounds that I hadn't got to the top.

'Just the camera angle, Colin. I got the 'Kilimanjaro Summit' certificate, I can assure you.'

After I had put the phone down, I found that Colin's comment still niggled. I had been quite correct in saying that I had got the certificate. We picked it up at the Tanzanian National Park office. I was so late getting down the mountain that my guide had to phone ahead asking the park people to keep the office open till I staggered in. The document clearly certifies that I have 'climbed Mount Kilimanjaro, having reached Gilman's Point (5,681 metres above Mean Sea Level or 18,710 feet)'.

Technically, though, I admit Colin had a point.

I hadn't on that first attempt actually reached the very highest point on Mount Kilimanjaro, which is Uhuru Peak. Uhuru Peak, at 5,895 metres (or 19,431 feet) is over 200 metres (more than 650 feet) higher than Gilman's Point.

Why hadn't I gone the whole hog, as it were?

The honest answer is that I was whacked by the time I reached Gilman's Point. I was late arriving at the rim of the crater that day. All the other climbers had been miles ahead of me. And it had begun to snow. My guide told me it would take another hour, maybe more, to trudge on round the crater to Uhuru Peak and back, and after that there would be the long haul down.

That was where matters stood until, a few months later, I received a call from a young woman called Emily, who worked for the Development Office of Exeter College, Oxford, my old college. In 2014, she told me, the College would be celebrating the seventieth anniversary of its foundation and it wanted to mark that occasion in a fitting manner. Some twenty Exonians would climb Kilimanjaro to boost Exeter College's 700th Anniversary Fund. She knew I had climbed the mountain before. Did I want to do it again?

I wouldn't say I jumped at the opportunity. I said 'no', I said 'yes' and then I said 'no'. But in the end, the idea of actually 'knocking the bastard off', as Sir Edmund Hillary put it when he and Tenzing 'conquered' Mount Everest in 1953, proved irresistible. Deep down, I knew that my line about there being more than one summit on Kilimanjaro was basically untenable. You can't have more than one prime minister. You can have a prime minister and a deputy prime minister. Ask Nick Clegg.

A few days later I received a solid information pack from Global Adventure Challenges, the company Emily had hired to organise our trek, telling me how to deal with altitude sickness (basically: 'if you can't stand the height, get off the mountain') and offering me the chance to do some practice climbs in the Brecon Beacons.

I wrote back by return to say that the dates proposed for the Welsh weekend didn't work for me and, anyway, last time round, I had just waltzed up Primrose Hill by way of preparation.

As it happened, my son Leo was launching his new book, *Turnaround Challenge*, in London on the scheduled departure day, so instead of heading for Heathrow, I went to Daunt's on Marylebone High Street for a well-attended party. But I caught up with my fellow Exonians a couple of days later. They had already pitched their tents on the lower slopes of the mountain and were enjoying a sing-song around the camp stove with the guides and porters.

I began to regret my lack of serious training. The men and women who shook me so warmly by the hand looked so young and fit. Yes, they had all gone to the same college as I had, but about four decades later! The chief guide, Mohammed, interrupted the festivities: 'Welcome to Kilimanjaro, Grandpa!'

Perhaps in deference to my seniority, I didn't have to share a tent. This made a tremendous difference. I could struggle with the zip on my sleeping bag without anyone else hearing my muttered curses.

From my point of view, the first couple of days were quite straightforward. We trekked across the high moorland scenery of the Shira plateau, climbing up to the Lava Tower at 4,600 metres, before descending to spend the night in camp at around 3,960 metres. The golden rule, so Mohammed told us, is 'Walk High, Sleep Low'.

The first real challenge came on Day Four when we came to the Great Barranco Wall. Even though I had climbed the mountain before, I had taken a different route and never had to tackle the GBW. I began to regret that I had passed up the opportunity to put in some training in Wales.

Global Adventure Challenges not only worked out the logistics of getting twenty people up Africa's highest mountain in one piece and all at the same time, they also provided us with a great leader in Anna Crampin, a young Scottish woman. As I was flailing around, trying to keep my balance while groping my way up what seemed to be a sheer cliff face, she called out encouragingly, 'Keep contact with the rock in at least three places, Grandpa! You don't want to fall off.'

The porters throughout were brilliant. They made the whole thing possible. Yes, we carried our daypacks and water bottles. But they did the heavy lifting.

Apart from all the other kit and caboodle they carried up the mountain, the porters hauled a large dining tent, together with

Looking for gorillas in the Democratic Republic of the Congo, 2004.

Chimanuka emerges from the jungle, Democratic Republic of the Congo, 2004

In the Brazilian Amazon, December 2004.

With an orang-utan, Tanjung Puting National Park, Kalimantan, Indonesia, 2005.

First visit to the
Galápagos, 2006.

Cuverville Island,
Antarctic Peninsula:
leopard seal captures
gentoo penguin, 2007.

With a grey whale in
San Ignacio lagoon,
Baja California,
Mexico, 2007.

Campaigning for Boris in the 2012 London mayoral election.

The hot-air balloon crash-landed, Masai Mara, Kenya 2009.

Champagne breakfast in the Masai Mara, Kenya, 2009.

With Dr Jane Goodall, Gombe, Lake Tanganyika, Tanzania, 2010.

Fifty years on: return visit to Machu Picchu, 2010.

With Max at the Great Wall of China, 2011.

With Jenny in Bhutan, 2008.

Wearing the traditional Bhutanese 'gho' at the coronation of Bhutan's King Jigme Khesar Namgyel Wangchuck, November 2008.

Celebrating the fortieth anniversary of the United Nations Environment Programme. Dr Achim Steiner, UNEP's executive director is on the left. Next to him is Donald Kaniaru, former UNEP senior official. Dr Mostafa Tolba, former UNEP executive director is in the middle. Amina Mohammed, then UNEP deputy ED, is second from right. On the far right is Professor Klaus Töepfer, another former UNEP ED and also former German Environment Minister. Nairobi, Kenya, 2012. I took the photo!

With Huli tribesmen,
Papua New Guinea, 2014.

With William Hague,
Foreign Secretary, Bogotá,
Colombia, 2014.

Boris Johnson's XI versus
Earl Spencer's XI, Althorp,
Northamptonshire, June 2014.
Kevin Pietersen, sixth from right
in cap, was our surprise 'ringer'!

The family gathers at Nethercote for my seventieth birthday, August 2010.

Team Johnson plays Winsford at cricket, August 2010.

From left to right: Jo, Leo, Boris, Stanley and Max.

Boris and Jo make runs but, on the Johnson side, Leo was top scorer!

With Rachel at the launch of her novel *Winter Games*, March 2013.

MAGAZINE OF THE YEAR

THE WEEK

4 MAY 2013 | ISSUE 916 | £2.80   THE BEST OF THE BRITISH AND FOREIGN MEDIA

Blond ambition
The irresistible rise of the Johnsons
Page 6

ALL YOU NEED TO KNOW ABOUT EVERYTHING THAT MATTERS   www.theweek.co.uk

The Week cover image, 4 May 2013.

Lois Sieff's ninetieth birthday celebration, February 2014. Jenny, Lois's daughter, is on the left. Adam Sieff, Lois's son, is on the right.

With David Cameron, Prime Minister, and Peter Tatchell, political campaigner, at the entrance to Downing Street, 8 April 2014. Prime Minister David Cameron promises us that the government will ban the use of wild animals in circuses. We are still waiting!

folding tables and chairs. Each day, they strode on ahead of us, laden to the gunwales. By the time we arrived at the next staging-post, the tent was already in place and the table set. The kettle had boiled and cups of steaming hot tea or chocolate were waiting for us, with dinner soon to follow.

After supper in the communal 'dining room' that last night, we headed off to our tents. The idea was to snatch an hour or two of sleep before setting out. I lay on my back with my eyes shut, wondering if I ought to make a 'last call' home. But I couldn't get a signal and anyway the battery on my phone was flat. (At least I hadn't left it on the plane!)

At around 10 p.m. on Day 8 we set off from the last campsite at Barafu Camp (4,600 metres) to begin the grindingly long ascent through the ice and scree to the crater's rim.

There was no moon, so we had to rely on our head-torches. Six hours or so later, the first rays of the sun streaked the clouds. And those clouds, I realised as I gazed back down the slope, were actually far beneath us! Even so, when I turned to look ahead, I could see that there was still, literally, a 'mountain to climb' ahead of us.

It was well after 8 a.m. before I reached the lip of the crater. At more or less this point, last time round, with a blizzard in the offing, I had decided to call it a day.

Anna, our leader, who had stayed behind with me, even as the others strode on, was concerned about whether I would make it.

'Are you sure you want to go on round the crater to Uhuru Peak?' she asked, as we paused to draw breath. 'It's a long haul and then you've got to get all the way back down to camp.'

I admit I was the last to arrive at Uhuru Peak but I made it in the end. Most of my colleagues were already heading back down the mountain by the time I reached the summit. But a small group had lingered and I arrived in time to enjoy one of the most extraordinary panoramas in the world. You can look north to Mt Kenya, east to the coast or west to the great forests of Central Africa. To the south, a mighty glacier dominates the view. The 'snows of Kilimanjaro' may be melting because of global warming but, to the untutored eye at least, they are still totally awesome.

When I finally staggered back into camp that afternoon, my feet were killing me but my spirits were as high as the mountaintop itself. I was already mentally composing a text to cousin Colin.

That particular 'high' didn't last. I had thought we were going to be able to spend the night at Barafu Camp, the 'summit assault' camp that we had left by now eighteen hours earlier. But other summiteers had arrived and we had to trek on down to a lower level.

I told Anna I could barely walk and that I really couldn't face another two-hour trek.

'They can run you down on the blood wagon,' Anna said. 'It's pretty uncomfortable, but they'll get you there.'

Uncomfortable was the word. They strapped me to a stretcher, then tied the stretcher onto a one-wheeled trolley and took me down the mountain at the double to the next camp, a thousand feet below. We hit boulders and crevasses en route and the trolley reared and bucked with me on it. I have never been so shaken up in my life.

A good night's sleep made the world of difference.

'Glad to see you're off your trolley today,' Anna Crampin said next morning when, poles in hand, I joined the group on its onward and downward march.

On the subject of trekking poles, having now climbed Mount Kilimanjaro twice within the space of three years, I would say that having a pair of stout trekking poles is absolutely essential. Actually, you need them more on the way down than on the way up. I'm sure there's a moral here somewhere.

Chapter Thirty

Father of the Mayor

I was sitting on the terrace of our house in Pelion, looking out at the calm waters of the Pagasitic Gulf. In the far distance, I could see Mt Parnassus, home of the gods. Out of the blue, a couple of jet fighters with swept-back wings swept low overhead. There's a military base near Volos, about 40 miles away. From time to time, the Greeks like to show the Turks that they still mean business in this part of the Aegean.

Sometimes (accidentally on purpose?), the Greek planes penetrate Turkish airspace – or vice versa – and everyone gets very steamed up about it.

Back in London, around the middle of July 2007, the Conservative Party was getting steamed up about the forthcoming London mayoral election. There was less than a year to go. They needed a candidate to challenge Ken Livingstone, the incumbent.

My mobile phone rang. It was Stuart Reid from *The Spectator*. Boris, he said, had just indicated that he was ready to run for the post of Mayor of London. There would have to be a Conservative 'primary' first, of course. Other candidates might put their hats in the ring too.

'Would you like to comment?' Stuart asked. 'If so, could I have, say, 1,100 words, by 7 p.m. tonight?'

I want to make it clear that I do not in any way consider myself to be a Joseph Kennedy figure, seeking by all means to promote the careers of my children. The idea is patently ludicrous. Joseph P. Kennedy was a man who wheeled and dealed his way to wealth and power. My career pattern, I would say, has been pretty much in the opposite direction.

That said, from time to time, I do what I can to help. I didn't imagine that an article by me in *The Spectator* would swing many votes in the upcoming Conservative primary, but what the heck...

I installed my laptop on a table by the pool with a glass of wine next to it and started typing.

I have never minded a short deadline. It's the thinking, not the writing, that slows you down.

Happily, Greece in July is an hour ahead of London, so I beat the clock fairly comfortably.

Here's how I began:

Boris was born in New York on 19 June 1964. I missed the birth since I had slipped outside for a moment to buy a pizza. When I first saw him he was bundled up in the hospital nursery with only the soles of his feet showing. These were completely black. This puzzled me. Had his mother, I wondered, somehow managed to give birth to the wrong baby?

I later discovered that in New York, for reasons of security, newborn babies' feet are dipped in black ink and an imprint taken for the record. Apparently there is no point in fingerprinting an infant as the skin on their tiny hands is too soft.

It didn't occur to me at that moment, just over forty-three years ago, that I might be looking at the insteps of a future Mayor of London. Like most new parents, my predominant emotion was gratitude that Boris had managed to emerge into the light of day with limbs and mental faculties apparently intact.

I have been in Greece for the last few days, so I have had to follow the mayoral saga at long distance. I knew that Boris was thinking about standing for mayor and, for what my tuppence was worth, urged him to do so. When I checked into the internet café in Milina, Pelion, Greece, on Monday morning, I learned from the BBC website that he had taken the plunge.

Over the years I have learned not to be surprised by Boris. As a parent, I remember attending a performance of *Richard II* in the Cloisters at Eton where Boris was playing the title role. It was fairly obvious that he hadn't learned the part, but he winged it splendidly, inventing on the hoof a sequence of nearly perfect Shakespearian pentameters.

There have been many streaks of sheer precocity in Boris's career. A few years ago, when most of us would have hung up our boots, I watched him score a brutally efficient try from a line-out (the *Daily Telegraph* rugby team was playing some north London side). He once wrote a superb parody of Dr Seuss's *Cat in the Hat* which is worth digging up from the archives. He takes after his mother in being a talented artist. Of course, I was thrilled when he won Henley to become a Conservative MP, less thrilled when Michael Howard sent him to Liverpool. Whatever else you may say about Boris, he is not a plodder.

Bursting with pride, I went on in that vein for several more paragraphs. Stuart had asked for 1,100 words and 1,100 words was what he got.

We all know the result of the mayoral contest in 2008 and the subsequent rerun of the Boris *v.* Ken Livingstone match in 2012. If I allude to these matters now, it is simply because the 'Boris phenomenon' as Conrad Black once put it, has definitely had an impact on my life (and, I suspect, on the lives of other members of the family) and it would be disingenuous of me to pretend otherwise.

From my point of view, I regard that impact as being totally positive. I am honoured to be known as Boris's dad. On the whole I don't go around looking for the downside where any particular turn of events may be concerned, and I frankly can't see what the downside is here. OK, people in cars occasionally shout jocund, even ribald comments when I'm riding my bicycle round Hyde Park Corner with my mobile phone to my ear. Bully for them, I say. If they can shout and drive, that's fine. Anything to liven up a dull day.

When I'm asked in the street what it's like being the 'father of the mayor', I don't brush people off or look shifty.

'Well actually,' I say, 'I regard myself as being tremendously lucky. Privileged. Totally privileged. Wouldn't you?'

Of course, things are not always totally straightforward. I am quite heavily involved at the moment in trying to stop the high-speed train known as HS2 going less than ten metres from our front door in London. Boris is Mayor of London and in favour of HS2. My third son, Jo, is MP for Orpington, and also a minister in 10 Downing Street, with responsibility for the government's policy unit.

I have to be tremendously careful not to talk to them about matters in which they have official duties and responsibilities. I have found that by far the best way is to communicate through the press, the radio and TV. *Urbi et orbi*, as it were. We all have to remember nowadays that under the Freedom of Information Act there is no such thing as a private communication even between consenting adults.

So everything I feel Boris or Jo ought to know about the HS2, for example, I put in the public domain as it were. I know this sounds tremendously pompous, but this is just one of the hazards of life nowadays.

Strangely, I have to be careful what I say to Rachel too. Having retired with full battle honours as editor of *The Lady*, Rachel is now a columnist for the *Mail on Sunday*. When I (briefly) wrote regularly for *The Guardian*, I used to take out a little red notebook when someone said something funny and write it down on the spot. Sometimes I would ask them to repeat it if I didn't get it down right. That, as I understand it, is what professional journalists are meant to do. Not that I've had any training as a journalist. I imagine that's fairly obvious.

Rachel is much more subtle. She is able to remember things without writing them down. You can make a perfectly good joke, a joke that, given care and attention, could probably be reused a fair number of times, and then – all of a sudden – it pops up in print somewhere.

People, even members of one's own family, can be pretty ruthless about using one's jokes without attribution. Take the line about being *pro*-secco and *anti*-pasto. I am sure I thought of that one first. I can put a date and a place to it. We were having a family holiday in a house near Gaiole in Chianti, in the summer of 1974. My mother was staying with us too. I had an old Super 8 camera and I took a film of us having lunch on the terrace, looking out over the Tuscan Hills. The camera had a recorder too.

'Here we are!' I say, with my eye to the camera's view-finder. 'Look at this groaning board. A typical Italian peasant feast. Granny Butter is just having a crack at the pasta. Pass Granny the wine, someone!' Pan to audience. 'I'm definitely *pro*-secco, but a bit *anti*-pasto…'

Chapter Thirty-One

Who Do You Think You Are?

A nother unexpected and, from my point of view, intriguing result of Boris's 'rise and rise' was the screening of the BBC's *Who Do You Think You Are?* documentary in April 2008 and the light that shed on the Johnson family history.

The production company behind the programme, one of a continuing series of that name, was called Wall-to-Wall. The energy they put into the project was truly phenomenal. They had researchers all over Europe digging around in dusty archives and coming up with all sorts of extraordinary facts.

For example, they plunged deeply into the 'de Pfeffel' connection.

My mother was always very proud of her French heritage. She had been born in Versailles, in a house that had once belonged to Madame Du Barry, Louis XV having presented it to his mistress. The house was at the time known as the Pavilion du Barry, though it has since found a new vocation as the seat of the Chambre de Commerce et d'Industrie de Versailles.

My French great-grandfather, the man who had bought Madame Du Barry's house at the beginning of the twentieth century was – I always thought – Baron Hubert Théodore Marie Charles Cretien de Pfeffel.

I was wrong! The Wall-to-Wall team, lavishly funded by tax-payers' money via the BBC, turned up some startling facts. The de Pfeffels were not French after all.

The researchers revealed that de Pfeffels weren't French – they were actually German. My great-grandfather's correct name wasn't Baron Hubert Théodore Marie Charles Cretien de Pfeffel. It was Baron Hubert Théodore Marie Charles Cretien *von* Pfeffel.

Of course, I was rocked by this revelation. In 1964, when I had registered Boris's birth at the British Consulate in New York, I had written his full name down as Alexander Boris de Pfeffel Johnson, my mother having promised the de Pfeffel silver to the first grandchild to bear that historic name. Now I realised I should have written von Pfeffel!

What might that have done, I wonder, to Boris's political prospects? But there were more shocks in store.

The programme made for riveting viewing. Boris, followed by a film crew, rushes about Europe trying to track down his ancestors. My sister, Birdie, is shown arriving at Boris's home in Islington with some vital documents.

An extraordinary paperchase ensues.

Baron Hubert's father, Karl von Pfeffel, marries Karoline von Rothenburg in 1836. Boris discovers that their wedding took place in the Bishop of Augsburg's private chapel, almost in secret, and the witnesses were no less than the president of the government and the Mayor of Augsburg. In a further twist, all the papers relating to the wedding were held by the bishop – something extremely unusual that suggested someone was trying to keep events under wraps.

It seems that Karoline was already pregnant when she was married – she gave birth four months later – which might account for the secrecy. But why would the wedding take place with such remarkable high-profile witnesses? The answer came in a note scribbled on the original marriage licence. In pencil the writer recorded that Karoline's father was Prince Paul of Württemberg, younger brother of the King of Württemberg.

'She was secretly connected,' explains Boris to the camera. 'It was important that when she became pregnant, she should get married.' It turns out that Karoline herself was illegitimate, the result of a liaison between the Prince and an actress, but it seems her father was still determined to look after her when she became pregnant.

From there researchers were able to rapidly discover more about our German roots. Prince Paul of Württemberg is the son of King Friedrich II of Württemberg who is married to Queen Auguste Caroline Braunschweig-Wolfenbüttel. Queen Auguste Caroline is the daughter of Augusta Hanover, the Princess Royal and she in turn is the daughter of Frederick Louis Hanover, the Prince of Wales. The Prince of Wales is, of course, the oldest son of King George II of England, though he died before he could accede to the throne.

At this point, Boris comments with tongue firmly in cheek, 'I would have been tremendously proud to have been a descendant of a German king, but I can't hide from it. Even in our common European home, I was particularly thrilled to find some link to British royalty!'

Boris then embarks on a rapid tour of southern Germany, as he puts it 'hovering up the schlosses' in which the ancestors lived. He strides through gilded salons, gazing at portraits of old red-faced gentlemen and their well-coiffed full-bosomed wives, only to calculate by the end of the programme that if King George II is his great x 8 grandparent, he shares that distinction with 1,023 other people!

My only regret watching the film was that I didn't try to stop my parents selling the 'de Pfeffel' silver that features in the film. I still have the catalogue of the Sotheby's sale, dated 21 July 1977, the 'de Pfeffel tea set' prominently displayed.

I was working in Brussels when my mother told me she planned to put the de Pfeffel tea set on the market. 'Pa and I want to go to Australia to see Hillie and Pete and the children,' she wrote. 'We think we need to sell the silver to pay for the trip.'

I felt a twinge of guilt. Boris's middle name was 'de Pfeffel'. Would he mind?

The sale was imminent. There wasn't time to consult. 'Of course you must sell the tea set,' I wrote back.

Looking back, I much regret that we hadn't looked for some other way to help my parents' make their long-planned trip to Australia.

The 'de Pfeffel silver' was very much a feature of my childhood. It had been kept in its special octagonal oak case in the 'middle kitchen' at Nethercote. As children, we used to sit around it, playing Cluedo or Monopoly on top of the solid oak surface. Once, when R. W. Powell, headmaster of my old school, Sherborne, was on a tour of the West Country and decided to 'drop in' for tea, my mother got the silver out of the case and we all spent the afternoon polishing it.

I had no idea – until the Wall-to-Wall researchers discovered the truth – that the 'de Pfeffel silver' had actually been presented by Prince Paul of Württemberg to his (illegitimate) daughter, Karoline von Rothenburg, on the occasion of her marriage to Karl von Pfeffel!

All efforts to find out what has happened to the 'de Pfeffel silver' since that Sotheby's sale have proved fruitless. Maybe someone will put it on eBay and we'll be able to buy it back.

If the BBC's *Who Do You Think You Are?* had, in its own way, been wonderfully funny as far as the 'de Pfeffel' side of the family was concerned, the reverse was true when it came to the Turkish sequences. They were sad beyond belief.

I described in the first volume of this memoir, *Stanley, I Presume*, how my paternal grandmother, Winifred, died of puerperal fever a few days after my father was born. I knew that, of course, even before the BBC film. Winifred had a sister, Viva, who lived in Geneva. She was very close to Winifred. I met her once at her home in Switzerland and she told me the whole sad tale.

'Your grandfather, Ali Kemal, thought it was too dangerous for your grandmother, Winifred, to stay in Turkey. He had too many enemies. She went to England to have the baby. She was heavily pregnant. She had to transfer from a small boat to the ship in the Bosphorus and maybe she suffered an injury. I was in Egypt when I received a message. "Come at once." I just had time to get to Bournemouth to see her before she died.'

As one of Boris's 'ancestors', I had a small walk-on part in the BBC programme. I am filmed showing Boris my father's birth certificate, which the BBC researchers had somehow located.

'Here it is,' I say. 'My father's birth is registered at the Bournemouth Register Office as Wilfred Osman Kemal, born 4 September 1909.'

Then I muse, 'If we had kept the Kemal name, Cameron would probably have put me on the A-list of Conservative candidates!'

I also described in *Stanley, I Presume* how, during my gap-year travels in 1959, I travelled to Turkey for the first time to meet my Turkish family. In Istanbul I met Sabiha, who married my grandfather, Ali Kemal, after his first wife, Winifred's death. I went on to Ankara where I met my father's half-brother, Zeki Kuneralp, a senior Turkish diplomat, Sabiha's only child, married to Neçla. I also met their two boys, my Turkish cousins, Sinan and Selim.

When Neçla was murdered by terrorists (they had been hoping to kill Zeki but they killed his wife instead), I flew out to Turkey for the funeral. I walked behind the gun-carriage as the cortège processed through the streets of Ankara. Later that day, I flew in a military plane with the Turkish high command to Istanbul, where Neçla was buried in a cemetery above the Golden Horn.

I shall never forget the moment when Sabiha came up to me after the funeral to say (in French), 'This is the second time in my life that I have lost a person most dear to me through an act of violence. First, my husband – your grandfather – was killed. And now my dear daughter-in-law, Neçla, has been taken away.'

My father almost never talked about his father. This is not so surprising. Turkey was on the 'wrong' side in the war. Ali Kemal was pursuing his journalistic and political career there. But my father, who had been born in England, was growing up in England too. He was a fourteen-year-old English schoolboy, with a love of cricket, when Ali Kemal was murdered. He never spoke of that event. I don't know if he had any actual memories of his father. If he did, he didn't speak of them.

What the BBC film did so brilliantly was to fill in the gaps of a story that, truth to tell, I knew only in outline.

For example, there is a moment in the film when my cousin, Sinan, himself a distinguished archivist, shows Boris, in a dusty Istanbul library, some newspaper reports of Ali Kemal's death. When the camera focuses on a photo of Ali Kemal hanging from a tree after being lynched by an angry mob, both Sinan and Boris are visibly moved.

'They removed his trousers before they hanged him,' Sinan gulps.

In 1918, the Allies occupied Turkey. Ali Kemal is made Minister of the Interior in the new regime. But he makes a big mistake. Mustafa Kemal has already embarked on his mission to revolutionise Turkey. He has set up a provisional government in Anatolia. He plans to advance on Istanbul and seize power from the Sultan and his government.

The researchers have been able to track down the actual cable that Ali Kemal sends to official government posts throughout the length and breadth of Turkey. The cable forbids any help or succour to be offered to the rebels.

In the film, Boris recognises that Ali Kemal's actions represent a 'serious political mistake', but he comments, 'Is it not possible that Ali Kemal just had the best interests of Turkey at heart? Maybe he thought, look, this guy – Mustafa Kemal – is trouble. All he wants to do is take on the French and the Brits, he's going to cause us no end of bother. All Ali Kemal wanted was diplomacy.'

A few days after the film was shown, I got a call from the *Daily Mail*. 'How did the Johnsons get their blonde hair?' the reporter asked. 'Was it the Turkish connection?'

I flew to Ankara with a *Daily Mail* photographer in tow. My cousin, Selim, now a senior diplomat with the Turkish Foreign Office, met me in Ankara and kindly offered to come with me to Kalfat, a town in eastern Anatolia where my great-grandfather Ahmet Hamdi came from.

'Does the Mayor of Kalfat know we are coming, Selim?' I asked.

'There may be a small reception party,' Selim replied.

This turned out to be the understatement of the year. The total population of Kalfat is probably around 2,000 and a high proportion seemed to be waiting for us that morning as we drove into the village. They had gathered in front of the mayor's office, ready to greet Selim and me. I must have shaken hands a hundred times that morning. As a matter of fact, as is the Turkish custom, I was frequently embraced on both cheeks. Some men actually kneeled to kiss my hand.

Selim whispered to me. 'Our great-grandfather was the first man from Kalfat to make the haj to Mecca. They are honouring you for that. He was known as Ahmet Hamdi *Haci*. Haci means someone who has made the haj.'

The Mayor of Kalfat made a speech of welcome in Turkish. My knowledge of that language being shamefully slight, Suat Kiniklioglu, the local MP, translated for me.

'He's saying how much the people of Kalfat welcome you and your cousin Selim here today. They are particularly proud about Boris becoming Mayor of London. He hopes that Boris himself may be able to come to Kalfat one day soon and he wonders if it might be possible for Kalfat to be twinned with London!'

I made a brief speech in reply, which Suat translated for the benefit of the rapt audience. I was very sorry, I said, that Boris himself had not been able to come. I had spoken to him by telephone that morning and he had sent his very best wishes. My cousin Selim and I felt honoured beyond measure by the reception we had received.

'As for Kalfat being twinned with London,' I added, 'I feel sure that London will be deeply honoured!'

I ended my remarks with one of the few Turkish expressions I know. '*Teshekur ederim. Chok teshekur.*' Thank you. Thank you very much.

They were simple but heartfelt words. As I stood there, surrounded by men (yes, all men) who under other circumstances might have been my compatriots, I felt profoundly moved. More than 150 years ago my great-grandfather had made the journey from Kalfat to Istanbul. What a lot of water had flown through the Bosphorus since then.

My reveries were interrupted when Suat turned to me. 'Stanley-bey,' he asked, 'the mayor would like to know whether you want to see Ahmet Hamdi's house and to meet the family.'

I couldn't believe my ears. I hadn't remotely imagined that Ahmet Hamdi's house might still survive or that my own relatives would still be around.

The whole village wanted to follow us down the street but the mayor waved them back. A reduced band of twenty or thirty of us walked a couple of hundred yards past the mosque, then turned right to come to a stop on a piece of open ground. Many of the houses in Kalfat today are of fairly modern construction. Turks don't seem to be as sentimental about old pieces of masonry as we are. Many of Kalfat's present residents have worked in Germany and, perhaps as a result of this, have been quite happy on their return to pull down their old homes and replace them with something more modern.

But the house we found ourselves standing in front of was of a kind I recognised from my previous trip through Anatolia, back in 1959, a solid stone and wood construction, with a splendid balcony. (The Turks have a saying: 'A man without a tummy is like a house without a balcony.')

Standing immediately next to it was another even older house in a state of some disrepair. A Turkish family was waiting to greet us. I recognised one or two of them as people I had already greeted that morning in the line-up outside the mayor's office.

Suat listened to the introductions, then summarised for me: 'These are Ahmet Hamdi's relatives, members of your Turkish family. This is Ahmet Demir, this is his wife, Aslihan Demir. This is Ahmet's father, Behir, and his wife. Behir's father was Riza and his grandfather was Haci Ahmet. They call him Haci because – like your great-grandfather, Ahmet Hamdi – he made the haj to the Holy Places. Haci Ahmet's father, Ali, was probably Ahmet Hamdi's brother.'

Suat saved the best till last. 'The family is still known in the village by the name they used to have before Ataturk introduced surnames to Turkey?' 'And what is that?' 'Sarioglangil ... the family of the blonde boys.'

Ahmet and Aslihan Demir had a three-year-old son, Ómer Berkay Demir. Young Ómer was presented to me. I held him in my arms while we had our photo taken. The sun shone from behind the minaret. Its rays caught the fine-spun white-gold hair. On the evidence, there was a whole clan of blondes here and one way or another they were all related to me.

I flew from Ankara to Istanbul on the way home. The journey across Anatolia that had taken my great-grandfather, Ahmet Hamdi, twelve days in 1850 took less than an hour. I was met at Istanbul airport by Selim's older brother, Sinan, a publisher. We spent the afternoon together tracking down some of the post-Kalfat landmarks of the Ahmet Hamdi story. In Istanbul, so the story goes, Ahmet Hamdi bought and married a young Circassian slave girl called Nanife Feride. And it was in this city, in the Suleimanye district, that their child, my grandfather, Ali Kemal, was brought up, together with his sisters.

Towards sunset on my last night in Turkey, Sinan and I walked down the famous Pera Street (now known as Istiklal Çaddesi or Independence Avenue). It was here, on 4 November 1922, in a barber's shop near the Cercle d'Orient Club, that my grandfather Ali Kemal was abducted.

'He was smuggled by boat that same night over the Sea of Marmara to Izmit,' Sinan told me, 'then brutally murdered on the orders of Nureddin Pasha.'

Today, Ali Kemal remains a controversial figure in Turkey. He opposed Turkey's entry into the First World War and was forbidden to speak out or publish while it lasted. After the war, he effectively signed his own death warrant by refusing to leave Istanbul even after the Sultan himself had fled. He was only fifty-three when he died.

Chapter Thirty-Two

Wild Animals

For the past ten years, I have spent a fair proportion of my time travelling round the world, writing about wild animals as a journalist or on behalf of the United Nations. (I am an honorary ambassador for the United Nations Environment Programme's Convention on Migratory Species.)

In May 2004, for example, I saw my first gorilla in the wild. I was visiting Kahuzi-Biega, a national park in the eastern Congo, with Greg Cummings, then the director of the Gorilla Organization, and Andrew Crowley, a *Daily Telegraph* photographer.

We had set off from the park headquarters at Tsivanga at about 10 a.m. and spent the next two hours following a wildly gushing watercourse upstream, climbing steeply all the time. The trackers, as usual, were somewhere up there ahead of us and messages were passed regularly on the radio.

After a particularly strenuous uphill stretch, when it seemed that we were dragging ourselves up a vertical slope clutching at roots and branches, we heard a sudden stentorian roar as a full-grown male gorilla burst out of the undergrowth. I knew what I was meant to do. The chief guide at Tsivanga, Robert Mulimbi, had briefed us. 'If a gorilla charges, stand still,' he said. 'Lower your head. Look submissive.' He looked pointedly at me. 'Better wear a hat. If they see your fair hair, they may think you're another silverback.'

Yes, I knew what to do all right. But when Chimanuka sprang from the bush in all his glory, I didn't stand my ground and lower my head. I jumped behind our pygmy tracker and held my breath.

This was a huge and magnificent animal. I had never seen anything like it before. We share 96 per cent of our DNA with gorillas. Man and gorilla may descend from a common ancestor.

Shock and awe. That's what you feel when you first see a gorilla in the wild.

Chimanuka must have charged us half a dozen times that morning. He seemed to enjoy it. The pattern went as follows: a charge would be followed by a period of chewing the cud. He would sit on his haunches, rolling his eyes and swiping the available vegetation with his long prehensile arms so as to grab any surrounding fruits or succulent stalks. After ten minutes or so, he would rise, turn away from us to show off his magnificent coat (it really is silver), before crashing off again through the undergrowth.

But he never went very far. It was almost as if he wanted us to catch up.

He seemed to wait for us. Perhaps that is what being 'habituated' means. At all events, our team of guards and guides would take out their pangas and thwack away and, a few minutes later, we would have the benefit of a repeat performance.

Paradoxically, even though there are still more Grauer's gorillas in the world (and all of them in the DRC) than mountain gorillas, the threat to the Grauer's may be more acute.

Take the eastern, more mountainous part of the Kahuzi-Biega National Park, the part we were in that day. In 1996, there were 254 gorillas there. Four years later, the number had fallen to 130. Today, there are probably fewer than 100. The continued presence of armed rebels in the park has been a major factor in this.

As far as the much larger western part of Kahuzi-Biega is concerned, the situation is even more dire. There are certainly substantial contingents of armed rebels inside the park. Another factor is the presence of as many as 8,000 'artisanal' coltan miners, mainly poor people who have made their way into the park to work the alluvial deposits of coltan or to quarry the minerals from the rocks.

As far as the gorillas are concerned, the combination of the two has been lethal. Nobody knows for sure how many Grauer's gorillas are left there. At one time, there were more than 10,000 in the lowland part of Kahuzi-Biega. Now the figure may be fewer than 1,000.

In September 2005, I went with Hylton Murray-Philipson to the Amazon, in the Brazilian state of Acre, near the Peruvian border. Hylton is a man of many distinctions. One of them is that, through his friendship with Tashka Yawanawa, he is a kind of 'honorary' member of the Yawanawa tribe.

We flew from Rio Branco to Tarauaca, a small town about 300 miles to the west, then another 80 miles in a small single-engine air taxi to a rough landing strip in the jungle. Then we canoed all day up-river.

River journeys in the upper reaches of the Amazon basin have their own rhythms and cadences. The helmsman stands at the back of the canoe watching the swirling water like a hawk. The river is full of floating trees and submerged logs. If you hit one, you can easily capsize. Or else, as the depth of the water changes from one second to the next, you can come to a shuddering halt on a sandbar. If that happens, you have to jump and try to manhandle the canoe over or around the obstacle, hoping that the piranhas and the alligators are looking the other way.

We spent the night in a hut on the river bank. By 5 a.m. the next day, we were back on the river and by noon we had reached the Yawanawa village of Mutum. This is the fiefdom of Tashka's father, Raimundo. Approaching his ninetieth birthday, Raimundo decided a year or two ago to hand over the chieftaincy to his son, Tashka, but in his own village he still called the shots.

As we sat there in his house, eating bananas and fending off mosquitoes, the old man started reminiscing about his wives and children. He had had seven wives altogether, although never more than four at a time.

'I had forty-seven children by my first three wives,' he said.

'Fifteen sons survived.'

'How many daughters?' we asked.

Raimundo didn't seem to know the answer to that question. He seemed disappointed when I told him I had only had two wives and six children.

'Does wife number two live in the same hut as wife number one?' asked Raimundo.

Hylton is a long-time supporter of Rainforest Concern. One of the projects the charity has been involved with is a new village school. This has been built along traditional lines, with a conical roof and open sides. The idea is to make sure that children learn the vital aspects of Yawanawan culture. The myths and legends have been written down.

It is in this kind of area that the old have such an advantage. Hylton, whose Portuguese is much better than mine, served as an amanuensis as Raimundo sat us down in front of him, just like schoolchildren, and told us about Yawanawan creation myths and symbols, about how each plant, each animal has its own importance, its own story to tell and how all must be treated with respect.

At one point, he held up the carved figure of an owl. 'The owl is not of this world. The owl hoots when someone is about to die,' he said. 'The owl asks: "Who is going to die?" And the Yawanawas answer: "Yes, it is true there is someone here who is about to pass over to the other side."'

Raimundo looked at us as we hung on his words. '"Give me the name," hoots the owl, "and I will look after him for ever."'

There are three great tropical forest areas in the world. The Congo Basin, the Amazon and the rainforests of south-east Asia.

One afternoon, in late 2005, I stood in a clearing in a forest in the heart of Kalimantan, the Indonesian part of Borneo. The equatorial sun shone through gaps in the tree canopy above us, creating a patchwork of light and dark on the forest floor. Our guide put a hand to his lips, warning us not to make a sound.

We waited three, four, five minutes, while a wild boar rooted around in the nearby brush and mosquitoes homed in unerringly on unprotected expanses of skin. Then we heard it: the low, haunting call of the male orang-utan.

I gazed up into the trees, trying to see where the sound was coming from. The forest seemed dark, impenetrable. Suddenly, high up in the canopy, I saw the branches move and as the sun pierced the foliage I caught a glimpse of a distant red-gold shape, heading our way.

There was movement to the left and right as well, as other orang-utans swung by. There must have been ten or twenty animals altogether, and for two hours that afternoon we were privileged to be able to watch them go about their extraordinary business.

Aside from humans, there are four types of great ape in the world: gorilla, chimpanzee, bonobo and orang-utan. I have seen them all in their natural habitat. For my money, the orang-utan, with its strength and subtlety, its luminous intelligence and, above all, its glorious russet beauty, must come at the top of the list.

How can it be, I asked myself, as I stood there in that forest clearing, that the human race, in its greed and vanity, is driving this magnificent creature to the edge of extinction? Once the number of orang-utans in south-east Asia could have been in the hundreds of thousands. Today, fewer than 60,000 orang-utans remain in the wild, and these are found only on the islands of Borneo and Sumatra, where they are classified as 'endangered' and 'critically endangered'. An estimated 5,000 of them are lost from the wild every year. You don't have to be a genius to work out that the orang-utan could be extinct within the next twelve years.

The most shattering aspect of this story is that a finger of blame can be pointed unerringly at food manufacturers and supermarkets in Britain and the products that they make and sell, and that we buy. Let's be clear about this. The biggest single threat to the orang-utan is the destruction of its forest habitat, and the most important reason for the destruction of the forest has been the spread of palm oil plantations in Borneo and Sumatra.

On our last weekend in Kalimantan, we drove upcountry to try to assess the extent of the palm oil threat to Tanjung Puting itself. There were rumours of massive new oil plantations being planned, with proposals to grant concessions for five palm oil plantations, totalling 16,000 hectares, inside the park. In addition, as much as 20,000 hectares of land could be lost outside the park. It might not be officially protected, but it is vital orang-utan habitat. Without it,

Tanjung Puting will be totally isolated, with the sea on one side and a desert of palm oil on the other.

After heading north for two hours on bumpy, potholed, tarmac roads, we turned east towards the Sekonyer River. The tarmac soon petered out, to be replaced by rutted dirt tracks. You begin to understand the sheer scale of the palm oil industry when you see the immense area of land in central Kalimantan, where primary forest has already been converted into plantation. More than once we passed long convoys of trucks loaded with bags of palm oil nuts, as well as lines of tankers carrying the processed oil from the refineries down to the coast.

Our worst fears seemed to be confirmed when, just before sunset, we finally reached our destination, a remote guard post at the northeast corner of Tanjung Puting. It was clear that palm oil plantations had already made substantial incursions into the park, and markers indicated that further, still deeper, incursions were planned.

That night we spread our maps on the floor of the hut. Stephen Brend, the Orang-utan Foundation's senior conservationist, explained the situation as he saw it: 'The marker stakes are now within a kilometre of the guard post here at Pos Ulin. If they go ahead, there will be palm oil plantations right in the heart of the park, within less than 20 kilometres of Camp Leaky itself.'

We all felt numb. The scale of the current incursions, as well as the projected further 'conversions', which seemed to be almost a fait accompli, left us stunned. The 'crown jewels' of Tanjung Puting were not just in jeopardy, they were being pillaged before our very eyes.

I have had the good fortune to have been able to visit the Galápagos twice in the past few years.

Towards the end of my first visit, I was walking with a guide on Española, one of the oldest islands of the archipelago. We were following a clifftop path that wound its way between nesting blue-footed boobies and Nazca boobies, past some rocky promontories, towards a headland where we could see scores of waved albatross, a species endemic to the Galápagos. Some of the albatross were nesting; some were in the air; still others were engaged in a strange courtship ritual involving much nodding of heads and stretching of vast wings.

I was so absorbed in the distant scene that I failed to notice the ground immediately ahead.

'Don't step on the iguanas!' the guide called out as he saw me about to place my feet on a thick mat of red-black marine reptiles that had spread themselves across the path.

When you find yourself about to stumble over a marine iguana warming itself in the morning sun before it heads out to sea and a breakfast of seaweed, you have to pinch yourself and ask, 'Can this be true?'

Then there were Darwin's beloved giant tortoises. We observed them on Santa Cruz Island on a wet and windy morning. Several hundred of them live in a vast forest reserve, where they are difficult to see. Happily, a score or more had emerged from the trees to graze on a nearby farmer's field, so we were able to watch them for an hour.

'Approach them from behind,' the guide instructed. 'That way you won't upset them.'

Once, when I came too close, a tortoise gave a low whooshing hiss, like lift doors closing, but on the whole they seemed quite content to ignore us.

Another image I have is of the blue-footed booby diving for food. When you are snorkelling, you will often hear a loud smack as a booby hits the water, beak outstretched, airbags extended, at 40mph.

Sometimes the bird splashes down just inches away from you and you wonder whether you are about to become a freak accident statistic: 'Snorkeller speared by diving booby!'

Seconds later, you might see the bird rise into the air with a fish in its bill. Apparently, diving birds such as boobies can go blind in the end, as a result of the effect of their repeated high-speed collisions with the surface of the ocean. This is indeed the survival of the fittest.

Perhaps my most vivid memory from that first Galápagos trip was when I peered down through my snorkel mask one day and in the blue depths below saw a huge turtle passing almost directly beneath me. It was a Pacific green turtle, doing a gentle breaststroke, with front and rear flippers moving in unison. I felt humbled in so many ways. Here was an animal that has existed since the age of the dinosaurs, certainly long before human beings made their appearance on the earth. And it is still around today.

One morning, when we were standing on deck, we had a grandstand view of turtles mating about 50 yards off the starboard bow. What surprised me, in the stillness of near-dawn, was the noise the turtles made – a strange bellowing sound. Other turtles swam around and even joined in the fun, offering – as far as one could tell – support and encouragement.

I had the same kind of thrill when seeing a shark at close quarters. I was snorkelling around the rim of a submerged volcano off Floreana Island when a 5-foot whitetip reef shark swam right in front of my face. Like the turtle, it was a creature from another age.

I mentioned that I have, for the past decade, been an ambassador for the United Nations Convention on Migratory Species (CMS). With Robert Vagg, I wrote a large coffee-table book called *Survival:*

Saving Endangered Migratory Species. One section of the book discusses desert antelopes. The CMS is trying to reintroduce the Arabian oryx, for example, in areas where it has become extinct.

One desert antelope species that is on the verge of extinction in the wild is the addax. The last known sightings were near the Termit Massif in Niger, that vast Saharan country lying to the north of Nigeria and to the west of Chad.

Termit Massif is a most unusual geographical and biological feature. Extending almost 80 miles (128km) north to south and in parts more than 8 miles (13km) wide, the rocky cliffs seem to rise hundreds of feet almost vertically from the desert floor. Here, if you are lucky, you will see Barbary sheep moving from crag to crag, desert tortoises, desert foxes and Dorcas gazelles. If you are very lucky, you might see a leopard or a Dama gazelle.

Of course, I was hoping desperately to see the rarest item of all, the addax, even if that meant driving on east from Termit into the vast Tin Toumma desert erg. That addaxes had been seen there in the past was not in doubt but the last sightings had been more than a year ago.

On our last evening at the Massif, we pored over the satellite maps. Greth remembered precisely where he had seen addaxes – nine altogether – three years earlier. He placed a finger on the chart. Newby measured off the distance.

'Fifty kilometres more or less due east,' Newby said. 'Let's go for it!'

Next day our convoy moved on into the heat of the desert. We drove for several hours that day along a transect, our vehicles rising and falling with the sand dunes. After 30 miles (50km), we turned 90 degrees south for 6 miles (10km), before returning on a track parallel to our original one.

Newby read out the coordinates from the GPS: '12 degrees 12 minutes east, 16 degrees 12 minutes north.' I'd like to be able to record that at precisely that moment we had our first sighting of a herd of addax, munching away on the unforgiving though still somehow nutritious desert grasses. But we had no such luck. The truth is that we were looking for a handful of animals in an area the size of Switzerland and it would have been almost a miracle if we had located them in such a short space of time.

The temperature in the desert dropped to 8°C that night and I was grateful for the shelter of my one-man tent. I lay with the flap open looking up at the stars.

Did it matter, I wondered, that we hadn't actually seen an addax? Surely not. It was enough to know that somewhere in that vast desert, they are still there. And if the CMS project for a Termit-Tin Toumma Protected Area comes to fruition, as I have every reason to hope it will, there is a chance that the world's last remaining population of wild addax will not only survive but prosper well into the future.

This will be good for the addax. And it will be a triumph for Niger as well.

When I came back from my first journey to Antarctica, back in early 1984, I felt sure that I would probably not have a chance to go there again. I was wrong. I went back again in 2007. One of my most visit memories is watching a leopard seal stalking a penguin.

There is nothing cuddly about a leopard seal. I was standing on a rock in an ice-strewn bay on Cuverville Island, just west of the Arctowski Peninsula, enjoying some of the finest scenery the Antarctic has to offer, when the seal surfaced – like a submarine – less than 10 yards away. It was a vast animal, 10 or 11 feet long, with a huge head and a snake-like body. When it lifted its head from the water to gaze balefully at me, I could see on its throat and belly the spots from which it derives its name.

Cuverville Island is home to a colony of gentoo penguins, one of the seven species of penguin found in the Antarctic. Gentoos are not particularly large – around 30–32in and 12–13lb – but what they lack in size, they make up for in numbers. There are several hundred thousand gentoos in Antarctica and quite a high proportion of that total seemed to be gathered that afternoon on that rocky beach.

It would be wrong to say that the penguins were totally undisturbed by the leopard seal's presence in the inshore waters where they were getting on with their daily business. They squawkingly registered its arrival, beating a hasty retreat from the water's edge.

The seal waited patiently, hull-down in the water with its nostrils just above the surface. When, a few minutes later, a gentoo decided to make a rash dash for the open sea, the leopard seal pounced. It grabbed the penguin in its mouth, like a gun dog retrieving a bird, and swam out with it into deeper water.

There then ensued one of the most extraordinary spectacles I have ever witnessed. The seal appeared to play cat-and-mouse with the traumatised bird, releasing it two or three times, then pouncing on it again before it could escape. Once the seal tired of this game, it settled down to the more serious task of preparing its meal. This involved thrashing the penguin from side to side in the water with such violence that the head eventually became detached from the body and the poor bird was, literally, turned inside out, so that it could be more conveniently eaten.

Nowadays, of course, we have all seen films in which animals – lions, leopards, cheetahs or whatever – seize and devour their prey. We know that nature is red in tooth and claw. But I have to say that this particular scene of a leopard seal catching and then eating its lunch on a brilliant sunny Antarctic day will stay with me for a long time.

'I can promise you the trip of a lifetime.' It was my first evening on board *Searcher* and the speaker was the vessel's captain, Art Taylor, a rugged fifty-year-old Californian. Four times a year for the past fifteen years, Art has been taking a maximum of twenty-four passengers on board his 95-foot vessel on twelve-day whale-watching and nature tours around Mexico's Baja peninsula, at 1,300km one of the longest and narrowest in the world.

During that first briefing session, Art ran through the essentials. The accommodation would be comfortable – with air-conditioned cabins. The food would be plentiful, the crew skilled and knowledgeable. For those of us who wanted to see a desert environment, Baja California was *sans pareil*. On half a dozen occasions, we would be landing from skiffs on the mainland or on one of the islands and we would have a chance to hike through the wilderness, keeping a wary eye out for rattlesnakes, scorpions, tarantulas, centipedes and sandflies.

As for those of us who wanted above all to observe marine wildlife, we would, Art hoped, return home satisfied.

He ticked off the species we would be most likely to encounter – seals and sea lions, dolphins, pelicans, ospreys, humpback whales...

'You may even get to see a blue whale,' he said. 'We usually do on these trips.'

I have to admit, when I heard that last claim I was incredulous. As far as I knew, the blue whale, the largest creature ever to exist on the planet, was effectively extinct, its population driven to such low levels by decades of commercial whaling that it could never recover.

Was Art joking, I wondered?

Five days later, we had just finished lunch in the salon when we heard the captain's voice over the loudspeaker.

'Blue whale on the surface. Two hundred yards at one o'clock.'

As I rushed to the bow, I heard a great swooshing noise. In the water just in front of the boat, I saw an immense blue-grey shape. The column of spray must have reached 30 or 40 feet into the air, rising straight up like some gigantic geyser.

We stayed with that blue whale for three-quarters of an hour that afternoon. It spouted two or three times more as it moved slowly through the water ahead of us. Rob Nowajchik, *Searcher*'s resident marine mammal expert and onboard lecturer, told us what was happening: 'After three or four spouts, he'll be getting ready to dive.'

I could see that the leviathan now seemed to be hunching its enormous back. The head was already under the surface and the dorsal fin had appeared.

'He's going to fluke!' Rob said.

A blue whale fluking at a distance of not much more than 100 yards is one of the most awe-inspiring sights I have ever witnessed. Ahead of us, the water boiled and churned and then, suddenly, we found ourselves once more looking at an empty ocean.

There is luck in this, of course. But there is also judgement. Experienced whale-watchers look for the whale's footprints, unnaturally smooth and glassy patches of water caused by the upward pressure of the flukes on the water column. With clear seas and an animal the size of the blue whale, you can actually see the outline underwater long before it rises to the surface.

Chapter Thirty-Three

More Wild Animals

A nyone who has read Jane Goodall's books, particularly *In the Shadow of Man*, her account of her early years at Gombe, will know how she first came here. But to hear her retell the tale right there at Gombe made it especially piquant.

Brought up in Bournemouth after her parents' divorce, Jane left school at eighteen, took a secretarial course and a couple of different jobs, before jumping at the chance to stay at a schoolfriend's parents' farm in Kenya. There, in Nairobi, she met Dr Leakey, who was the curator of what is now the Nairobi National Museum, and was offered, with one other girl, the opportunity to accompany Leakey and his wife, Mary, on one of their annual paleontological expeditions to Olduvai Gorge in the Serengeti plains.

It was Leakey who told Jane about a chimpanzee population at Gombe, suggesting that she might undertake an unprecedented study of them in the wild. In those days before women's liberation, the proposal must have been highly unusual. The (then colonial) authorities certainly felt so. They were not happy about an unaccompanied white woman camping for months in the bush. But Jane had wanted to live with animals since reading the Tarzan books as a child, and she had the support of her mother, Vanne, who told her, 'If you work hard and really want something and never give up, you'll find a way.'

What an extraordinary journey it has been for her! The 26-year-old dragging up her boat onto the shore, with 'one ex-army tent, one pair of lousy binoculars and a couple of tin mugs and plates', has turned into a star of the international circuit. Hectic as her life now is, she doesn't want to be known simply as 'the chimpanzee lady'. In 2002, Kofi Annan, the then Secretary-General of the UN, appointed her, with other notable personalities, as a Messenger of Peace. She told me, 'I was the only one who actually showed up in New York for the ceremony.'

As the whisky bottle went round again, Jane remembered the moment in May 1975 when the Congo exploded into their lives.

'It was the middle of the night. The kidnappers came in by boat, parked on the beach down there' – she waved towards the spot. 'They grabbed four of the students. They sent one of them back almost at once with a message. The parents came out. I think money was paid, because the next two were released. I think the figure was $250,000. But the fourth didn't come back for some time.'

She was evidently deeply marked by that event. In practical terms, it meant she had to give up full-time residence at Gombe. 'We had to go: the authorities wouldn't let us stay.' But even without the abductions, one wonders how long Jane and Hugo could have remained. Kidnappers were not the only menace. They had a son, Grub, to bring up, and Gombe is not safe for an infant. Jane had noted early on that chimpanzees were omnivores. She showed me 'Grub's cage': a wire-netting enclosure, it was designed to protect the boy, but was not a long-term solution.

Next day, I took a trek up through the Gombe hills to find a group of chimpanzees located by trackers earlier that morning. 'That's Freud,' Anthony Collins, a director of the Jane Goodall Institute who was visiting Gombe, told me. 'He used to be the alpha male, but he's been supplanted by Ferdinand. And here comes Frodo, watch out!'

I had put my backpack on the ground and Frodo was out to get it. He had also been an alpha male and was now making a bit of a comeback.

A mother and daughter chased each other around a tree. Groups of chimpanzees called to each other across the clearing, 'pant-hooting'. The alpha male shook the trees and the females submitted to his will. 'If they don't come at once,' said Anthony, 'Ferdinand will beat them up.'

When we met up with Jane, we gave her a full account of the day's events. The last chimpanzee of those she first met in 1960 died three years ago, so she has known all 106 of the current Gombe chimpanzees since their birth. Her thinking about her extended family has evolved over the years. If she ever idealised them, she has moved on. She has witnessed terrible internecine fighting, as one group all but obliterated another. She watched a deadly rampage as one female took her daughter on a killing spree, murdering and devouring any infant chimpanzees they came across.

When we told her that Frodo had charged my backpack, she shook her head. 'I'm afraid to go out now if Frodo's around. He makes a beeline for me and tries to knock me down. He almost killed me once, dragging me to the edge of a cliff and pushing me over. Mind you, I think he knew there were trees that would block my fall.'

Despite such fears for her safety, even today she insists on walking the hills alone, hour after hour. I remarked that nobody wants to hear on the news that she is dead. She smiled. 'It would be quite a story, wouldn't it? I wonder what it would do for the cause of conservation, "Jane Goodall killed by chimpanzee!"'

In 2009, fifty years after I had first visited Machu Picchu, I made a return visit. In 1959, I had been the only tourist on the train. Now, in April, when my wife and I went there, all the compartments were packed, with passengers being limited to hand luggage. And the little station that serves Machu Picchu has itself been transformed. From my earlier visit, I remembered a tiny wayside stop, where you disembarked to climb up to the citadel. Today, the town (known as Aguas Calientes or Machu Picchu Pueblo) has more than 2,000 people. I can't recall where I spent the night when I first went there but, since I was travelling on a shoestring, I am sure it was a fleapit hostel. Today you can stay in splendour at the five-star Inkaterra hotel on the edge of town or in the Sanctuary Lodge Hotel right outside the entrance to the archaeological site.

In 1959, there weren't any other tourists in Machu Picchu. I look at my old photographs and I cannot see a single human being. Today, if you stand on Machu Picchu ('Old Mountain') and take a wide-angle shot of the ruins with Huayna Picchu ('Young Mountain') as a backdrop, you will on an average day find scores, if not hundreds, of tourists in view.

If there weren't any tourists in 1959, there weren't any tourist guides, either. Looking back I rather regret that. We certainly benefited from having a knowledgeable escort this time around.

At the end of our first morning in Machu Picchu, we found ourselves standing in front of a tall circular structure with three trapeze-shaped window openings looking out to the east.

'This is the Sun Temple,' our guide, Ivanov, told us. 'At precisely 7.22 on the morning of the winter solstice [21 June], the sun will shine through the central window to illuminate that huge white granite rock.' I knew from my photo album that I had seen precisely the same structure in 1959, without understanding the astronomical significance.

I suggested to Ivanov that if the Incas had been anything like the Aztecs they would have marked the occasion with a sacrificial victim or two. Ivanov shook his head.

'We don't find any evidence of human sacrifice at Machu Picchu. At Cusco, however, there is such evidence. It was regarded as a great privilege to be chosen as a sacrificial victim. Upper-class families competed for the honour!'

We learned such a lot that day. Ivanov told us, for example, that the alignment of the great Inca towns reflected iconic images of Andean wildlife. Cusco, he told us, is designed in the shape of a puma and 'the Incas built their great citadel of Machu Picchu in the shape of a giant condor so that, at death, they could fly to the Milky Way'.

Our guide left us after lunch to return to Cusco. Jenny and I spent the afternoon walking around the ruins. As the early crowds dispersed, I found myself reliving the grandeur, mystery and excitement of the place I had known in my younger days. In the whole world, there is nothing quite like Machu Picchu. Even 5,000 tourists a day can't change that.

Will I go back again? You bet I will. I have promised myself that, some time before that giant condor flies me off to the Milky Way, I will return. With any luck, I will still be fit enough to hike through the mountains along the Inca Trail, and sleep under the stars.

Ranthambore is one of the loveliest of India's national parks. With its tenth-century fort perched on a hilltop looking out over deep forests, it is straight out of Kipling's *Jungle Book*. Though in the '90s poaching led to a collapse in Ranthambore's tiger population, it seems that since then there has been a recovery.

When Jenny and I arrived at our lodge, just outside the boundaries of the park, we were briefed by a ranger: 'We believe there are about thirty tigers in Ranthambore today.' We went out four times in the canters – open-sided vehicles riding high off the ground for good viewing. We enjoyed the magical setting: the lakes, the battlements and the jungle backdrop. We saw a mass of wildlife – monkeys, peacocks and an abundance of sambar deer and spotted deer, herons and kingfishers – but the tigers remained elusive.

From time to time a tracker would point out a print, but this would be followed by a shaking of the head and a clicking of the teeth. '*Acha*! This is not a fresh print. Tiger was here this morning. Now gone very far!'

Finally we came to the end of our last ride on our last day in Ranthambore. I was sitting up front with a tracker, Shivraj, next to me. Shivraj was deeply despondent. It was as though he felt his own honour was impugned by his inability to produce a real live tiger for us.

Then, as we were getting ready to call it a day, a message came through on the radio that a tiger had been seen at a waterhole a few miles away. With our driver, Vijay, breaking the speed limit by a considerable margin, we careered off through the forests only to find that the tiger, if there was one, had moved on.

Finally we had to head for home, still lickety-split, since we were out of time and the park gates had already closed. We were travelling, I guess, at almost 30mph on a bumpy track when we were all but sideswiped by a Jeep containing a party of tourists. What interested Shivraj, as we took rapid evasive action, was that the Jeep wasn't heading for the exit; it was heading towards another part of the forest.

'Follow that Jeep!' Shivraj told the driver.

So we belted after the Jeep and, as luck would have it, arrived a few minutes later at a fork in the road where three or four vehicles were already gathered. A female tiger came out of the bush and crouched in the road right alongside one of the vehicles. We could hear her growling. Seconds later, a male tiger followed her.

The female's growls grew into snarls. By now I was standing up, holding on to the windscreen, trying to focus my camera.

'They are going to mate,' Shivraj whispered to me. 'That's why the female is snarling.'

I would like to report that we saw the tigers mating, but suddenly Shivraj told the driver to reverse and beat a retreat.

'We are illegal here!' he told me as we drove back. 'This is Route No. 5. Ours is Route No. 4. If the park officials catch us, our canter can be impounded, and the rangers can be suspended and fined.'

We drove back to the lodge, tired but happy. Like the Battle of Waterloo, it had been a damn close-run thing.

For as long as I can remember, I have wanted to see a giant panda in the wild. Not in a zoo. Not in a research station. In the mountains of central China, the only place on earth where they survive. Giant pandas once inhabited much of China, but nowadays they are to be found in only three provinces: Sichuan, Shaanxi and Gansu. In the mid-1980s, I visited Sichuan, taking a cargo boat down the Yangtze through the Three Gorges. While my fellow passengers filled their breakfast bowls with rice from a pail, I'd pop up on deck with my eyes skinned, hoping that, just as the sun was rising, I might see a giant panda having its own breakfast on the banks of the river. No such luck…

In the spring of 2011, I finally had a chance, being invited to visit the Foping Nature Reserve in Shaanxi Province.

Our first full day in Foping was perfect for tracking. The sun shone as we headed towards the first of the several valleys we would explore. The panda is on the whole a solitary animal. The general rule is one valley per panda. We were joined by guides He, Pu and Hu. Pu and Hu were authorised to scout in the mountains around and above us. If they spotted a panda, they would summon us by mobile phone. It seemed a fine system, but the call from the spotters never came.

Pu and Hu were still out in the field when He checked his watch. It was around 6 p.m. and the sun was beginning to set. We were heading back to base camp when suddenly He overtook me on the narrow track. 'They've seen a panda in a tree!' he hissed. 'Go back! Back up the hill!'

We retraced our steps and He gestured that we should go down a slope through the bamboo, then up the dry bed of a creek. Moments later, I saw the animal: a large white mass of fur, 40 feet up a tree, almost directly above us. From time to time, it waved a paw but otherwise it remained motionless. Our presence seemed not to bother her in the slightest.

But the best was yet to come. March is mating season for pandas. Seconds later, a fully grown male panda poked its head out of the bamboo 20 yards away and gazed balefully at me. The size of the animal stunned me (an adult male can reach 5 feet when standing and weigh more than 20 stone), but so did the fact it was there at all. Not only was there a female panda directly overhead, but a large male panda, looking decidedly grumpy, was heading in my direction. I was so shocked I completely failed to take a photograph. I pointed my camera at the approaching male, tried to press the button for the zoom, but somehow turned the camera off instead.

An added bonus, on that particular visit to China, was that I was able to see Max, then working in Beijing. One afternoon, we climbed up the Great Wall. I couldn't help remembering my first visit to the Great Wall, back in 1957 when Mao was still alive and the Gang of Four were in China. China had been a very different country then. You couldn't in those days, for example, take a toboggan chute all the way down from the top of the Great Wall to the car park at the bottom where the tour buses are waiting.

But Max and I did precisely that. We had booked dinner that evening at a smart Italian restaurant off Tiananmen Square and we didn't want to miss our reservation.

In February 2012, I visited Mindanao, the Philippines' most southerly province to report on horse fighting for the *Sunday Times*. I was less than 5 miles from a town called Midsayap when, over to the right, off the road, I saw flags flying and banners waving and heard a loud-speaker blaring with what was obviously a running commentary. A huge sign, depicting two rearing stallions engaged in mortal combat, waved over a makeshift arena. Two or three hundred spectators were pressed up against the railings. This was clearly a great family occasion. Young and old, men and women, all had turned out.

Police were present in case of trouble. Horse fighting may be a proscribed activity in the Philippines in the sense that it is banned by law, but the spectacle I was about to witness, illegal though it might be, had actually been licensed by the Mayor of Midsayap. The local constabulary was present to see that things didn't get out of hand.

We parked the car. Nobody paid us much attention. They were too busy concentrating on what was going on in the arena. Someone offered me a chair to stand on so I could look over the heads of the crowd.

The scenes I witnessed that afternoon were almost surreal. Inside the ring, two stallions, already lathered in sweat and blood, tried to fight each other to a standstill. They reared, they gouged, they kicked, and they slashed, all the while competing for the tethered mare. At times they came to a trembling halt, and almost nuzzled each other, before launching once more into a horrific attack. At other times, they raced around the arena at full speed, causing the referee and officials to step smartly aside or even slip quickly under the railings and out of harm's way.

For the most part the stallions that are entered in these local derbies are not reared specifically as fighters. They are animals that, when they are not fighting, are being used as beasts of burden or as a means of transport.

As I looked around that afternoon, it was quite obvious that the spectators were deeply involved in the fight. They are 'aficionados' of the sport. If they didn't themselves appreciate the finer points of the contest, the broadcast commentary put them straight. But there is far more to horse fighting than the horse fight itself. The real reason these fights continue to take place, even though they are banned under the law of the land, seems to lie in the money that changes hand.

Yes, the owner of a winning horse will earn a tidy sum. If he has several winners, claiming the 'Derby Champion' title, he will gain a small fortune. But even more important are the bets placed by the spectators. Markers – 'cristos', as they are called – make a mental note of the wagers shouted out by the crowd as the fight runs its course. For a few minutes at the end, the exits are blocked so that bets can be collected and money paid out. Yes, the police are on hand to make sure there is no violence. But they are there too, perhaps more importantly, to see that no one slips out of the venue without paying up.

As it turned out, the horse fight I watched that afternoon in Midsayap was the last of the day. I don't know when the fight actually started but by my watch the two stallions in the ring fought each other for over forty minutes before one of them was declared a winner.

The rules, as I understood them, are quite precise. If a stallion fails to challenge another, he can lose a point. If he runs for the exit-chute, he can also lose a point. Once he loses two points, the other horse wins. En route to the verdict, there are lashings of blood and gore. One horse may gouge the other's leg or testicles. It may bite the other's neck and sides. No, it is not a pretty sight.

Dino, the vet who had accompanied me that day, was as much concerned for the welfare of the mare as for the stallions.

'That mare,' he explained, pointing to the quivering animal roped in the middle of the arena, 'has been out there in the sun all day. There may have been ten or twelve fights. She will have been mounted as many times. That's the winner's perk. You might say she's "gang-raped". And she will also be bitten and scratched and kicked as the stallions fight it out. For me,' Dino concluded, 'there is nothing noble or natural about the horse fight. This is a purely induced anger.'

As I stood there among the crowd, absorbing the spectacle, we encountered more than a few curious glances. There are few, if any, European or American faces to be seen in this part of Mindanao, and certainly not at these underground and 'illegal' events.

But Dino had already prepared a cover story for us. After the last fight of the day was over, he took us around and introduced us to the referee and the other officials.

'Meet Mr Johnson,' he urged them. 'He is a big businessman from America. From Texas! Soon he will be introducing horse fighting in the rodeos over there!'

I did my best to look the part. 'Y'all have a great day,' I said, doffing my hat.

I had no sooner returned to England from the Philippines than I was despatched to Tanzania to write an article for *Condé Nast Traveller* about the great animal migrations in the Serengeti.

That particular trip was almost aborted on take-off. I got to Heathrow Terminal 4 in plenty of time for the 10.20 a.m. Kenya Airways flight to Nairobi. I had booked in online and printed out my boarding card but anyway had to drop off my bags. Actually, I didn't have much luggage. There was a 15kg limit on the flight from Arusha to Kogatende, the airstrip in the heart of the Lamai Wedge, the relatively unfrequented part of the northern Serengeti where I was heading.

To my surprise, I had been given an upgrade so I found the business lounge near Gate 10, poured myself a coffee and sat down with my laptop to clear some last emails. I put a smug out-of-office notice on my Hotmail account. 'I will be in the Serengeti, in Tanzania, for the next few days and may not be able to reply immediately to your message.'

For some reason, when the time came to board the plane, I failed to check which boarding gate I should be heading for, but instead homed in on Gate 10 where the flight was already boarding. The man at the door gave my boarding card a cursory look.

'Seat 1A,' I said firmly.

The man took a closer look. He seemed puzzled. 'This is the Continental flight to Houston, Texas. You're going to Nairobi on Kenya Airways.'

When finally I arrived, panting, at the right gate, I was greeted by the kindly Kenya Airways airport manager. She was tremendously sympathetic but there was nothing she could do. I had missed my plane and my bag had been offloaded.

In the end, I was rebooked on the evening flight. I caught up with *Condé Nast Traveller* photographer Hugo Burnand and his assistant

Radu Brebene, in Nairobi next morning as we waited to board the plane for Kilimanjaro in Tanzania.

'Sorry, chaps,' I said. 'I know I almost blew it.'

Things could only get better. After we landed at Kilimanjaro international airport, we were transferred by car to the smaller, local airport at Arusha. Then we boarded a twelve-seater Cessna Caravan.

'First stop will be Lake Manyara,' the pilot announced. 'Flying time will be twenty-two minutes. It may be a bit bumpy. In an emergency always exit by the back, away from the propellers.'

There is nothing automatic and predictable about the great migration, except that it happens. The precise timing of the movement of the herds seems to be dictated by the animals' own sense of the pattern of rainfall and the prospect of nutritious grazing. It is hard to be precise about the numbers. As we drove out from camp that evening on our first game drive, Chedi, the guide who looked after us while we were staying at Lamai Camp, told us there might be 1.5 million migrating wildebeest, along with 150,000 zebras and perhaps half a million elands and gazelles.

'Of course, not all of them will go all the way. Not all of them will make the crossing.'

The crossing! Let's be frank about this. However amazing the sheer spectacle of several thousand wildebeest and zebras and their accompanying outriders churning up the dust on the plains may be, the 'money shot', as Hugo put it, has to be that extraordinary moment when the animals gather by the banks of the Mara River and, after waiting for hours or even days, finally decide to cross.

As far as actually seeing the river-crossings, we were – I believe – extraordinarily lucky. On our first full day at Lamai we had set out early in our Toyota Land Cruiser. Around noon we were driving along the south bank of the Mara River when we saw a herd of wildebeest gathering on the other side. It was not a large herd, maybe two or three hundred animals. But through the binoculars we could see a mass of other animals in the distance, which also seemed to be heading for the river. In the end a kind of irresistible pressure seems to build up as the newcomers add their weight to the scrum.

Chedi parked several hundred yards away from the river. 'We have to be careful not to put them off. They may be getting ready to cross and we mustn't block them.'

Experienced hands like our guide Chedi are well aware that it is impossible to predict just when a crossing will take place. As we sat there, our eyes glued on the distant scene, he told us, 'It's just luck if you're there when they start crossing. The first ones across may make it, but the crocodiles hear the noise and will gather in no time. As a matter of fact, the crocodiles are there already.'

We looked where he pointed to see a line of brown reptiles looking like large logs half-submerged in the muddy but fast-flowing water.

On that particular occasion, after an hour or so waiting, we decided to head back to camp. But we returned in the afternoon to take up our position once again. By then, the herds on the bank opposite had grown considerably in size. There seemed to be a lot of tension in the air as the animals pranced around the steep banks and the crumbling surfaces that led down to the river.

'Even when they are actually in the river,' Chedi said, 'you can never be sure they are going to cross. I've seen them get halfway across and then turn back.'

In the event we saw not one but two crossings that afternoon. Once the crossings have actually started, your driver gets to the river's edge as fast as he can since, if the herd on the far bank is small, the crossing may be over in minutes.

Of course, we didn't – and couldn't – make a precise count but I would say that on both occasions that afternoon the number of animals that took the plunge, as it were, was in the hundreds, not thousands. During the first crossing we saw a young wildebeest taken by a crocodile. The crocodile lunged to grab the animal's leg before pulling it under. On the second crossing, a bit further downstream, the same thing happened but this time the crocodile, having drowned the wildebeest, simply let the carcass float away downstream.

'Basically, the crocodiles are not very hungry at the moment,' Chedi explained. 'There is a lot of water in the river and a lot of animal carcasses around.'

Whereas at the Mara River crossings in Kenya's Masai Mara, you can get forty or fifty vehicles on the riverbank, jostling for a view, in the Lamai Wedge you can find yourself virtually alone. There may be one or two other vehicles but seldom more than a handful. You really do feel privileged.

When we left Lamai Camp, having seen two river crossings and a host of other wildlife – elephants, giraffes, hippopotamuses, lions, baboons, eagles, vultures etc. – we already felt that we had had more than our fair share of good luck. We shook hands with Titus, our guide, and the other camp staff and when we said 'Asante-sana!' we really meant it.

We moved on to the second of the two permanent camps in the Wedge, Sayari Camp. Whereas the Lamai Camp is built on an elevation, Sayari – by contrast – has been set up on the plain, less than half a mile from the river. Hippos have been found in the camp's swimming pool. At night, you can hear the wildebeest moving around, not to speak of leopards and lions. If you want to move from your tent to the communal dining area, you have to use the walky-talky to call for an askari to escort you.

Because the camp is so close to the river, we decided – on our first day at Sayari – to go back to base for lunch. The plates were just being cleared when word came that a crossing had just started. At Sayari we had a new guide, also called Titus, who doubled up as a driver. Though we had already seen two crossings, we certainly were ready to see another. Titus drove like a maniac down to the river, and then followed the track bank.

'They're at crossing number eight!' he shouted to us. The most-used river-crossing points are numbered from one to eight, going upstream from west to east. (The Mara flows through Kenya into Tanzania and then into Lake Victoria.)

I felt sure it would be all over before we got there, but it wasn't. That afternoon the herd that had gathered on the other side was truly enormous. Titus reckoned it must have contained four or five thousand animals. The riverbanks opposite were, literally, heaving with wildlife as the wildebeest jostled each other before leaping into the foaming tide. Oddly enough, the crocodiles seemed to have taken the afternoon off. Or maybe even they were daunted by the sheer size of the cloven-hoofed army that confronted them.

The herd was still crossing a full twenty minutes after we arrived at the river. Later, determined not to lose sight of them, we followed the animals as they headed south. Once we even got ahead of them. I shall never forget the sight of thousands upon thousands of wildebeest and zebras heading at the gallop towards our parked Land Cruiser, and then veering aside at the last moment, to pass us less than a hundred yards away.

Chapter Thirty-Four

Bhutan: Gross National Happiness

There were relatively few foreigners present at the coronation on 1 November 2008 of Jigme Khesar Namgyel Wangchuck as Druk Gyalpo, or King of Bhutan, and I am ready to bet that not one of them actually walked 40 miles over the mountains to attend that extraordinary event. But my wife, Jenny, and I did precisely that. Admittedly, we had not planned it that way.

Back in June that year when we made the arrangements to visit the Himalayan kingdom of Bhutan, the precise date of the coronation was still under discussion. Soothsayers still needed to be consulted and entrails examined. So our aim at the time was simply to trek from Paro (where the plane from Delhi would land) to Thimpu (the capital) and to do some sightseeing once we got there.

The plan was for us to have a couple of days to acclimatise in Paro, before heading off over the mountains. I work at the top of our house in London and Jenny has a study on the ground floor so I emailed her the details of the trek.

'I don't think we're going to do any very high-altitude stuff,' I wrote, 'so I'm sure you'll be OK.'

Men are from Mars. Women are from Venus. Jenny pinged an email back.

'I see we're camping at 3,750 metres on Day 3. How high is that?'

'Not quite sure of the actual altitude in feet,' I replied. 'Should be a piece of cake anyway.'

Well, some pieces of cake are more edible than others.

Trekking in Bhutan is not like trekking in Nepal. Everything you need is carried on horses, donkeys or mules rather than by porters. To help Jenny and me across the mountains from Paro to Thimpu required the assistance of (a) our guide, Sonam Norbu, an engaging and humorous 25-year-old Bhutanese from the east of the country, (b) one head cook, named Kunzang, (c) one assistant cook, Tashi, (d) one horseman, Tshering, and (e) seven pack animals, namely three horses, three donkeys and one mule.

Jenny and I met our full team, pack animals included, early one morning at the agreed rendezvous. As vantage points go, this was superb. The Paro valley stretched out below us, dominated by the magnificent Paro Dzong. (The dzongs, found throughout Bhutan, are unique Bhutanese fortresses, built in commanding defensive positions and used for both both civil and religious purposes.) For the next hour, as we climbed up through the forest, the image of the dzong down in the valley below grew steadily smaller. Eventually, as the path entered the trees, it passed from our view.

Our travel guide's itinerary had spoken of a 'long but not steep' climb for this first day's trekking. 'Long' and 'steep' are really subjective terms. I have to admit that Jenny and I found the going tough. One might have thought that with seven pack animals at our disposal we might somehow have managed to grab on to a passing horse's tail. But that's not the way it is. In Bhutan the horses don't accompany you as you climb. Each morning you just walk out of the camp, leaving your team to pack everything up. You don't have to dismantle the tents or even roll up your sleeping bag. That's all done for you. You might have been trekking for two or three hours before you hear the tinkling bell of the lead horse coming up fast behind you.

This is the moment to step aside, unhook your water bottle and take a deep swig, as the animals pass. Our horseman, Tshering, brings up the rear. The paths over these hills are narrow. To the untutored eye, the way is often not clearly marked, with several options on offer.

I ask Sonam, our guide, how the horses keep to the track.

'They know the way,' Sonam replies.

Sometimes, we pass a convoy coming in the opposite direction. Once I noted that the lone horseman had a sling in his hand.

Sonam elaborates, 'If the horses go in the wrong direction, the horseman can fire a sling-shot at the lead animal to set it back on the right track.'

On the whole, we didn't do much talking that first day. Jenny and I were seriously winded. As the track got steeper and rockier, we found ourselves counting out the paces.

'98 ... 99 ... 100', I would pant. 'OK, let's do another hundred before we pause.'

By the time we reached a spot of level ground where Tashi had spread out a copious lunch, I was ready to admit – at least to myself – that it would have been advisable to have spent a bit more effort getting into shape before we left London. We could have climbed up to the top of nearby Primrose Hill once or twice, for example.

In many ways, the first day was the worst. Even if we had been fit, it was not easy going. The fact is, with horses the dominant means of transport in these parts, the narrow paths get quite churned up. They can be slippery as well as rocky.

We camped the first night at almost 3,700 metres, just below the sixteenth-century monastery of Jili Dzong. We might still have been in the sixteenth century except for the fact that, in the stillness of the evening, we could hear the sounds of a transistor radio, the monks' only contact with the outside world. At that altitude it was seriously cold. The food warmed us up a bit. My notebook records that we had noodles, pork, broccoli, rice and potato curry, followed by apple custard. But still, that first evening, Jenny and I felt totally exhausted. By 8 p.m. we were inside our tent and tucked up in our sleeping bags. As we lay there, we could hear the voices of our team outside, as dinner was cleared away and the horses hobbled for the night.

'We only hobble the naughty horses,' Sunam had explained during supper, 'the ones who may lead the others astray.'

Jenny had packed some head-torches. We switched them on, like miners' lamps, to study the next day's itinerary. I tried to sound encouraging.

'It's downhill all the way tomorrow.'

Jenny was not reassured. 'Downhill can be even harder. It can put a tremendous strain on the knees.'

'Just lengthen your poles,' I advised.

Bhutan is the country that famously has, as its national goal, the pursuit not of ever-increasing Gross National Product (GNP) but of Gross National Happiness (GNH). As we began the second day of our trek from Paro to Thimpu, I began to glimpse the reality behind the slogan. We walked through tiny villages that had never seen a car (there mostly aren't any roads in Bhutan anyway), where quantities of green and red chillies were spread out to dry on the roofs of the houses, and teams of oxen pulled wooden ploughs around the small terraced fields. We came to a watermill where the wheat was being ground into flour. A small boy showed us how the system worked and I wanted to give him a dollar. Sonam gave him a stick of chewing gum instead. 'It will be more use to him,' he said.

At a tiny hamlet called Jedika, where we stopped for lunch, the women were washing clothes in the stream below an ever-turning prayer wheel.

'The water is always turning the wheel. It never stops,' Sonam explained.

'Who earns the merits then?' I asked. By then we had been in Bhutan long enough to know that in this deeply Buddhist country the accumulation of merit is a vital consideration – at least if you want to avoid being reincarnated as, say, a dog in the next life.

'The man who built the prayer wheel over the stream earns the merit,' Sonam explained.

The sun shone brilliantly that day, as it did throughout the whole of our trek. The scenery was spectacular. Though we were walking down through forests of fir trees, we almost never lost sight of the distant Himalayan peaks, many of them rising to over 6,000 metres.

Whereas Nepal has been invaded by mountaineers, Sonam explained that Bhutan has closed its mountains to adventurers of every sort.

'Why so?' I asked.

'Out of respect for the gods,' Sonam replied as though this was the most obvious thing in the world.

We spent most of our third day climbing once again. That's the way it is in Bhutan. Up 1,000 metres, then down 1,200 metres, then up, say, another 1,250 metres. Late in the afternoon, when we were heading for the camp site at Phajoding, another sixteenth-century mountain monastery that actually overlooks the Thimpu valley, we saw two golden eagles, circling on the thermals. At one point they soared almost directly above us and I grabbed my camera. I caught a distant image of one of the birds as it powered overhead. I know the resulting photo won't win a prize, but still it means the world to me.

Gross Personal Happiness! That's how I would describe that moment on the mountain pass, as the golden eagles flew overhead with the valley of Thimpu spread out far below and the sun beginning to set on the far mountain peaks.

We spent the last morning walking down to Thimpu. After a while, the conifers gave way to deciduous trees. Can you have a cacophony of colour? I'm not sure, but that's how it felt. The forests were streaked with autumn hues. I shall never forget the pink bloom of the Himalayan cherry trees we saw that morning on our way down.

Around two o'clock that afternoon, when we had reached more or less level ground and the horses were being unloaded for the last time, I heard some astonishing news. The Bhutanese authorities, who keep a close track of all visitors to this mountain kingdom, had apparently spotted my name on some list and while we were up in the mountains had decided that I was to be issued with a press invitation to the coronation.

Our trip to Bhutan had been arranged by Choki Dorji of Blue Poppy Tours and Treks; his English wife, Naomi, came out in person to the mustering point on the outskirts of Thimpu to inform us of the sudden change in plans.

'The Prime Minister is holding a press conference this afternoon at three o'clock and you're expected to attend. The coronation itself is actually going to take place tomorrow in Thimpu Dzong.'

I have to admit that I reacted to this development with mixed emotions. On the one hand I was delighted to be issued with a press pass to what would undoubtedly be a unique event. Though King Jigme Singye Wangchuk, King Jigme Khesar's father, had stepped aside in 2006, the handover would not be complete until this week's ceremonies were over. We couldn't have timed our arrival better.

On the other hand, I had absolutely nothing suitable to wear. Apart from a pair of black leather shoes that I had thrown into my case at the last moment, trekking gear was all I had.

'Can I buy a suit in town?' I asked Naomi.

Naomi looked doubtful. 'The Bhutanese don't do suits, and even if they did, I am not sure they would have one to fit you.'

There was no time to sort out the problem that afternoon. While Jenny went to the hotel, I went to the Prime Minister's press conference. Though a fair number of Bhutanese journalists were present, as far as I could see the international contingent consisted of Reuters' New Delhi correspondent, a German lady from *Glamour* magazine, and me. The reason for the absence of the international press corps seemed to be the fact that the coronation coincided with Barack Obama's election as the forty-fourth (and first black) President of the United States. Journalists, who might otherwise have come to Bhutan, had stayed away to cover that historic event.

Back in 1968, Heinemann had published my second novel, *Panther Jones for President,* about the election of America's first black president. The plot involved an incumbent president, modelled on Lyndon Johnson, cynically selecting a Black Power activist as his running mate. The president is duly re-elected. When he goes to Guam to greet some returning US astronauts on their Pacific 'splash-down', Congress passes a resolution on 'Back-Contamination from Outer Space'. The president is duly quarantined for five years, so Panther Jones succeeds him as president in a bloodless coup!

My novel might have been a hit, if Lyndon Johnson had not announced, on the very day the book was published, 31 March 1968, that he would not stand for re-election!

I was right about the lunar astronauts, I reflected. They landed on the moon the following year. But I was half a century too soon in predicting the election of an Afro-American to the nation's highest office.

Sitting in the second row of the stalls that afternoon in Thimpu, I was able to observe the Bhutanese Prime Minister Lyonchhen Jigme Y. Thinley at close quarters.

Though Prime Minister Lyonchhen had vast experience of Bhutanese politics, he had actually only been in his present job since March this year when Bhutan's new constitution came into force.

His reverence for the institution of monarchy was almost palpable. He started by explaining the key role of the previous King, Jigme Singye, the current King's father.

'The King gave us democracy. Democracy has come to Bhutan not by the will of the people, but by the will of the King.'

He went on to assert that the new King would be a unifying force: 'The King will be the force to ensure the long-term sustainability of democracy.'

Someone – was it the lady from *Glamour* magazine? – asks the Prime Minister how he intends to promote Gross National Happiness in practice.

'Gross National Happiness,' replies the PM, 'is never far from our minds. With every project we undertake, we ask ourselves, will this project enhance the happiness of our people?'

Cynic that I am about much of politics, I none the less found myself engaged at that moment in what Samuel Taylor Coleridge once called 'the willing suspension of disbelief'. I had seen enough of Bhutan so far – the beauty of the country, the demeanour of the people, the reverence for tradition and the Buddhist way of life, the deep-rooted respect for and veneration of the monarchy – to be ready to concede that the Prime Minister truly, madly, deeply meant what he said.

None of that, of course, helped me in my key dilemma of what to wear at the following day's ceremony where, so the Prime Minister announced, the press would have unique privileges. We would be admitted to a special platform in the courtyard of the great Thimpu Dzong and would have an unrivalled view of the arrival both of the dignatories and of the King himself as he made his way to the throne room. Later in the day, another vantage point had been prepared so that we could witness at close quarters the passage of the royal party across the courtyard to the temple where the ceremony would continue.

Happily, Yeshey Dorji, Bhutan's Foreign Secretary, who had been sitting alongside the Prime Minister for the press conference, came to my aid.

As I left the room at the end of the conference, he signalled to an aide, who presented me with a carefully wrapped parcel. 'You may find this useful tomorrow,' Yeshey Dorji said tactfully.

I have no idea how he knew that I was several sizes larger than the average Bhutanese, but he obviously did. When I got back to the hotel and unwrapped the parcel, I found a magnificent Bhutanese gho, the national dress, first introduced in the seventeenth century and a must for all formal occasions. All the trimmings were there too: the long white scarf to be worn over the left shoulder, the white shirt with the long sleeves that you fold back on to the outside of the gho, the belt to pull it tight, the long socks to keep the draught off bare legs.

Sonam, our guide, came to the hotel at six o'clock the next morning to help me dress. I didn't begin to understand the subtleties: how much white shirt could be glimpsed at the neck of the gho, how deep the skirt could drop below the knee without giving offence? Was it OK to wear underpants? (I decided it was.)

By 7 a.m. I was on the viewing platform in the dzong's courtyard, together with the rest of the press corps. We watched as Pratibha Patil, the President of India, arrived, followed by Sonia Gandhi, President of India's Congress Party. Next came the ancillary royals, notably King Jigme Singye's four wives, all sisters. (Apparently, a fifth sister was also invited to become his wife, but she politely declined the honour.) At 8.30 a.m. there was an extra stir of excitement as the young King, Harvard and Oxford-educated, took his seat on the dais next to his father.

I looked at King Jigme Khesar Namgyel Wangchuck sitting on his throne, surrounded by his family and courtiers. I took in the staggering beauty of the setting: the trumpeters on the roof of the dzong, the giant tapestry, or thondril, hanging from the tower in the middle of the courtyard. I watched the masked dancers perform their rituals before Their Majesties. A line from Hamlet came into my mind as I watched. 'There's such divinity doth hedge a king...' I have to admit that I couldn't help thinking at that moment that Shakespeare had got it right.

King Jigme Singye Wangchuck was only sixteen when he acceded to the throne in 1972 and only fifty-two when he handed over to his son. Jigme Khesar, the new King or Druk Gyalpo, was only twenty-eight, still unmarried. Who can tell when the next coronation will be? It might be half a century from now.

Will Bhutan, that magical mountain kingdom, the Shangri-la archetype, still be the same fifty years hence? Will it have managed to retain the qualities that make it unique among the nations of the world? Will the pursuit of Gross National Happiness remain the official goal?

Though sandwiched between those giants of our time, India and China, Bhutan, with barely 700,000 people, has so far miraculously managed to retain its own unique identity. Will it continue to do so?

From what I have seen I am sure that, under the constitution developed and sponsored by his revered father, the new King's government and parliament, and indeed the vast majority of the Bhutanese themselves, will do their level best to ensure that this is the case.

And if in the end they don't succeed, it will – I suspect – not be through their own fault. It will be a result of global forces, largely beyond their control. Bhutan versus the rest of the world? I know which side I'm on.

Chapter Thirty Five

The Yasuni Initiative

The flight from Quito to Coca, a small oil town in the Ecuadorian Amazon, takes off a couple of hours late, so we don't reach Coca until around noon. Then we have to take a helicopter up the Napo River to reach Añangu, in the heart of Yasuni, the extraordinary national park that is among the most biodiverse places on the planet.

If all had gone to plan, we would have been in our seats long before the President and his party arrived. As it is, as we hover over the endless jungle, I can see that the President's own helicopter, a tough-looking military model, is already parked in a clearing in the forest, and the show has started.

Ana Alban, Ecuador's former Environment Minister, and at that time (February 2013) her country's ambassador in London, had explained before we left England, 'Now that the election campaign has started, the Vice President, Lenin Moreno, becomes President for the duration of the campaign. He is planning to make a televised address to the nation from the Amazon region in the last week of the campaign and we hope to meet him there. This will be his last national broadcast before he retires. He is not standing for re-election.'

Apart from the ambassador, my fellow guest on the trip this morning is Genoveva Casanova, director of Spain's Casa de

Alba Foundation and honorary ambassador for the UN High Commission on Refugees.

Alban urges us both to hurry, so we duck under the still-whirring rotors and make our way to the front of the crowd, where seats have been reserved for us. The President has obviously been well briefed, because he pauses in his fluent oration long enough to greet each of us by name as we take our seats. The cameraman has clearly been briefed, too, because he zooms in on us as our names are mentioned and, when we look up, we can see our own faces on a giant screen. We can also glimpse behind us the serried ranks of Quechua people who have come in from Añangu and the surrounding area for what, for them, must be the event of a lifetime.

Lenin Moreno, the man sitting just a few feet from me with a microphone in his hand and a warm smile on his face, is one of the most remarkable men in South American politics. Born in 1953, he was pursuing a successful career as a businessman in Quito when, in 1998, he was the victim of a car-jacking. Shot in the back and confined to a wheelchair ever since, he came to terms with his disability and took up a political career, being inaugurated as Vice President in 2006. Much of his energies have been devoted to improving the lives of disabled people in Ecuador and, boy, did they need improving. At the time of his shooting, it was rare to see people in wheelchairs in public. In rural areas, those with severe handicaps were treated as outcasts, sometimes confined to sheds and chicken coops.

But Moreno has actively changed all that. Wheelchair ramps have sprung up across Ecuador. People with severe disabilities now receive $300 monthly stipends from the government. And Moreno has helped draw up a law that compels Ecuadorian companies to set aside at least 4 per cent of jobs for people with disabilities. He recently pledged that the government would reach out to all disabled people who needed help. That, he said, amounted to a revolution.

Last year, Moreno was nominated for the Nobel Peace Prize for his work. More than 2.5 million signatures were collected endorsing him, and 180 countries signalled their support. In the event, the prize was awarded to the European Union – a decision greeted on most sides with distinctly underwhelming enthusiasm.

One of the reasons we have all gathered in the remote heart of the rainforest this February morning is undoubtedly Moreno's wish to demonstrate that his disability is not going to prevent him from going wherever he is needed and doing whatever he has to do. And that includes going to the Amazon. In a sense, he is returning to his roots: he was born and raised in the Amazon, at Nuevo Rocafuerte on the Ecuador–Peru border. Coming back to the Amazon to give the last speech of his career (for now at least) is obviously of great personal and symbolic significance.

But it is more important than that. Far more important. Moreno speaks about Pacha Mama, the goddess of planting and regeneration widely worshipped among the Andean peoples. The concept of environmental protection is enshrined in Ecuador's constitution, and Moreno is here to tell us that the Yasuni initiative is central to Ecuador's plans to save the Amazon. And the future of the Amazon, he says, is vital for the future of Ecuador. Indeed, it is vital for the future of the world.

Now, Moreno is not averse to hyperbole. He has written books, he has composed songs. He is a performer in every sense of the word. Yet when he goes on to tell his audience, 'If there are no jaguars or pumas, we shall all die', I get absolutely no sense that he is merely putting on a show.

After a while, the President calls on Ivonne Baki, the Secretary of State for the Yasuni-ITT Initiative, to come to the dais. A striking figure, Baki takes the microphone, sits beside the President and addresses the audience. 'Ecuador is a developing country,' she says. 'It's really tough for us. Electricity, infrastructure, schools, health, hospitals. We are starting from zero. We need everything. Yet we have to preserve the environment as well. It's written in our constitution.'

The country faces an impossible dilemma, she continues. The Yasuni National Park is one of the most biodiverse locations in the world: home to 596 species of birds, 2,274 species of trees and bushes, more than 382 species of freshwater fish, at least 169 species of mammals, 141 species of amphibians and 121 species of reptiles. 'There are also more than 100,000 species of insects per hectare, the highest number in the world.'

Yet, with savage irony, it is here in Yasuni that some of Ecuador's most valuable oil reserves are to be found. 'You may have 900 million barrels of oil – that's 20 per cent of the oil of Ecuador. It could be more. They say it could be 1 billion, or even 5 billion barrels.'

So what should the country do, she asks. 'Should we keep the oil in the ground or take it out?' Can Ecuador somehow manage to have its cake and eat it?

In a nutshell, the answer is yes. Baki explains that the Yasuni-ITT Initiative, for which she is responsible, is the emblematic project of the Ecuadorian government. To avoid the environmental destruction caused by oil exploration in one of the areas with the greatest biological and cultural diversity of the Amazon, the government has committed itself to a permanent ban on oil production in the Ishpingo-Tambococha-Tiputini (ITT) oil fields, located in Yasuni.

To make good on that commitment, the Ecuadorian government has agreed to forego 50 per cent of the oil revenues, currently estimated at more than $12 billion, that it would otherwise have received. This is a colossal sacrifice – and one the government is ready to make. But, Baki explains, Ecuador cannot afford to go it alone. 'The government of Ecuador, in the spirit of shared responsibility, is seeking contributions of $3.6 billion over thirteen years – corresponding to half the value of exports foregone in 2007 – from international public and private contributions. This initiative will promote the conservation of the world's most valuable biodiversity.'

Baki points out that conserving Yasuni's forest will also avoid the emission of approximately 1.2 million metric tons of carbon dioxide, since deforestation is one of the principal sources of CO_2 emissions. And she ends on a note of optimism: to date, the amount raised by, or committed to, the Yasuni-ITT Initiative is $330 million.

But what will the money be spent on? Here, too, Baki explains, the concept is visionary. 'We want to build Ecuador's economy on the basis of renewable resources, not fossil fuels.' The funds under the Yasuni-ITT initiative are administered by the Multi-Partner Trust Fund Office of the United Nations Development Programme. The first project, a mini-hydroelectric station – at Huapamala in Loja in southern Ecuador – has just been launched.

We later have lunch in a lodge built by the Quechua people to encourage wildlife tourism. I find myself sitting next to Diego Zorilla, the United Nations Development Programme's representative in Ecuador. It is clear that he is a passionate believer in the Yasuni-ITT initiative. Indeed, he thinks some potential benefits may have been understated in Minister Baki's presentation. As far as climate change is concerned, for example, it is not just a case of the reduction in CO_2 emissions resulting from lower rates of deforestation. There is the crucial role, now being explored by scientists, that the vast Yasuni forest plays in the hydrological cycle of the whole Amazon Basin. 'And if the Amazon Basin dries out thanks to deforestation and flips over to savannah, what does that mean for the whole world's weather patterns?' Zorilla asks.

For one reason or another, I have been visiting the Amazon on a regular basis for more than fifty years, ever since that first trip to Brasilia, which I described in an earlier chapter. I have crossed it, by road or in the air, from north to south and from east to west. There was a time, back in the 1960s, when you could fly in a jet plane hour after hour and see nothing but a great green expanse below. Those days are gone. The need to preserve what is left of the Amazon from the various threats that assail it – oil exploitation, cattle, logging, soya, palm oil and so on – is more urgent than it has ever been.

In this context, the amounts of money asked by Ecuador to 'save' the Yasuni seem derisory, a tiny fraction of the amount of money we have thrown at the banks since 2008. People who deprecate Ecuador's initiative for this park, calling it 'blackmail' or 'greenmail', need their heads examining. This is an idea whose time has come.

As our lunch draws to an end, I have an opportunity to talk to the President in person. More accurately, after I have presented my compliments in stilted Spanish, I have a chance to listen to Lenin Moreno as he reminisces about his Amazonian childhood. By now, I am flagging from the effort of keeping up with all the quickfire Spanish, but Genoveva Casanova, who has been sitting next to him throughout the meal, helpfully fills in the gaps.

'He says that one day,' she tells me, 'a puma was attacking his uncle's cattle. His uncle called the men in the family to come and help hunt the animal. Suddenly the animal jumps out of the bush and everyone starts shooting. One of the cousins had a very old gun. When the animal is dead, they realise it is the man who has the very old gun who has shot the beast. The President tells us that his uncle gave him the skin of the puma and he kept it for years. He really cherished that skin.'

I ask Casanova to ask the President whether he has ever seen a jaguar. I myself have seen wild animals all over the world in my time, but never a jaguar. The President nods. Yes, he has seen a jaguar. I am green with envy.

I have a feeling that the President is ready to stay in that Quechua village for hours, reminiscing about his childhood in the Amazon, but it is time for him to go, and he is wheeled to his helicopter. The members of the Cabinet who have accompanied him to Yasuni gather to pay their respects. As the squad of soldiers salute and the tribespeople gaze in wonder, the great green beast takes off and roars back to Coca, where the presidential jet awaits. We feel the downdraft as the helicopter passes overhead.

When the President and his party have gone, and all the Quechua have dispersed, some to their village houses, others to a greater distance, our local guide, Remy, escorts us through the forest to a boat that is waiting to take us to another jungle lodge, downriver, where we are booked to stay the night.

Baki, who accompanies us, explains that for the final two hours, we will be paddling down a creek – a *quebrada* – with no outboard motor. The Napo Wildlife Center, where we are heading, is on a lagoon. On the way we see several caiman and the tracks of a tapir, as well as five species of kingfisher, several striated herons, a cluster of hoatzin, and an owl butterfly, to name but a few.

On the way back the next day, I see a family of giant river otters and a boa constrictor in a tree, waiting to catch parrots flying into a nearby clay lick. As we sit there, looking at the 7-foot-long reptile coiled around a high branch with its head in the air, ready to strike, Remy tells us, 'A boa constrictor needs to eat only one parrot a month.'

After a while, we get out of the boat and walk along a trail through the forest to another clay lick, where hundreds of parrots have gathered. 'They need the clay to clear the toxins in their diet,' Remy explains.

For the record, the various birds we see that morning include dusky-headed parakeets, white-eyed parakeets, blue-eyed parakeets, blue-headed parrots, yellow-crowned and Mealy Amazon parrots.

We also see a scarlet macaw, which brings an abrupt end to the spectacular show when it spots a large hawk approaching. It issues a loud squawking alarm, the birds panic – and suddenly they are off, in all directions.

Chapter Thirty-Six

I Could Have Been a Contender

The last time I was in Rio was in June 2012, exactly twenty years after the Rio 1992 Earth Summit. I had been invited by Achim Steiner, the executive director of the United Nations Environment Programme (UNEP) to attend the conference, otherwise known as Rio+20, as part of UNEP's delegation. Steiner was then and is now UNEP's executive director. At Steiner's invitation, I've just written a long account of international environmental policy over its forty years. The official title of the book is *UNEP: The First 40 Years*.

The average layperson might think that 'forty years of UNEP' is about as dull a topic as anyone could conceivably imagine. Well, the average layperson would be wrong. In fewer than 150,000 words (148,929 to be precise) I romped through ozone depletion, climate change, toxic waste, biodiversity, trade and the environment etc. All the key issues, in fact. And I reckon I did so in a lively readable way, mainly because I was present in one capacity or another at most of the key events, beginning with that first Earth Summit held in Stockholm in June 1972, when we all paraded at midnight through the still-bright streets of the Old Town carrying banners saying SAVE THE WHALE!

My UNEP book had been officially launched in Nairobi at a jolly fortieth anniversary dinner held in a large tent on the lawn of UNEP's headquarters in Gigiri. Multitasking as photographer as well as author, I had taken some splendid photos of UNEP's former executive directors using a ceremonial sword to cut a vast cake adorned with forty flaming candles.

After that we all decamped to Rio where, among other assignments, I had agreed to give a talk about my new great work at an early morning 'side event' to be held at the Rio Centre. (At these big Earth Summits the fringe events are often more rewarding than the plenary meetings.)

The evening before I was due to give the talk, I went to a reception at one of the hotels on Copacabana Beach. When the party was over, I walked down to the ocean's edge.

I put my shoes on a convenient mound of sand, rolled up my trouser legs to walk barefoot at the water's edge. What a mistake! The very next wave roared past me, sweeping my shoes off their perch before I had time to grasp them.

If I had brought a spare pair of shoes with me, I might have laughed it off. But I hadn't brought a spare pair. I didn't even have any sneakers with me. I couldn't imagine how I could possibly find new footwear before I had to leave for the meeting.

Admittedly, people at that Rio conference (and at its precursor twenty years earlier) were turning up in all sorts of gear. The indigenous Yanomami, for example, paraded around the conference hall wearing huge wooden plugs to distend their lower lips. Some of them didn't seem to be wearing anything at all, except a grass skirt and a penis gourd. But I was representing UNEP! I was going to talk about forty years of international environmental policy! People who made the long trek out to Rio Centro (an hour by bus if you were lucky) expected to see a man with shoes on his feet as well as some brains in his head.

Amazingly, I managed to rescue one shoe when it was suddenly thrown by a wave in my direction. I collapsed on the beach. Oh

God, I thought, what a total shambles! Here I am over seventy years old, planning to present an important book at a major international venue in my best chalk-striped suit, but I'm going to be wearing only one shoe, and a very soggy shoe at that!

I really mean it. I was seriously upset. I started to hyperventilate. And then, miraculously, another wave rushed in and I caught a glimpse of a bobbing black object. Could it really be? By God, it was!

When I walked into the meeting room at Rio Centro the next morning to give my talk, my shoes felt cold and clammy. Disgusting, actually. But at least there were two of them. And they were on my feet!

Back in London, WWF – the World Wide Fund for Nature, as it now is – launched my UNEP book for the 'third' time, and presented me with a WWF silver medal for 'services to conservation'. Of course, there's no such thing as a free launch and quite soon I was able to return the compliment by addressing a group of 'high net worth donors' over an elegant WWF-sponsored dinner in Mayfair.

I had hoped to show my photos of the leopard seal eating the penguin in Antarctica or the crocodiles sinking the young zebra in the Mara River or that (as I felt) amazing shot of the boa constrictor in the tree in the Amazon with its jaw open to catch its monthly parrot.

As a matter of fact I had some other wholly new pictures to show as well as these old favourites. At the time of that WWF dinner, I had just returned from two weeks in Papua New Guinea. I had some splendid images of the Huli tribesmen with their extraordinary headdresses and – amazingly – a brilliantly clear photo of the ribbon-tailed astrapia, one of PNG's loveliest birds of paradise, actually in flight.

Alas, for some reason, the projector wasn't there or else it didn't work. Instead of showing pictures, I had to talk. Much harder work!

Even more recently, I have been to Colombia. The British ambassador, Lindsay Croisdale-Appleby, very kindly invited me to dinner at the Residence the night I arrived. By some strange coincidence, the Foreign Secretary, William Hague, was there for dinner that night too.

Hague vividly remembered the occasion when he was hosting *Have I Got News For You* and I forgot – momentarily – the name of my youngest daughter.

'That was very amusing,' he said. 'We all had a great laugh.'

'I think the audience found it funnier than I did,' I said.

While the Foreign Secretary flew on to Manaus, I joined a Bristol Zoo team on a mission to Colombia's Central Magdalena region. Now that the FARC are negotiating with the government, large areas of Colombia are opening up. Much of the Central Magdalena region has been out of bounds till recently, but – thanks to the efforts of the embassy, the Colombian government and some local NGOs – we managed to get into the forest near Barrancabermeja. I was longing to see a jaguar, but we saw only the pawmarks, some jaguar scat and a brilliant jaguar 'selfie' taken by one of the camera traps.

So jaguars, in the wild, are still on my 'to see' list.

Polar bears, on the other hand, are at last in the bag. Jenny and I had a ten-day trip round Svalbard, north east of Greenland, in the summer of 2013 and saw, in total, three polar bears, including one at close range. There are actually around 3,000 polar bears in Svalbard, out of a total world population of, say, 20,000. So the survival of those bears is desperately important. The trouble is, with global warming, the seas are no longer freezing around Svalbard. If the polar bears can't get out on the ice, they can't hunt the seals. So they starve. Nigel Lawson may think global warming isn't a problem. Tell that to the polar bears!

A lot of people nowadays are campaigning for polar bears. I officially unveiled a giant statue of a polar bear in Sloane Square, before it was moved to the zoo in Regent's Park. That particular event received some coverage in the press. But one swallow doesn't make a summer. Around 600 polar bears each year are still being killed in the Arctic, and their skins traded. Shamefully, even though Britain pleaded for a trade ban, the EU failed to back the proposal when CITES discussed the issue last year in Bangkok. A positive EU vote might have done the trick. Maybe David Cameron should put this one on his EU-negotiating list.

Talking about politics, whatever happened to my political career? Were my few well-chosen remarks to my supporters after my defeat in Teignbridge really my last word on the subject? Could I still, in my eighth decade, be a contender, as Marlon Brando put it?

Well, if I may paraphrase Michael Heseltine, I cannot foresee a situation where I would once again seek elective office.

When Boris resigned his seat in Henley, having been elected Mayor of London, the Conservative hierarchy apparently made it clear that elder Johnsons need not apply for the vacated seat, David Cameron having – according to the BBC – make a personal visit to the constituency to ensure that the shortlist was to his liking.

I was disappointed but not deterred. When, a few months later, Paul Goodman, the Member of Parliament for Wycombe, in leafy Buckinghamshire, announced his intention to stand down, I started sniffing around.

Local knowledge, as I saw it, wasn't really an issue where Wycombe was concerned. I used to bomb up the old A40 from Oxford to London all the time. What was the name of that pub in Beaconsfield?

I was in a hot-air balloon above the Masai Mara in Kenya when Lady McAlpine sent me a text message inviting Jenny and me to drinks and dinner ('John Madejski is coming') the following week at the McAlpine estate in the Chilterns.

I sent a message back. 'Delighted!'

Once back in England I found myself plunged into the middle of a political controversy that went to the core of the relationship between the Conservative Party's leadership and the 'party in the country', as embodied in the party's local constituency associations.

To explain: as the chairman of Wycombe Conservative Association had himself decided to put in for Paul Goodman's seat, Sir William McAlpine, the Association's President, had taken over as chairman of the selection committee.

But while I was on my way back from Africa, things had, as Lady McAlpine subsequently explained, begun to go wrong. 'From the very beginning that particular selection process was skewed. At the local party meeting held to select the selection committee, a cohort from Central Office had arrived to say: "We have new rules: You must select three men and three women. You are not allowed to interview even your final selection. The chairman must deliver us the list of names three weeks from today."'

Lady McAlpine, Judy, always a colourful personality, went on to say, 'It seems the young man learned some new expletives and was sent back with messages he probably chose not to deliver. When asked "When were these rules agreed?" the answer was "5 p.m. today"!'

'A week later,' Judy continued, 'on the Sunday before the first meeting scheduled for the Monday evening, each member of the committee received two ring-binders, one with details of a few hundred male candidates and the other a few hundred female candidates. No photos, no ages, no religion.'

Sir William McAlpine, his wife said, 'wondered how the hell you judge someone from a few lines on a piece of paper'.

Everyone diligently read all night, went to work the next day then turned up at the McAlpines' armed with their personal list of 'possibilities'. Two more meetings produced a shortlist of about twenty names and all agreed they could go no further without interviewing or at least meeting the people they were trying to judge.

Lady McAlpine told me about the decisive intervention she had made at this moment.

'The selection committee had reached a point where they couldn't continue without meeting the candidates. I said to them, "Two of your list are already due to come here for dinner next Friday: invited ages ago; nothing to do with politics at all ... so why don't we ask the rest of them – and you – for drinks before dinner but only the original dinner guests are staying on?"'

Some sixth sense told me that there might be trouble ahead, but if we hadn't specifically declined the dinner invitation – and we hadn't – then I didn't see how we could do so now. Besides, I was looking forward to meeting Sir John Madejski, the man who owned the Madejski Millennium Hotel, the Madejski Stadium and Reading Football Club. Not that I knew anything about football. We played rugger at Sherborne. My last year on the XV we were unbeaten, though we drew against Downside. And it was always good fun at the McAlpines' anyway.

When Jenny and I arrived at the appointed hour at the McAlpines' home in the Chilterns, Judy was on the phone and clearly in the middle of a tremendous row with CCHQ or Conservative Campaign Headquarters, as Conservative Central Office was now called.

'I fail to understand why you think you have any right to dictate who I invite into my home as guests. If I believe members of the local association should be offered an informal drink with some potential candidates, I will invite them. It is none of your business. Surely it is up to us to decide who our candidate is to be! We certainly do not need to be dictated to by some apparatchik at Central Office, especially one with such appalling manners as yours.'

Judy McAlpine slammed down the phone. She saw us standing there.

'Ah, Jenny, Stanley! Come on and have a drink on the terrace.'

We stepped out into a lively drinks party and forgot all about Judy's telephone anger.

I vividly remember the other guests. They included Rory Stewart, Bob Stewart, Dominic Raab, Dr Philip Lee (all of whom would find seats later, though not in Wycombe) as well as Victoria Borwick, married to Sir William's nephew, Jamie Borwick. Victoria would later be elected as the statutory Deputy Mayor of London. We were not specifically introduced to the members of the selection committee but it was clear they were keen to give us the once-over, like inspecting the horses in the paddock before the race.

When dusk fell, and the red kites that had swooped and swirled all evening over the vast estate had finally realised the sausages had run out and had folded their wings, Judy McAlpine rang a bell to indicate that this was the *exeunt omnes* moment. But the *omnes* didn't include us! Jenny and I tried to fade into the bushes while goodbyes were said. But it was pretty obvious dinner was imminent: the table was laid, the candles were lit – guests were required.

We were about to tuck into the first course when the doorbell rang. Dominic Raab appeared looking flushed and irritated.

'We can't get out of the gate at the end of the drive. Is there some code for us to punch in or something?' he asked.

I could sense his quick brain registering the fact that, while all candidates in the modern and inclusive Tory Party were meant to be equal, some were invited to stay on for dinner.

I'll never know who it was – and, when asked by Judy, all who had been there swore blind it wasn't them – who 'sneaked' or 'snitched' to the powers that be at Conservative Central Office. Nor do I know who they complained to. Was it Andrew Griffiths, Eric Pickles's sidekick, Pickles being the man then in charge of candidates? Was it Pickles himself? And what further conversations ensued? Was the party leader, David Cameron, himself contacted? You don't cross the McAlpines lightly. They used to run the Conservative Party.

All I know is that at 8 a.m. the following Tuesday, Bill McAlpine rang me in London: 'Central Office has cancelled the whole selection process.' He sounded furious. 'They're starting again from scratch with a new chairman, a new selection committee and a totally new slate of candidates, which *they*, not we, are going to choose.'

Judy later told me precisely what had happened. 'The selection committee, having met ALL the candidates, had just unanimously agreed on the list to go to head office when a young man began screaming at me on the telephone that he must speak to Sir William, saying they must STOP the selection process immediately.'

When he finally spoke to the 'screamer', Sir William returned to the room 'shaking with rage', something his wife had never witnessed before.

A few days later, Judy sent me a copy of the letter she had written to David Cameron. As *Private Eye* used to put it, 'Phew, what a scorcher!'

Realistically, Wycombe was probably my last best chance to catch the eye of the selectors. I knew the writing was on the wall. Nonetheless, when Orpington came up, a few months before the election, I thought I'd at least investigate.

After all, my own maternal grandfather, Stanley Williams, had lived with my French 'de Pfeffel' grandmother in nearby Bromley before he retired to Cornwall. My mother and father were actually married in Bromley and I myself had learned to swim in Beckenham Baths!

My mother had laid a ten-shilling note at one end of the swimming pool, promising that I could have it if I swam the whole length. Ten shillings meant a lot in those days. Tenuous though they might seem, I was ready to make the most of these local connections.

In the end, I decided that I would not, in the classic phrase, 'let my name go forward' to Orpington. Realistically, I reckoned that if I did let it go forward, it would not get very far, not much further than Blackheath I imagined. The truth of the matter was that I would be only a few months short of my seventieth birthday, come the most likely date for the next general election (May 2010). Wasn't this the moment to hang up my boots?

So I put Orpington firmly out of my mind until, around 10 p.m. a few weeks later, a received a most mysterious text message from my old friend, Jonathan Isaby.

This is what it said. 'Congratulations! Jo selected as Conservative candidate for Orpington on sixth ballot!'

'Jo? Jo who?' I said to myself. Not Jo Johnson, surely? To the best of my knowledge Jo Johnson wasn't even on the candidates' list. If he was, he certainly hadn't mentioned it. Of course, we Johnsons operate a 'need to know' policy as far as intra-family communications are concerned, but this was surely pushing it.

But if the 'Jo' of Isaby's message was not Jo Johnson, my third son and fourth child, why on earth was I being texted late at night? Besides, most often Jo, in the masculine version anyway, is spelled with an 'e' at the end.

I couldn't get hold of Isaby, so I fired off a text myself.

'Fantastic news! No idea you were even in the running! Love Dada.'

Chapter Thirty-Seven

What Next?

Quite a few chapters ago, I trotted out an ancient Chinese proverb: 'When one door shut, other door open.'

Are there still other portals out there? My TV career, such as it was, seems to be on hold. I have had occasional feelers from TV producers who would like me to eat worms in the Australian forests or go on *Big Brother* but whenever these overtures have seemed likely to turn into hard offers, a 'family veto' has been applied. Frankly, I never mind making a fool of myself. That's what I do for a living. But there are other people, near and dear to me, who do mind. Sometimes, you have to take other people's feelings into account.

A year or two ago, I made regular appearances on an hour-long BBC One show (strictly speaking, there were four 'pilots') called *This Is Britain*, hosted by Julia Bradbury and Nick Knowles. I was responsible for the 'candid camera' sequences. I had no fewer than three cameramen with me, all secretly filming away under cover while I travelled round the country trying to persuade people to do silly things.

For example, we went to a shopping centre in Bradford just before Christmas. Why Bradford? Why Christmas? I asked.

Doh! Parts of Bradford nowadays, I was told, were 'basically 100 per cent ethnic'.

'What you have to do,' the producer said, 'is go into the shopping mall, find some likely local and tell him that unfortunately Santa Claus is late – some incident with the reindeer maybe – and would he mind just dressing up in this Father Christmas outfit, you know red coat and hood, white beard and so forth, and go into the grotto. Tell him the kids will be extremely disappointed if Father Christmas doesn't show up. If you can persuade him to say "Ho ho ho!" as well, that would be fantastic!'

'Are you sure the kids' mums are going to happy to let their kids into the grotto with a man they don't know?' I asked.

This was before the Jimmy Savile scandal broke so the man from the BBC was fairly relaxed about it. 'Just keep an eye on things,' he said.

The BBC's basic thesis, in commissioning these candid camera sequences, was that, nowadays, everything had gone to the dogs and you couldn't get people to help out in an emergency.

'You'll probably have to talk to half a dozen people or more before you find one ready to dress up as Santa and go into the grotto,' the producer said.

How wrong he was! Every single person I asked seemed only too delighted to take time off from their busy schedule, dress up as Santa, and spend half an hour in the grotto saying 'Ho ho ho!'

For some reason, the candid camera team always headed north on its excursions out of London.

One day we added an actress to the team. The job specification was very precise.

'Pretty, if possible. People have to want to help her,' the producer insisted. 'But above all, she has to be short, in the sense of "not tall".'

We all trundled up to Birmingham, or wherever. Our 'short' actress was to go into a supermarket, struggle to reach the top shelf, and persuade another shopper to grab the cornflakes or whatever for her.

'Ideally,' the producer explained, 'they'll load her trolley, help her to the check-out, then push her trolley to her car, load her car, then actually get into the car, and drive it for her, so she can get out of the car park without bumping into other vehicles. Any questions? Let's roll!'

We took bets on how far the young lady would get before the 'helper' decided to call it a day.

Well, we all lost our bets because all the 'helpers' our 'short' young lady approached were only too keen to reach down the goods from the shelf, help through the check-out and push the trolley to the car. Some of them even offered to drive, not just out of the car park, but all the way home!

After a while, *This Is Britain* came off the air, and I came off the air with it.

The good news is that, at the time of writing, I've just appeared on *Pointless*, another BBC One TV show that goes out at 5.15 every afternoon and apparently has between five and six million viewers. The family don't mind my appearing on *Pointless*.

Jenny explained it to me. 'You need to get the lowest possible score, not the highest.'

I thought of all those letters I used to write home from school. '*Dear Mummy and Daddy,*' I could have said, '*you will be very pleased to hear that I came bottom again this week.*'

In the event, *Pointless* was tremendous fun. My partner was Kate Adie, the BBC's former chief news correspondent. Though Kate and I didn't win by coming bottom, we weren't knocked out in the first round either. We very much hope to be invited back.

If a TV career seems improbable, I am sure I will remain fully committed on the environmental front. I am now President Emeritus of the Gorilla Organization, having handed over the chairmanship to Ian Redmond, an amazing man who has devoted his whole life to conservation. I remain an ambassador for the United Nations Environment Programme's Convention on Migratory Species (CMS) and have just joined the Council of the World Land Trust, which helps protect the world's most biologically important and threatened habitats acre by acre.

I was very pleased, in November 2012, to be invited to give the Aurelio Peccei lecture to the Club of Rome's EU chapter in Brussels. My brief was to take a 'broad bird's-eye view of forty years of environmental policy and action' since the publication in 1972 of the Club of Rome's influential report on 'The Limits to Growth'. I began by paying tribute to my old friend Edward Goldsmith, founder of the *Ecologist* magazine. For my money, 'Teddy' Goldsmith and the Club of Rome – with their emphasis on the need to curb both population growth and economic growth – were spot on. Without such curbs, we are all spitting in the wind.

Finally, for those who haven't heard quite enough about the Johnsons as it is, here is the latest family update (as of summer 2014).

Boris is still Mayor of London. Marina, his wife, is a barrister, specialising in human rights. Rachel is an author and journalist. Ivo, Rachel's husband, is the head of the National Trust's London area office. Leo is an environmental consultant and entrepreneur. Taies, Leo's wife, works for the World Bank. Jo is a Member of Parliament, Minister of State in the Cabinet Office and currently in charge of the 10 Downing Street policy unit. Amelia Gentleman, his wife, works for the *Guardian* newspaper. Julia, having gained a first in Classics at UCL, teaches Latin and has just released her second solo album. Calum, Julia's husband, works for a film company. Max, with an MBA from Tsinghua University in Beijing, works for Goldman Sachs in Hong Kong.

Towards the end of June 2014, when I was working on the final draft of this book, I was telephoned by Paul Clements, deputy features editor of the *Sunday Telegraph*. President Obama, he said, in a recent interview with CNN, handed out some free advice for parents. 'Tell your kids to bath, eat their peas, pick up the toys off the floor,' Obama suggested. As a man with some experience, what was my advice on parenting, Clements asked? He was ringing around to gather some reactions to the President's remarks.

I said that in so far as I had any ideas on the subject worth recording, it would be along the lines of: 'Always agree immediately and enthusiastically to whatever schemes or proposals are being advanced by your children.'

Clements asked for an example so I gave him one.

'September 1984. I am in my office in Brussels. The phone rings. Rachel is calling reverse-charge from Israel, where she is doing some gap-year work on a kibbutz, before going up to read Classics at Oxford. She tells me she has met an Israeli shepherd called David. "I'm not going up to Oxford next month," she says. "I'm going to stay here on the kibbutz for the next few years."'

'Wonderful, darling! Totally brilliant!' I say. 'Don't forget to tell New College you won't be coming. They'll need to know. Say "Shalom!" to David.'

'And what happened?' Clements asked.

'Rachel in due course arrived in Oxford in time for the beginning of term,' I replied. 'I don't know what happened to David.'

If this is an example of 'long-distance' as opposed to 'helicopter' parenting, I plead guilty. But there must be something to be said for it.

My eleven (so far) grandchildren are motoring ahead with their own lives. For the record, and to prove I can still do it in the right order, they are: Ludo, Lara, Milo, Milly, Oliver, Cassia, Theo, Rose, Lula, William and Ruby Noor. I look forward to being 'lapped' by some or all of them too in due course!

As Horace put it, '*Exegi monumentum aere perennius.*' I have raised a monument more lasting than bronze.

To mark my seventieth birthday on 18 August 2010, a Johnson XI took on a Winsford XI at Winsford in a close-fought cricket match. The Johnsons batted first and scored a respectable 172, with Leo (my second son) clocking up the top score of 37. I thought we were in with a chance, but the 'home' side, viz. Winsford, laid on a tremendous spread for tea. I see now this was part of a devilish plan to sap our energies when we went out to field.

Jo, captaining the Johnsons, decided that every player on our side, except the wicket-keeper, should have the chance to bowl two overs. Winsford were still forty runs behind, with only four overs left to play, when it was Theo's turn to bowl. Theo, Boris and Marina's young-est child, was only twelve years old at the time. He did his best, but unfortunately, Winsford's captain, Andrew Blackmore, coming in at number 8, decided to let rip. He scored twenty-five runs off Theo's first over, which brought Winsford's score to 154 for 7. It still seemed to me that, even if we didn't win, we might achieve a draw provided Theo didn't give away too many runs on his second over.

But Blackmore was determined to give no quarter. He carted the first ball of Theo's second over for six, followed by two fours. A second six delivered the 'coup de grace'.

A few weeks later, when Winsford Cricket Club were having their annual dinner in the Royal Oak, and I was giving the 'President's Address', I duly congratulated the Winsford team on its victory over the Johnsons.

'Mind you,' I turned to Blackmore, 'I think you were a bit tough on a twelve-year-old kid, Andrew. I'm not sure you really had to cart Theo out of the ground like that.'

We are planning a return match in due course.

In the meantime, I have had some useful practice. On 15 June 2014, a Johnson XI, captained by Boris but with technical advice provided by Jo (who played for Eton), took on a team brought together by Earl (Charles) Spencer at Althorp, the Spencer family seat in Northamptonshire. The pitch was in perfect shape. Cows, sheep, geese, ducks and peacocks looked on with interest, as well as spectators taking a break from the increasingly popular Althorp Literary Festival then in full swing. The stately home, virtually overlooking the ground, was bathed in the summer sun.

The agreed format for this 'needle' match was the ever more popular 20:20. The Johnson side consisted of eight 'Johnsons', viz. Boris, Leo, Jo, Rachel, Milo, Oliver, Stanley and Calum with Theo on duty as a 'runner'. Our wicket-keeper was Bob Swerling, one of Boris's contemporaries at Oxford, who performed his difficult task with tremendous enthusiasm. Will Walden, the Mayor of London's director of communications, proved a useful bowler.

Our secret weapon, however, was Kevin Pietersen. Yes, *the* Kevin Pietersen, known to all and sundry as 'KP'!

A friend of Boris's, Pietersen flew in by helicopter in time for the pre-match lunch. His arrival caused consternation among the Spencer contingent. On other such occasions, Earl Spencer himself has been known to spring unwelcome surprises on the opposition. But on this occasion, the table had been well and truly turned.

The Spencer XI won the toss and batted first. In the course of their twenty overs, they knocked up the very respectable total of 188. Rachel took a glorious one-handed catch on the boundary off KP's bowling.

In spite of my less than spectacular performance at Winsford four years earlier, Boris was kind enough to ask me to open the Johnson innings, with his elder son, Milo, at the other end. With Pietersen coming in first wicket down, I understood perfectly what my role was. Get runs or get out.

Normally, I lash out when confronted with an incoming missile, but at Althorp, conscious of the prestige of being an 'opener',

I took things steadily. Milo, who rates an entry in *Wisden* as a school-boy cricketer (Westminster), was going great guns. Our combined run rate wasn't too bad, but I knew we had to do better. When I decided to go for a quick single, my right calf went into a spasm. Theo nobly came on as a runner but after an over or so, I knew it was time to call it a day.

As I hobbled off, I removed my glove and shook hands with the incoming Pietersen. I didn't feel he needed any tips about how to play the bowling. Nor from me anyway. So I contented myself with a brief nonchalant comment.

'You may want them to move the sight-screen,' I said. 'There are some cows behind the bowler's arm.'

KP quickly scored 80 with one hand tied behind his back. In the end, he skied the ball deliberately and walked. It was time to let the tail-enders finish the job. We were still twenty runs shy of the total when we ran out of overs.

Minutes later, as we tucked into the Pimms, KP's 'chopper' flew low over the pitch. We waved and raised our glasses. What a great man! Couldn't have been nicer. Why did people make a fuss about KP? A perfect day in so many ways.

As far as the wider family circle is concerned, my sister Hilary and her husband have just celebrated their fiftieth wedding anniversary in Australia. My elder brother Peter, a town planner, has retired to the Lake District. My younger sister, Birdie, has finally left Nethercote and now lives in Sussex though she still, I notice, has the *West Somerset Free Press* sent to her each week.

Jenny's mother, Lois Sieff, at ninety-one, remains the life and soul of the party. If I want to get a table at, say, the Wolseley, Colbert, Sheekeys, the Delaunay or wherever, I just have to say, 'I'm Lois Sieff's son-in-law.'

'Mrs Sieff? Of course, sir,' comes the reply. 'She was here only last evening.'

I hope I am half as sparky and funny when I get to her age, a couple of years from now.

Which, of course, brings me – last but not least – to Jenny.

Jenny and I have now celebrated more than thirty-two years of marriage. She has been and continues to be my prop and general support in every conceivable way. I know that she finds me difficult at times, probably most of the time, in the sense that I'm always zooming around and having ideas and she would possibly like a quieter life. She certainly deserves it. Plus, we disagree about most things. She's very left-wing, for example. She believes in helping other people. I spend most of my time thinking about animals and the need to protect them from mankind's ravaging.

As Elizabeth Barrett Browning put it: 'How do I love thee? Let me count the ways.'

Frankly, without Jenny, I don't know how I would have managed these past three or more decades. Yes, I put on a good show. I talk a good game. I add half a line each year to the CV if I'm lucky. But Jenny is the one who makes it all possible. And she does so while pursuing her own intellectual and professional pursuits. She sits on lots of committees. And I've lost track of how many degrees Jenny has or what the subject is. I know she has a BA from Oxford and an MA from London and a BSc from somewhere else. I wouldn't put it past her to be working away on a PhD without letting on.

It's true, I admit, that I have taken some massively bad decisions that have had a major impact on our lives. I know, for example, that I shouldn't have had Aston Chase (or was it John D. Wood?) round to the Rocking Horse House that day when she was out of town.

'I could tell from your voice that something was going on. I knew you had the estate agents there when I rang you from the train,' she told me later.

In self-defence, I would argue that we weren't to know when we sold the Rocking Horse House on Primrose Hill, in order to 'downsize', that the house we moved to would turn out to be less than ten metres from the route the high-speed train – HS2 – will take out of Euston and that the Rocking Horse House would be resold virtually the next day for a multiple of our asking price!

Only the other day I was looking at the photos of the time Jenny and I went to Rome with all the newly elected Conservative MEPs to meet His Holiness Pope John Paul II. There is Jenny in her mantilla. There is the Pope, holding out his hand. There is Jim Scott-Hopkins, apparently fumbling for words.

'This is Mr Johnson, Holy Father,' Jim says, 'and this is ... er ... er...'

'Holy Smoke!' I think, as I look at that photo. Jim hasn't really forgotten Jenny's name, has he? He's a smart politician. Remembering names is what you do.

Scott-Hopkins is setting it up for the Pope! He just wants to be sure that we – Jenny and I – get a proper papal blessing. Good old Jim!

And does the Pope play ball? Is the Pope Catholic? You bet he does! He helps Scott-Hopkins out, just as Jim hopes he will.

When Jim says, 'This is ... er ... er ... in point of fact', His Supremely Serene Holiness says, 'Well, this is Mrs Johnson, I suppose?'

Then he folds Jenny's hand in his. The rest is history.

As for the point about having a pizza in the piazza after that papal audience, way back in Chapter Two, I'm pretty sure I've remembered it right. And I've checked with Julia, who says you would definitely expect to get anchovies with a 'pizza napolitana'.

Index